Dressmaking with

LIBERTY

by Ann Ladbury

BEAUFORT BOOKS, INC.

NEW YORK

Library of Congress Cataloging in Publication Data

Ladbury, Ann.
   Dressmaking with Liberty.

   1. Dressmaking.   2. Textile fabrics.   I. Title.
TT515.L144   1984   646.4'304   83–25849
ISBN 0–8253–0215–3

Published in the United States by Beaufort Books, Inc., New York.

Colour photographs by Tony McGee
Black and white photographs by Ian O'Leary
Designed by David Fordham
Tissue patterns printed by Maudella Patterns Co. Ltd
Line illustrations by Jil Shipley

Phototypeset by
Falcon Graphic Art Ltd
Wallington, Surrey

Printed in Great Britain by
R.J. Acford, Industrial Estate,
Chichester, Sussex

10 9 8 7 6 5 4 3 2 1

First American Edition
First published in Great Britain
in 1984 by Sidgwick and Jackson Limited

Contents

Acknowledgements

I should like to thank all the people who have helped me with this book, especially Cheryl Owen for working so hard on the patterns and also, for making the outfits for photography,

Dawn Cloake
Margaret Brearley
Sue Lemon
Eileen Amos
Dorothy Longden
Joy Baker
Myra Davidson
Valerie Ibbett
Mary Peacock

Glossary

Readers in the United States may find helpful the following list of alternative terms and dressmaking products.

Bias strip: *crossway strip*
Cut on the cross: *cut on the bias*
Fold-a-Band: *use Fuse 'n' Fold in the appropriate weight, or Waist-Shaper for waistbands*
Frill: *ruffle or flounce*
Machine: *machine stitch*
Machine fell seam: *flat fell seam*
Neaten: *finish*
Open seam: *plain seam*
Petersham: *Grosgrain ribbon or Milliner's ribbon*
Press stud: *snap*
Rouleau: *tubing*
Round: *around*
Snip: *clip*
Tack: *baste*
Turning: *seam allowance*
Vilene: *Pellon*
Wundaweb: *use Stitch Witchery or Save-a-Stitch*
Zip: *zipper*

How to Use this Book

The book contains complete patterns for making up all the outfits shown in the colour photographs and dozens of variations as well. Some of the patterns are full size, printed on tissue and enclosed in the envelope at the back of the book. The rest are drawn as diagrams to be scaled up following the measurements given – see patterns. The adult patterns are from size 8 up to size 20, that is bust 80cm (31½in.) to 107cm (42in.); the girl's dress pattern is from 1 to 6 years, and the romper suit for a 6 to 12-month-old baby. Select your usual size for making up, but if you are unsure of your best size consult the measurement chart on page 6.

Once you have chosen an outfit or a variation of it, prepared the appropriate pattern pieces (see pages 14 and 15) and obtained the necessary fabric and items of haberdashery, (see the charts on pages 10-13), look at the order of construction in the section beginning on page 75. This is a brief outline which provides not only a guide to how to tackle the sewing, but also an indication as to how much sewing, and therefore time, is involved. The sewing techniques that apply to several garments are described in detail in the alphabetical section at the back of the book. This arrangement allows you to proceed quickly through the processes with which you are familiar, but also ensures that you have ready access to those you have never tackled.

THE DESIGNS

The book contains patterns for a classic shirt, six skirts, four dresses, trousers and a jacket, lingerie, a child's dress, and a baby's romper suit. All the designs are classic yet with fashion features, simple but with the opportunity to use your sewing and creative skills, and above all they are clothes you will want to go on making for a long time in different versions. The basic patterns can all be varied in many different ways. In addition to the versions photographed the fabrics can, of course, be different, but also style features like collars, necklines, belts, sleeve lengths and decorative features are interchangeable. For example we made up and photographed the basic shirt in seven different ways and there are probably at least a dozen more possibilities for that one pattern alone.

Just to give you an idea, you could for instance put the jacket with the straight skirt in the same fabric; you could shorten the straight dress and put it with the trousers to make pyjamas; you could lengthen the jacket and quilt it to make a housecoat; you could make the gathered dress floor length as a winter dinner dress; you could wear the V-neck top with the shirt over it as a jacket; and for stunning simplicity you could make the shirt in white crêpe de chine and the trousers in black.

A number of decorative techniques are included amongst the sewing techniques, all of which can be successfully applied to any of the patterns, to any variation, and to any of the fabrics suggested. Read the instructions for the feature you select in order to find out whether it really will produce the effect you want and also to discover what you need in the way of additional haberdashery. You will also get an idea of how complex the process is and how long it will take to work.

A few suggestions as to how these techniques might be used are shown in the photographs, but the further possibilities for combining fabric, pattern and sewing techniques in various ways are almost endless and you will find it satisfying and exciting to create beautiful, individual clothes that reflect your taste as well as your skill.

Beginners and those with limited experience will also find this book exciting, but not at all difficult to use. Any of the patterns can be made successfully, starting with simple versions to gain confidence. Absolute beginners would be advised to start with trousers or shorts, the T-shirt top and the V-neck top, progressing to the gathered skirt and the simple dress, leaving the clothes with collars, cuffs, buttons and decoration to a later stage.

All the designs made up to perfection in Liberty fabrics. For a full list of the fabrics we chose, with sewing and washing instructions see page 56. For a chart suggesting which types of fabric generally are suitable see page 57.

BODY MEASUREMENTS

The patterns have been made to the body measurements shown below. Check your measurements against the list and use the pattern nearest to your size. If you fall between sizes choose the smaller pattern unless you have one prominent feature e.g. large hips, full bust. The actual pattern pieces will, of course, measure more.

Ease for movement has already been allowed so you can safely select your size from this chart without making any further calculations.

All patterns are given from size 8 to 20. Choose tops by your bust measurements, straight skirt and trousers by hip measurements and full or gathered skirts by waist size.

PATTERN	SIZE	CHEST		WAIST		BK NECK TO HEM	
Child's Dress		cm	in.	cm	in.	cm	in.
	1	51	20	50	19½	50.0	19¾
	2	53	20⅞	51	19⅞	53.5	20⅞
	3	56	22	52	20¼	55.5	21½
	4	58	22¾	53	20¾	58.5	22⅞
	5	61	24	55	21½	63.5	24¾
	6	64	25¼	56	21¾	67.5	26¼

PATTERN	SIZE	BUST		WAIST		HIPS		BK NECK TO HEM	
Shirt		cm	in.	cm	in.	cm	in.	cm	in.
	8/10	80-83	31½-32½	64	25	88	34	65	26
	12	87	34	67	26	92	36	65	26
	14	92	36	71	28	97	38	65	26
	16	97	38	76	30	102	40	65	26
	18	102	40	81	32	107	42	65	26
	20	107	42	87	34	112	44	65	26

The Basic Patterns

SHIRT

An easy-fitting classic style with a buttoned front band, saddle yoke and slightly extended shoulder with deep, comfortable armhole. The long sleeve can be gathered into a cuff, left straight and loose at the wrist or simply made plain and short. There is a choice of classic shirt collar set into a neck band, or a Peter Pan collar, and the neck band on its own provides yet another neckline style. One or two patch pockets can be put on the shirt front. The collar and cuffs can be made in contrast fabric; they can be made double; they can be bound or piped; or they can be cut on the cross.

Use small buttons on the band, spacing out 5, 6 or 7 no bigger than 1cm (⅜in.) in diameter, and make corresponding vertical buttonholes in the centre of the band. The cuffs and band have been cut the correct width to be interfaced with light Fold-a-Band (Fuse 'n' Fold); use light or soft iron-on or sew-in Vilene (Pellon) in the collars with two layers in the band if extra crispness is required.

Make the shirt in printed, yarn-dyed or plain Tana lawn, Country cotton, Jubilee or crêpe de chine, or even in Varuna wool for winter.

The shirt can be matched or contrasted with any of the skirts or with trousers or shorts.

Variations
Lengthen the front, back and band to thigh length or mid-calf for a robe or nightshirt (see page 110), to below the knee for a classic button-through shirtwaister (see page 112), or shorten it to the cut-off line and attach it to the low-waist skirt provided to make a low-waisted loose smock (see page 104). Add front patch pockets or side seam pockets to the longer versions as alternatives to a top pocket.

STRAIGHT SKIRT

A calf-length figure-fitting skirt with front panel and pleats. The skirt fastens at the back with a zip (zipper) and a button or Velcro. The band has been cut the correct width for firm Fold-a-Band (Fuse 'n' Fold); alternatively petersham (grosgrain or milliner's ribbon) or other waistband stiffening can be used. The knife pleats are crisply pressed and top-stitched. Pockets can be inserted into one or both side seams. To line the skirt, cut the back pattern in lining, cut the front pieces in lining but omit the pleats, leaving a slit in the lining the same depth as the pleat.

Make the skirt in plain or yarn-dyed Liberty Varuna wool, or in Liberty Wandel. Wear it with any version of the shirt or with the V-neck top.

Variations
The front pleats may be omitted. Stitch the panel seams, press and top-stitch. You may need more room for movement in the hem of this version — if so, add extra fabric at the centre back seam when cutting out and make a kick pleat.

A-LINE SKIRT

A softly styled flattering skirt with gentle gathering at the waist (see page 97). It fastens with a zip and button at the centre back, using the same waistband as for the straight skirt. Seam pockets can be inserted in the sides or perhaps patch pockets on the front. To line the skirt cut the front and back pattern in lining fabric.

Make the A-line skirt in Varuna wool or in Country cotton, crêpe de chine or Wandel.

Wear it to match or tone with any version of the shirt or with the V-neck top.

Variations
Cut full length and make with a hemline slit in the left side seam for evening wear (see page 101).

GATHERED SKIRT

A full dirndl-style skirt gathered into a waistband, with zip at centre back and side seam pockets (see page 103).

Make the skirt in Tana lawn or Country cotton and wear it with any version of the shirt or with the V-neck top.

Variations
The possibilities for variation and decoration are endless. Just adding a belt or cummerbund in a plain fabric, or perhaps a sash of another toning Liberty print, will give a matching skirt and blouse quite a different look. Changes to the skirt itself might include an elastic waistband, patch pockets, hemline tucks, hemline frill (flounce), two layered skirts, an apron skirt over the basic skirt (see page 100), and so on.

CIRCULAR SKIRT

A swirling circular skirt gathered into a waistband with zip at centre back and pockets in the side seams (see page 111). Make it in Tana lawn or Country cotton.

Variations
Omit the zip, cut the waistband longer than the pattern and attach it in the usual way but without interfacing. Thread wide elastic through the band and pull it up to waist size. Make the skirt shorter and attach a deep frill (flounce) at hemline or use a frill to lengthen the skirt to mid-calf.

Variations in decoration are wide and include a bound hem, narrow ribbon tucks on the frill, patch pockets with tucks, binding or lace edging. Wear the skirt with the shirt or top in matching or contrasting print; add a wide sash or make a stiffened cummerbund.

JACKET

A side-fastening jacket with shaped stand collar, dropped shoulder and deep armhole (see page 98). It fastens with rouleau loops and buttons on one corner of the lapel.

Make the jacket unlined or lined in quilted fabric (see page 99), Varuna wool, crêpe de chine or Tana lawn. Bind the outer edges with matching or contrasting fabric or with matt or satin binding. Wear it with a skirt or trousers.

Variations
Make the jacket in print using a contrasting fabric for the front facings and inside the collar; the sleeves could also be faced in contrast to make turn-back cuffs.

Wear it buttoned, loose or belted, with one or both lapels turned back. Lengthen the hem to cover the hips, to coat length, or even to ankle length.

TROUSERS

Easy-fitting straight-legged trousers with elasticated waist and side seam pockets (see page 99). To line the trousers cut front and back pattern pieces in lining, join the seams and hold both fabrics together at the waist.

Make the trousers in plain, printed or yarn-dyed Varuna wool, in Country cotton, in crêpe de chine or in Wandel. Wear them with the jacket or V-neck top or with the shirt.

Variations
Cut-off lines are shown for shorts, long shorts and knee-length shorts and French knickers; or crop the trousers above the ankle in Varuna wool or Country cotton.

V-NECK TOP

An easy top with shaped neckline and bust darts for a good comfortable fit. The neck and armholes are faced.

Variations
The neck and armholes may be finished with matching or contrast binding. A panel of decoration can be added to the centre front by working vertical pin tucks, flat tucks or twin-needle stitching, or by attaching lines of lace or ribbon. Work the decoration before cutting out if possible as the amount by which the fabric is drawn up will vary.

Make the top in Tana lawn, Country cotton or crêpe de chine. Wear it with trousers, shorts or any of the skirts, or make a drop-waist sundress by attaching the low-waist skirt (see page 105).

GATHERED DRESS

A loose-fitting, round-yoked dress with full skirt and sleeves (see page 109). It has a tie neckline and the yoke fastens with buttons and rouleau loops. Pockets can be inserted in the side seams.

Make it in printed Varuna wool with plain contrast piping round yoke and cuffs, in Country cotton, or in plain Varuna wool.

Variations

This style can be elegant and sophisticated or casual and pretty. You can shorten the dress to tunic length and make it with three-quarter sleeves and plain round neck; or with a detachable collar and wear it over a gathered skirt (see page 103).

The possibilities for decoration on any version of this dress are legion. Quilt the yoke and cuffs, or pad part of the print and add beads. The hem can be bound or tucked; add patch pockets or rows of narrow ribbon or both. Attach the wide flat collar or add a lace crochet collar. A band of smocking could be worked on the sleeves above the cuffs.

The dress could be shorter still and worn with trousers or it can be made ankle length. It is also an ideal pattern for maternity wear.

STRAIGHT DRESS

A simple shape with optional wide flat tuck across the front, extended shoulder and deep armhole (see page 102). It can be made sleeveless or with three-quarter-length sleeves. The dress fastens at the left shoulder seam with 3 buttons and rouleau loops, or with Velcro. To line it use the same pattern pieces and hold together at the shoulder seams. Omit the tuck from the lining.

Make the dress in Varuna wool, Country cotton or crêpe de chine.

Variations

Make the dress ankle length with hemline slit and omit the sleeves (see page 111). Make it in crêpe de chine or Country cotton and wear it with a wide ribbon or fabric sash.

The pattern can also be made tunic-length and belted over trousers or the straight skirt, or a glamorous cowl-back tunic can be made using the dress front pattern (see page 101). Seam pockets may be inserted in any versions.

BIKINI

A brief bra top and pants with bound edges and rouleau straps (see page 129), which can be worn as lingerie or for the beach. Although like all the patterns the bikini is sized up to 20, there may be insufficient support in the bra for a large bust. Cups can be inserted in a bikini top but it would not be advisable for large sizes to wear this pattern as lingerie. Use double thickness Tana lawn with contrast bindings, or the bikini could be made in Country cotton as an alternative fabric.

ROMPERS

Practical baby's rompers for the six- to twelve-month age group with short bound sleeves and collar. The leg section is gathered on to a yoke and fastened with 3 buttons at the back. Make the rompers in Jubilee or Tana lawn. Contrast piping can be inserted in yoke and outer edge of collar. See page 108.

CHILD'S DRESS

Size 1-6 (Age 1-6)
A little girl's classic dress with yoke, gathered skirt, full sleeves and Peter Pan collar for ages one to six years. The dress fastens at the back with 3 buttons on the yoke and an opening in the skirt. Sleeve edges are bound and have elastic in the wrists. Make the dress in Tana lawn or Jubilee. See pages 104 and 112.

Variations

The skirt is full and allows for smocking; select stranded embroidery threads to match or tone with the fabric.

The sleeves can be short, the neckline can be plain bound, hemline tucks can be added to the skirt; a long version for parties or for a bridesmaid can be made by cutting the skirt to ankle length and adding a wide sash.

Use the same skirt pattern to make a pinafore with the yoke pattern in tissue; make the yoke double and omit the collar, add frills to the armholes and replace the back buttons with fabric ties. The pinafore can then be worn over the dress and, if the pinafore hem is tucked, it shortens it attractively above the dress hem.

Fabric Quantities and Haberdashery

The first chart below shows the amount of fabric required for each pattern size for the clothes shown in the photographs. Remember to adjust the quantity you buy when making your own variations.

The easiest way to make the calculation is to use a cutting board. The board will be marked with various fabric widths and with metres (yards) on the longer edge. Lay out the pattern pieces you intend to use, already adjusted for length, and matching straight grain arrows to lengthwise lines on the board. If some pieces of pattern have to be cut twice it is worth making another copy of that piece to make sure it is not forgotten. Read off the amount of fabric required at the edge of the board.

The second chart gives a comprehensive breakdown of haberdashery and other 'extras' needed for making each garment as shown. Your own variations may require other items.

SHIRT

Long sleeve; shirt collar; pocket — Page 75

in.	cm	8/10	12	14	16	18	20
36	90	3.10 / 3⅛yd	3.15 / 3¼yd	3.15 / 3¼yd	3.20 / 3½yd	3.25 / 3⅝yd	3.30 / 3⅝yd
45	115	2.10 / 2¼yd	2.15 / 2⅜yd	2.25 / 2½yd	2.30 / 2½yd	2.35 / 2⅝yd	2.45 / 2¾yd

Short sleeve; round collar — Page 132

in.	cm	8/10	12	14	16	18	20
36	90	2.45 / 2¾yd	2.50 / 2¾yd	2.50 / 2¾yd	2.55 / 2¾yd	2.60 / 2⅞yd	2.65 / 2⅞yd
45	115	1.90 / 2⅛yd	1.90 / 2⅛yd	1.95 / 2⅛yd	2.00 / 2⅛yd	2.10 / 2¼yd	2.20 / 2¼yd
54	137	1.50 / 1⅝yd	1.50 / 1⅝yd	1.50 / 1⅝yd	1.60 / 1¾yd	1.60 / 1¾yd	1.70 / 1⅞yd

Long sleeve; two pockets; contrast collar and cuffs — Page 115

in.	cm	8/10	12	14	16	18	20
36	90	2.60 / 2⅞yd	2.65 / 2⅞yd	2.70 / 3yd	2.75 / 3yd	2.75 / 3yd	2.80 / 3⅛yd
45	115	1.95 / 2⅛yd	2.05 / 2¼yd	2.10 / 2¼yd	2.20 / 2⅜yd	2.30 / 2½yd	2.35 / 2⅝yd

STRAIGHT SKIRT

Front panel; seam pockets — Page 118

in.	cm	8/10	12	14	16	18	20
36	90	1.70 / 1⅞yd	1.70 / 1⅞yd	1.70 / 1⅞yd	1.70 / 1⅞yd	1.75 / 1⅞yd	1.80 / 2yd
45	115	1.70 / 1⅞yd	1.70 / 1⅞yd	1.70 / 1⅞yd	1.70 / 1⅞yd	1.70 / 1⅞yd	1.70 / 1⅞yd
54	137	.95 / 1yd	1.00 / 1⅛yd	1.05 / 1⅛yd	1.15 / 1¼yd	1.30 / 1⅜yd	1.50 / 1½yd
60	150	.95 / 1yd	.95 / 1yd	.95 / 1yd	.95 / 1yd	.95 / 1yd	.95 / 1yd

Pleats; seam pockets — Page 115

in.	cm	8/10	12	14	16	18	20
36	90	1.70 / 1⅞yd	1.70 / 1⅞yd	1.70 / 1⅞yd	1.80 / 2yd	2.05 / 2yd	2.25 / 2½yd
45	115	1.70 / 1⅞yd	1.70 / 1⅞yd	1.70 / 1⅞yd	1.70 / 1⅞yd	1.70 / 1⅞yd	1.75 / 1⅞yd
54	137	1.40 / 1½yd	1.50 / 1½yd	1.60 / 1¾yd	1.65 / 1⅞yd	1.75 / 1⅞yd	1.80 / 2yd

A-LINE SKIRT

Below knee — Page 75

in.	cm	8/10	12	14	16	18	20
54	137	1.70 / 1⅞yd	1.70 / 1⅞yd	2.10 / 2⅜yd	2.10 / 2⅜yd	2.10 / 2⅜yd	2.10 / 2⅜yd

Ankle length; hemline slit — Page 85

in.	cm	8/10	12	14	16	18	20
36	90	4.85 / 5⅜yd	4.85 / 5⅜yd	5.10 / 5⅝yd	5.10 / 5⅝yd	5.10 / 5⅝yd	5.10 / 5⅝yd

BUTTON-THROUGH DRESS

Bias band and cuffs — Page 135

in.	cm	8/10	12	14	16	18	20
36	90	4.50 / 4⅞yd	4.55 / 4⅞yd	4.60 / 5yd	4.75 / 5⅛yd	4.85 / 5⅜yd	5.00 / 5½yd

ROBE

Band collar; ankle length; pockets and belt — Page 127

in.	cm	8/10	12	14	16	18	20
36	90	4.65 / 5⅛yd	4.70 / 5⅛yd	4.90 / 5⅜yd	4.90 / 5⅜yd	4.95 / 5½yd	5 / 5½yd

STRAIGHT DRESS

Seam pockets; sash; sleeveless; long length — Page 131

in.	cm	8/10	12	14	16	18	20
36	90	3.45 / 3¾yd	3.55 / 3⅞yd	3.80 / 4½yd	3.80 / 4¼yd	4.65 / 5¼yd	4.65 / 5¼yd

Long sleeves — Page 88

in.	cm	8/10	12	14	16	18	20
54	137	3.50 / 3⅞yd	3.55 / 3⅞yd	3.55 / 3⅞yd	3.60 / 4yd	3.60 / 4yd	3.60 / 4yd

Tunic; cowl back; belt — Page 85

in.	cm	8/10	12	14	16	18	20
36	90	3.25 / 3⅝yd	3.25 / 3⅝yd	3.45 / 3¾yd	3.45 / 3¾yd	3.55 / 3⅞yd	3.55 / 3⅞yd

V-NECK TOP

Front pin tucks; faced neck — Page 84

in.	cm	8/10	12	14	16	18	20
36	90	1.75 / 1⅞yd	1.80 / 2yd	1.85 / 2yd	1.90 / 2⅛yd	1.90 / 2⅛yd	2.00 / 2⅛yd

SUNDRESS

Gathered skirt; patch pockets — Page 113

in.	cm	8/10	12	14	16	18	20
45	115	3.70 / 4¼yd	3.75 / 4½yd	3.75 / 4½yd	3.75 / 4½yd	3.80 / 4½yd	3.80 / 4½yd

JACKET

Quilted — Page 80

in.	cm	8/10	12	14	16	18	20
54	137	1.70 / 1⅞yd	1.70 / 1⅞yd	1.75 / 1⅞yd	1.75 / 1⅞yd	1.80 / 2yd	1.80 / 2yd

Print with contrast facings — Page 78

in.	cm	8/10	12	14	16	18	20
45	115	1.80 / 2yd	1.85 / 2yd	1.85 / 2yd	1.90 / 2⅛yd	1.90 / 2⅛yd	1.90 / 2⅛yd

Contrast

in.	cm	8/10	12	14	16	18	20
36	90	.70 / ¾yd	.75 / ⅞yd	.75 / ⅞yd	.75 / ⅞yd	.75 / ⅞yd	.75 / ⅞yd

in.	cm	8/10	12	14	16	18	20
GATHERED DRESS							
Seam pockets; tie neck; long sleeve							Page 124
54	137	4.40 4⅞yd	4.40 4⅞yd	4.55 5⅛yd	5.40 5⅞yd	6.05 6⅝yd	6.05 6⅝yd
Short; patch pockets; ¾ sleeve							Page 90
36	90	5.10 5⅝yd	5.20 5¾yd	5.20 5¾yd	5.50 6yd	5.65 6¼yd	5.75 6⅜yd
GATHERED SKIRT							
Skirt							Page 90
36	90	4.00 4⅜yd	4.00 4⅜yd	4.00 4⅜yd	4.00 4⅜yd	4.00 4⅜yd	4.00 4⅜yd
Overskirt							Page 83
36	90	3.40 3¾yd	3.40 3¾yd	3.40 3¾yd	3.40 3¾yd	3.40 3¾yd	3.40 3¾yd
BANDEAU TOP AND LONG SHORTS							
All versions							Page 113
36	90	3.25 3⅝yd	3.25 3⅝yd	3.30 3⅝yd	3.30 3⅝yd	3.35 3¾yd	3.35 3¾yd
CIRCULAR SKIRT							
Seam pockets							Page 113
36	90	4.10 4½yd	4.10 4½yd	4.10 4½yd	4.10 4½yd	4.10 4½yd	4.10 4½yd
45	115	4.10 4½yd	4.10 4½yd	4.10 4½yd	4.10 4½yd	4.10 4½yd	4.10 4½yd
54	137	4.10 4½yd	4.10 4½yd	4.10 4½yd	4.10 4½yd	4.10 4½yd	4.10 4½yd
Elastic waist; patch pockets							Page 92
36	90	4.10 4½yd	4.10 4½yd	4.10 4½yd	4.10 4½yd	4.10 4½yd	4.10 4½yd
45	115	4.10 4½yd	4.10 4½yd	4.10 4½yd	4.10 4½yd	4.10 4½yd	4.10 4½yd
54	137	4.10 4½yd	4.10 4½yd	4.10 4½yd	4.10 4½yd	4.10 4½yd	4.10 4½yd
DROP-WAIST DRESS							
Peter Pan collar; short sleeve; pockets							Page 93
36	90	4.10 4½yd	4.15 4⅝yd	4.35 4¾yd	4.60 4⅞yd	4.60 4⅞yd	4.65 4⅞yd
TROUSERS							
Seam pockets							Page 80
54	137	2.35 2⅝yd	2.35 2⅝yd	2.40 2⅝yd	2.50 2¾yd	2.50 2¾yd	2.60 2⅞yd
Cropped							Page 78
60	150	2.05 2¼yd	2.05 2¼yd	2.05 2¼yd	2.15 2⅜yd	2.20 2½yd	2.20 2½yd

in.	cm	8/10	12	14	16	18	20
Long shorts with pockets; facings							113
36	90	2.05 2¼yd	2.05 2¼yd	2.15 2⅜yd	2.15 2⅜yd	2.20 2½yd	2.20 2½yd
45	115	1.50 1⅝yd	1.50 1⅝yd	1.50 1⅝yd	1.55 1⅝yd	1.85 2yd	1.85 2yd
French knickers							127
36	90	1.10 1¼yd	1.10 1¼yd	1.10 1¼yd	1.10 1¼yd	1.50 1⅝yd	1.50 1⅝yd
BIKINI							
Lined in self fabric							Page 129
36	90	1.80 2yd	1.80 2yd	1.90 2⅛yd	1.90 2⅛yd	2.00 2¼yd	2.00 2¼yd

Contrast 80cm (⅞yd) all sizes.

in.	cm	8/10	12	14	16	18	20
DETACHABLE BOW							Page 76
36	90	1.35 1½yd	1.35 1½yd	1.35 1½yd	1.35 1½yd	1.35 1½yd	1.35 1½yd
45	115	1.35 1½yd	1.35 1½yd	1.35 1½yd	1.35 1½yd	1.35 1½yd	1.35 1½yd
CUMMERBUND							Page 20
36	90	.25 ¼yd	.25 ¼yd	.25 ¼yd	.25 ¼yd	.25 ¼yd	.25 ¼yd
45	115	.25 ¼yd	.25 ¼yd	.25 ¼yd	.25 ¼yd	.25 ¼yd	.25 ¼yd
T-SHIRT							Page 83
36	90	1.70 1⅞yd	1.80 2yd	1.80 2yd	1.80 2yd	1.85 2⅛yd	1.85 2⅛yd
CHILD'S DRESS							
Collar; long sleeve. Sizes 1-6 years							Pages 93 and 135
36	90	2.00 2¼yd	2.15 2⅜yd	2.45 2⅝yd	2.50 2¾yd	2.65 3yd	2.90 3¼yd
Collar; short sleeve							Page 95
36	90	1.80 2yd	1.95 2⅛yd	2.00 2¼yd	2.25 2½yd	2.45 2⅝yd	2.60 2⅞yd
CHILD'S PINAFORE							
Frilled armhole; hemline tucks							Page 135
36	90	1.70 1⅞yd	1.85 2yd	2.15 2⅜yd	2.20 2⅜yd	2.40 2⅝yd	2.45 2⅝yd
ROMPERS							ONE SIZE
Collar; short sleeve 6-12months							Page 121
36	90	1.05 1⅛yd					

LININGS THROUGHOUT

As for main fabric but omit sleeves

NOTIONS AND HABERDASHERY

Allow 2 reels of thread each; more if the design includes tucks

Garment	Version	Vilene (Pellon)	Fold-a-Band (Fuse 'n' Fold) for bands, cuffs, pocket tops	Waist-banding	Elastic	Zip (zipper)	Buttons	Fastening	Extras
SHIRT	Shirt collar, Long sleeves, pocket	Collar & pockets 50 x 20cm (20 x 8in.)	2m 10cm (2¼yd) soft				9 x 7mm (¼in.)	1 press stud (snap)	
	Short sleeves, Peter Pan collar	35 x 20cm (14 x 8in.)	1m 30 (51in.) soft				6 x 1cm (⅜in.)	1 press stud (snap)	Narrow ribbon
	Shirt collar, pocket, bow	50 x 20cm (20 x 8in.)	1m 30 (51in.) soft				7 x 1cm (⅜in.)	Velcro for neck bow	
	Band collar, pocket	50 x 10cm (20 x 4in.)	2m 10 (2¼yd) soft				6 x 1cm (⅜in.)		Cuff links or 4 extra buttons
STRAIGHT SKIRT	Pleated, pockets	for pockets 30 x 35cm (18 x 15in.)	for pleats 110cm (43in.) soft	waist length		20cm (8in.)	1 x 13mm (½in.)	Large hook or Velcro	Wundaweb (Stitch Witchery) for hem
	Panelled, pockets	for pockets 36 x 35cm (18 x 15in.)		waist length		20cm (8in.)	1 x 13mm (½in.)	Large hook or Velcro	Wundaweb (Stitch Witchery) for hem
BUTTON-THROUGH DRESS	Long sleeve, shirt collar, pockets	50 x 20cm (20 x 8in.)	2m 70 (3yd) soft				12 x 13mm (½in.)	1 press stud (snap)	Belt backing 1m (39in.); clasp or buckle
DROP-WAIST DRESS	Short sleeve, Peter Pan collar, pockets	65 x 30cm (26 x 12in.)	1m (39in.)				6 x 6mm (¼in.)	1 press stud (snap)	Embroidery thread
GATHERED SKIRT	Layered		Waist length					Large hook or Velcro	
	Elastic waist	30 x 35cm (12 x 14in.)			Waist length 2-3cm wide (¾-1¼in.)				
CIRCULAR SKIRT		30 x 35cm (12 x 14in.)	Waist length			20cm (8in.)		Large hook or Velcro	Optional ribbon 3mm (⅛in.) wide
COWL TOP		40 x 13cm (16 x 5in.)					3 small ball buttons		1 small dress weight for cowl
STRAIGHT DRESS	Sleeveless, pockets	50 x 40cm (20 x 16in.)					3 small ball buttons		
	Tuck; long sleeves, pockets	50 x 40cm (20 x 16in.)					3 small ball buttons		
T-SHIRT		45 x 25cm (18 x 10in.)							
GATHERED DRESS	Long sleeves, full length	45 x 45cm (18 x 18in.)					11 x 10mm (⅜in.)	1 small hook	
ROBE	Band collar, 2 pockets	48 x 10cm (19 x 4in.)	3m 20 (3yd 8in.)						
JACKET	Quilted	70 x 60cm (27 x 24in.)					3 x 13mm (½in.)	Small piece of Velcro 1 press stud (snap)	4m 50 satin binding (4⅞yd)
	Print	70 x 60cm (27 x 24in.)					1 x 15mm (⅝in.)		
V-NECK TOP							3 x 6mm (¼in.)		
SUNDRESS			38cm (15in.)						

Garment	Version	Vilene (Pellon)	Fold-a-Band (Fuse 'n' Fold) for bands, cuffs, pocket tops	Waist-banding	Elastic	Zip (zipper)	Buttons	Fastening	Extras
TROUSERS AND SHORTS		30 x 35cm (12 x 14in.)			Waist length 2.5cm (1in.) wide				Wundaweb (Stitch Witchery) for hems Lace edging for French knickers
BIKINI	Bra and pants				2.50m (2¾yd) narrow				
A-LINE SKIRT		30 x 35cm (12 x 14in.)	Waist length			20cm (8in)			
	Smock ¾ sleeves	85 x 55cm (33 x 22in.)	Approx 80cm for cuffs (32in.)				6 x 10mm (⅜in.)	1 small hook	Optional narrow ribbon for trimming
CHILD'S DRESS		25 x 25cm (10 x 10in.)			15cm (6in.) narrow		3 x 6mm (¼in.)	2 small press studs (snaps)	Optional: Narrow ribbon, stranded embroidery thread for smocking, lace edging
PINAFORE									Stranded embroidery thread for smocking
ROMPERS		25 x 25cm (10 x 10in.)			25cm (10in.) narrow		6 x 6mm (¼in.)	2 small press studs (snaps)	
RABBIT		15 x 15cm (6 x 6in.)							Felt or wool, embroidery thread, Kapok or stuffing
SEPARATE ROUND COLLAR FOR SMOCK		35 x 48cm (14 x 15in.)							Narrow ribbon

Using the Tissue Patterns

The tissue patterns in the back of the book are printed and they are multi-size. The advantage of this is that they can be used for more than one person and also if you are out of proportion you can use a differently sized top and skirt to achieve a better fit.

Once you have selected the garment and are quite sure of the appropriate size, locate the pattern pieces required as listed for the garment and cut them out, trimming accurately on the printed line using old or blunt scissors or those that you keep for cutting paper.

BALANCE MARKS

Balance marks or notches are indicated by printed diamonds: cut through them, keeping a smooth edge to the pattern piece. It is time consuming and unnecessary to cut them outwards. Transfer the essential balance marks to the fabric after cutting out.

Smooth each piece of pattern with a cool dry iron immediately before placing on the fabric – it will adhere slightly and lie flatter than when cold.

If the patterns are likely to be needed in other sizes do not cut up the tissue but trace off the pieces using a pencil and sheets of pattern drafting paper or greaseproof paper, or better still using light-weight sew-in Vilene and a felt-tip pen. Use a ruler for all straight lines. Curves are easier to draw as dotted lines although a French curve is a valuable tool. Copy on to each piece all the information printed on the tissue including the size you have traced.

Cut the pieces out and place on the fabric ready to pin in position, following the layout diagram shown or the one you have worked out for your own variation.

How to Cut Patterns from Diagrams

Diagram patterns are drawn to scale. Each square on the grid represents 2.5cm (1in.). All measurements are to the nearest 5mm (¼in.).

You will need a supply of large sheets of paper. This can be graph paper or plain paper on which you rule a grid of 2.5cm (1in.) squares, or have one sheet of printed graph paper and use it as a grid, pinning plain paper over it on which to draw the patterns. An even better alternative, if you are going to make patterns frequently, is to buy a folding sewing board and put sheets of plain paper over the grid. This has the added advantage of providing a large, smooth, firm surface for making patterns as well as for cutting out and sewing.

Use a pencil or felt-tip pen with a long ruler. It is also useful to have a French curve to help with necklines and armholes.

With all patterns it is vital to work logically, starting by copying the points at the edges of the diagrams and drawing in any obviously easy parts such as straight lines. However, all the diagram patterns in the book are simple and loose or full so it will not prove disastrous if your lines are not quite perfect. Some inaccuracies will also be corrected when you cut the paper. After cutting the pattern pieces, check that seam edges to be matched are equal in length. If it is the first time you have copied diagram patterns and you are unsure of your skill, it is worth pinning up the main pattern pieces to see how the fit looks and to try it on before cutting the fabric. In any case, tack up and fit the garment.

After drawing all the pieces copy all markings and notes shown in the book, including straight grain lines, balance marks or notches and dots, centre front, centre back, fold, etc. Identify each piece clearly and include your size.

Making Up the Diagram Patterns

This section gives specific information relating to making the diagram patterns, and also the additional belts, bows and sashes shown in the colour photographs on pages 97-112.

THE A-LINE SKIRT

Select the size and length required from the chart.

Size	A-B		Shorter skirt A-C		Long skirt A-D		Shorter skirt extend to E		Longer skirt extend to F	
	cm	in.	cm	in.	cm	in.	cm	in.	cm	in.
8/10	41	16¼	76	30	107	42¼	4.5	1¾	6	2¾
12	42.5	16¾	76.5	30¼	108	42½	as above throughout		as above throughout	
14	44	17⅜	77	30⅜	108.5	42¾				
16	45.5	18	77.5	30½	109.5	43				
18	47	18½	78	30¾	110.5	43½				
20	48.5	19¼	78.5	31	115.5	44				

The skirt back and front are alike, so put two pieces of paper on top of each other. Taking measurements shown above, draw lines A-B, A-C or A-D and complete the rectangle. Extend the line to E for short skirt or F for long skirt.

Add pocket extension 5cm (2in.) from B. Extension is 1.5cm (⅝in.) wide and 19.5cm (7¾in.) long.

The back has a centre back seam. The front is cut to a seam or a fold depending on fabric width.

THE GATHERED SKIRT

Length of skirt 71cm (28in.). If you want the skirt to be longer or shorter adjust the figures given.

The pattern is simple and can be made in paper or cut directly in fabric.

Draw the centre line on the paper 78cm (30⅜in.) from A-B. Rule a horizontal line from there 88cm (35in.) long. Complete the rectangle. This is the basic length. If you wish to add tucks then make it 7.5cm (3in.) longer from A-B. Add the pocket extension 5cm (2in.) down side seam edge. The extension is 1.5cm (⅝in.) wide and 19.5cm (7¾in.) long. Cut out the pattern.

PATTERN FOR OVERSKIRT

Cut the overskirt the same width as the main skirt but omit pocket extension and make it 10cm (4in.) shorter. The back skirt is cut to a fold and the front to a seam.

PATTERN FOR SKIRT WITH FRILLED HEM

Cut the skirt as for main skirt but only 50cm (20in.) long. For the frill cut a pattern on 4 pieces of fabric 25cm (10in.) deep and the full width of 90cm fabric.

THE TROUSERS AND SHORTS

Decide on the version you want and copy the diagram for the front and back in your size. If making the long shorts make the front and back hem facings.

Mark grain lines, balance marks and label each piece.

If making long or cropped trousers check that the length is right. Cut out the pattern pieces.

Pockets
In our versions the trousers had seam pockets and long shorts were planned with small patch pockets on the back, but they can be varied as you wish. You will find both pocket pattern pieces on the full-size tissue in the back of the book.

THE V-NECK TOP

This top can be worn with any of the skirts and trousers, or the pattern can be combined with the gathered skirt from the full-size tissue patterns to make the drop-waist sundress shown on page 105. Neck and armholes are faced, the facings being finished on either the right or wrong side of the top.

Select your size and copy the front and back patterns. Mark the width of facing on the neck and armholes as shown. Trace off the neckline facing pieces and cut out. Make the armhole facings in one piece by tracing them off with shoulder lines together and overlapping by 3cm (1¼in.) to remove the shoulder seam allowance. Mark the straight grain down centre front and centre back of neckline facings and parallel with underarm seam of the back on the armhole facing.

THE SKIRT PATTERN FOR CHILD'S DRESS

Select the size required and copy the diagram shown. Mark grain lines and fold, etc. The pattern pieces for the back and front yoke, the sleeve and collar are included on the tissue patterns in the back of the book.

THE CHILD'S PINAFORE

The skirt pattern pieces are the same as for the dress, but follow the broken lines for centre back and armhole edges.
   The back and front yoke patterns and the armhole frill pattern are from tissue.

AN ANKLE-LENGTH DRESS AND PINAFORE

Lengthen the skirt pattern pieces by the following amounts when cutting out, or measure the child and extend the length appropriately.

Size 1 cut skirt back and front 1.5cm (⅝in.) longer
Size 2   3.5cm (1⅜in.)
Size 3   6cm (2½in.)
Size 4   6cm (2½in.)
Size 5   6cm (2½in.)
Size 6   7cm (2¾in.)

Cut three pieces of fabric for the hemline frills on the dress 90cm (36in.) long x 18.5cm (7¼ in.) wide.

THE CIRCULAR SKIRT

Begin at one corner of the pattern paper and measure 16.5cm (6½in.) and 90cm (36in.) and mark both quarter circles. Draw a line 1.5cm (⅝in.) inside one edge and add the pocket extension 5cm (2in.) down. This produces a skirt 70.5cm (27¾in.) long. If you want it shorter measure a shorter distance. If you want to add hemline frills measure to only 70cm (27½in.) from the corner.

Frills (flounces) can be cut as follows:
90cm (36in.) fabric: 90cm × 26cm (36in. × 10in.) cut 10 pieces
115cm (45in.) fabric: 115cm × 26cm (45in. × 10in.) cut 8 pieces
137cm (54in.) fabric: 137cm × 26cm (54in. × 10in.) cut 7 pieces

The skirt can be cut directly in fabric. Four sections as shown make one circular skirt. Either fold the fabric and cut the pattern twice to a fold or, with a pronounced one-way fabric, cut each quarter separately and make centre seams.
   The waistband is made to fit using Fold-a-Band (Fuse 'n' Fold) as a guide. The skirt pattern is one-size and gathered into the waistband.

THE GATHERED DRESS

Select your size and draw the pattern pieces for front back and sleeve. To make a complete yoke back pattern, fold the paper before drawing the pattern. Cut tie collar on double paper. Mark all grain lines, balance marks, centre lines, folds etc. Also mark-cut off lines on sleeve, back and front. Draw collar pattern against fold of double paper to make a complete pattern. The collar may be attached to the dress or made detachable.
   You will also need pieces of fabric for loops, piping etc., but there is no need to cut pattern pieces for these. Measurements are given with the making-up instructions.

THE BIKINI

Both bra and pants are made in double fabric, so cutting out will be simplified if you draw the pattern on a folded sheet of paper to produce a complete pattern. Draw the pants with the centre front and centre back edges against the fold and open out after cutting.
   Mark straight grain on all pattern pieces and label them. It will also help to mark the edges of the bra to distinguish side and lower edges.
   Remember that if you do not conform to average shape you can cut a different size top and bottom for a better fit.

THE STRAIGHT DRESS

The front and back are alike, so put two sheets of paper on top of each other and draw the pattern including the back neckline. Draw pattern to length required. Cut out, outline both pieces together. Label one piece back. On the other draw and cut the front neckline and label the piece front.

Draw facing pieces for front and back neckline. For a sleeveless dress draw armhole facings; for a dress with sleeves draw sleeve pattern. Mark all pieces with grain lines etc., label, and cut out.

Both versions of the dress shown in the photographs have side seam pockets cut from the tissue pattern in the back of the book but they may be omitted if you wish. Sash and button loops can be cut directly in fabric without making a pattern piece.

To make the straight dress with a tuck below the shoulder (see page 88), make the pattern for the dress, marking the tuck position on the front as shown. Cut the pattern on this line, open out the pieces and pin to the fabric inserting 10cm (4in.) between the cut edges. Cut out the fabric. Mark the tuck with tailor tacks.

Draw the sleeve pattern. Use the back and neck facings from the other version.

A third version of the straight dress has the same front and sleeve as the long dress but is cut off at the line at hip level to make a tunic top. Draw a new back pattern as shown which drapes into a lovely cowl. The centre section of the back is cut on the cross and the section below that has a centre seam.

The T-shirt top can also be made from the front and back pattern of the long dress but cut off on the hip line. Omit loops and buttons. Sleeve facings are optional. Our version had a narrow hem.

THE COWL TOP

The front pattern and the front neck facing are the same as for the straight dress, but taking the pattern to hip level only. The sleeve is a simple rectangle set into the extended sleeve to provide length to the elbow. Cut the lower back and cowl pieces as shown, marking the straight grain correctly. The neckline has a fold-back facing.

THE RABBIT

Draw the pattern pieces as shown, cut them out and place matching pieces together, e.g. front leg against back leg, body front to body back, trimming the edges level before cutting the fabric.

DETACHABLE BOW

This was made in crêpe de chine, but Tana lawn could also be used. The bow is cut on the cross and stitched to a straight band. The bow slides out for ease of pressing.

Making up

1. Cut out. Cut band and loop on the straight but the bow on the cross. For a bigger bow simply cut it wider.

2. Press light iron-on Vilene to wrong side of neck band. Fold band right sides together and stitch, leaving a gap. Turn through and press. Stitch the gap. Put round neckline of garment under the collar and fit. Sew a Velcro circle to the end to fasten.

3. Join ends of loop. Fold in half and stitch side, leaving a gap. Turn loop right side out and press. Stitch the gap. Stitch back of loop to centre of the neck band.

4. Fold bias tie right sides together, stitch along side and across ends, leaving a gap. Turn right side out; press; stitch gap. Fold tie into a bow and slide it into the loop.

DOUBLE TIE

An optional tie (not illustrated) can be made in any fabric but as there are four thicknesses at the centre it would probably be too bulky in Varuna wool.

Cut a strip of fabric on the cross 125cm (49in.) long and 15cm (6in.) wide. You may have to cut two pieces and join them in the middle. Fold fabric right sides together and stitch across the ends and down the long side leaving a gap. Trim edges, turn tie right side out through the gap. Stitch the gap. Press. Fold tie in half for a distance of 28cm (11in.) at the middle and machine the edges together. Turn through so join is hidden. Press. Wear under the collar of a blouse or dress and tie as a tie or as a bow.

TIE BELT

The belt is 150cm (59in.) long and 6cm (2⅜in.) wide. Make up a pattern, or cut directly in fabric. To make plain ends, cut at an angle of 45° with fabric or paper folded. To make fringed ends make 2½m (96in.) of narrow rouleau, cut it into 14 equal lengths. Place seven at each end of the belt on the right side with raw edges level with belt end and either single or folded double with beads threaded on. Machine in place. Fold belt right sides together, stitch across ends and along side. Trim and turn right side out. Press. Free ends can be knotted or have beads attached.

BOUND TIE BELT WITH ROUNDED ENDS

On double fabric use tailor's chalk and a ruler to draw a rectangle on the straight grain 1.50m (60in.) × 8.5cm (3¼in.). Drawing round a circular shape, such as a saucer, round off the ends. Baste between the chalk lines. Cut out the rectangle but cut *beyond* the rounded ends.

Cut bias strips in matching or contrast fabric to bind the outer edge 3.20m (3½yd) × 2.5cm (1in.). Attach bias to one side on the chalk line. Make the join 20cm (8in.) from the centre on one side. Trim surplus fabric and hem. Press.

SASH

Cut a single piece of fabric on the straight grain 1.50m (60in.) × 8.5cm (3¼in.). Turn a narrow hem all round, stitch and press.

FRILLS

Frills for hemline of gathered skirt are cut as follows:
90cm (36in.) fabric
90cm × 26cm (36in. × 10in.)
Cut 8 and join
115cm (45in.) fabric
115cm × 26cm (45in. × 10in.)
Cut 6 and join
137cm (54in.) fabric
137cm × 26 cm (54in. × 10in.)
Cut 5 and join

THE BANDEAU TOP

Simple tie top in Tana lawn Jackanory lined with plain lawn and bound round the outer edge, worn twisted at the front and tied in a knot at the back.

Cut 2 pieces of fabric on the straight grain 127cm × 20cm (50 × 8 in.) and sufficient bias strips 2.5cm (1in.) long to go all around outer edge.

Making up

1. Cut out. If you make the bandeau with contrast lining it is extravagant of fabric; you could economise by making it from double fabric instead of lining it with plain lawn.

2. Place fabric wrong sides together and machine stitch around outer edge 1cm (⅜in.) from raw edges.

3. Binding. Join the strips. Begin 20cm (8in.) from one end and attach to right side, stitching 1.5cm (⅝in.) from edge. Trim. Join the binding. Finish on wrong side by hemming into machining. Press.

FLAT COLLAR

Making this collar detachable means the gathered dress can be worn in a wider variety of ways, for example, with the buttons open, or with a shirt underneath.

Make collar pattern from diagram, cutting the whole collar by drawing it on folded paper. Cut out. Attach light iron-on interfacing to wrong side of one piece. Tack collars wrong sides together. Bind outer edge with contrast plain fabric. Attach two rows of narrow ribbon 3mm (⅛in.) apart and 6mm (¼in.) from edge. Use remainder of contrast bias fabric to bind neck edge and make ends into long ties, cutting a strip 2m (2¾yd) long and 2.5cm (1in.) wide.

PUFFED BOW

Make in Tana lawn and wear it under the collar of shirts or dresses. Copying the diagram on page 54, either make pattern or cut directly in fabric.

Join the seam at the centre back with a French seam. Roll a narrow hem all round the outer edge. Stitch and press. Fold the back neck section in half before putting it round your neck.

CUMMERBUND

Made in Tana lawn with bound edges, ribbon trim and rouleau streamer, it can be worn over any of the full skirts. Interface it with pelmet Vilene and fasten with large hooks or Velcro.

Diagram pattern
Remember to make a bigger size than your waist measurement to allow for the width of the cummerbund.

Making up

1. Cut 2 pieces of fabric and one of Vilene. Cut 3.5m (4¼yd) of bias strip 2.5cm (1in.) wide.

2. Place Vilene between the two pieces of fabric, baste round edge. Bind the outer edge, mitre the corners and join the ends of the binding at one corner. Attach narrow ribbon to right side, placing it in the seam of the bound edge.

3. Make remaining crossway strip into rouleau. Make a bow and stitch to centre of cummerbund. Knot the ends.

Try on cummerbund. Attach fastening.

EMBROIDERED CUMMERBUND

The distinctive and colourful Liberty print Darlington used for the straight dress (page 102) has a majestic symmetrical motif that makes a focal centrepiece for a cummerbund.

Use the basic cummerbund shape, but before cutting out mark round the part of the motif you want to use with chalk or tacking. Cut out the fabric allowing at least 8cm (3in.) extra all round the selected shape, or more if you are using a hoop. Tack fabric to soft sew-in Vilene. Begin outlining the print design from the centre, using colours that are slightly stronger than those on the fabric. Work lines with stem stitch and use satin stitch for solid areas. Beads can be added to flowers; ends of swirls can be seeded, areas can be filled with French knots.

Make the cummerbund by re-measuring and marking the outline. Cut another piece of fabric the same size and baste pelmet Vilene between the two. Bind the outer edge with contrast fabric. Fasten the back with large hooks or Velcro.

The A-Line Skirt

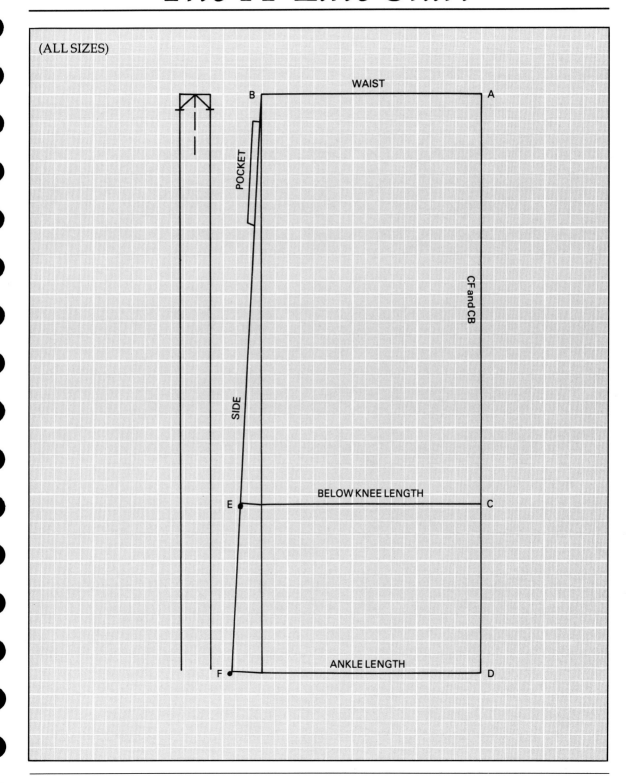

The Gathered Skirt

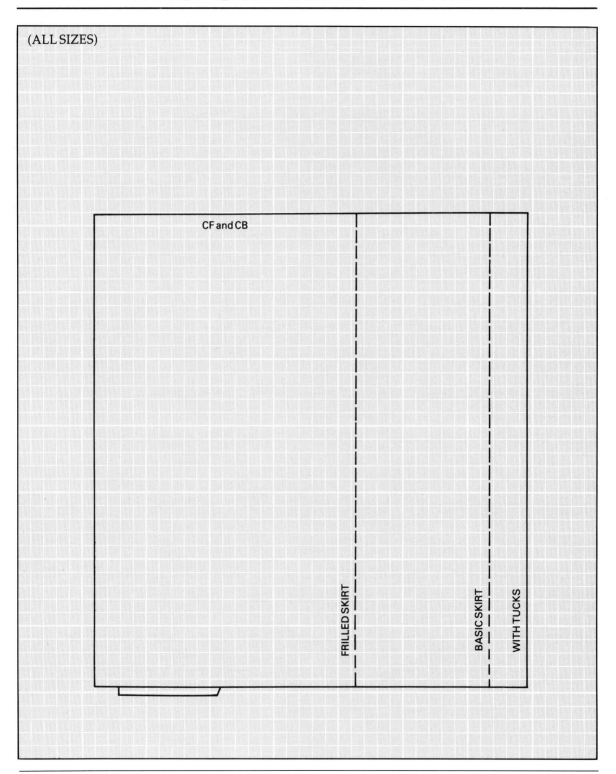

(ALL SIZES)

CF and CB

FRILLED SKIRT

BASIC SKIRT

WITH TUCKS

The Trousers

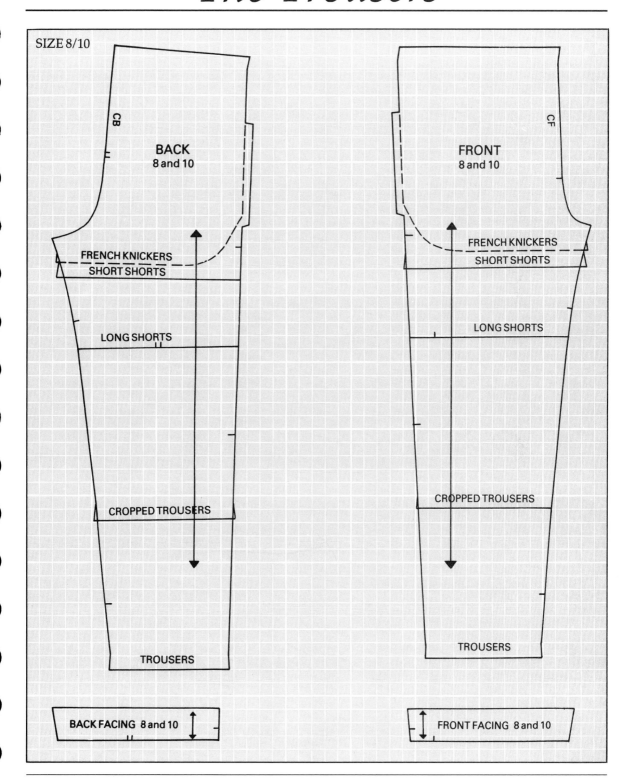

SIZE 8/10

CB

BACK
8 and 10

FRENCH KNICKERS
SHORT SHORTS

LONG SHORTS

CROPPED TROUSERS

TROUSERS

BACK FACING 8 and 10

CF

FRONT
8 and 10

FRENCH KNICKERS
SHORT SHORTS

LONG SHORTS

CROPPED TROUSERS

TROUSERS

FRONT FACING 8 and 10

The Trousers

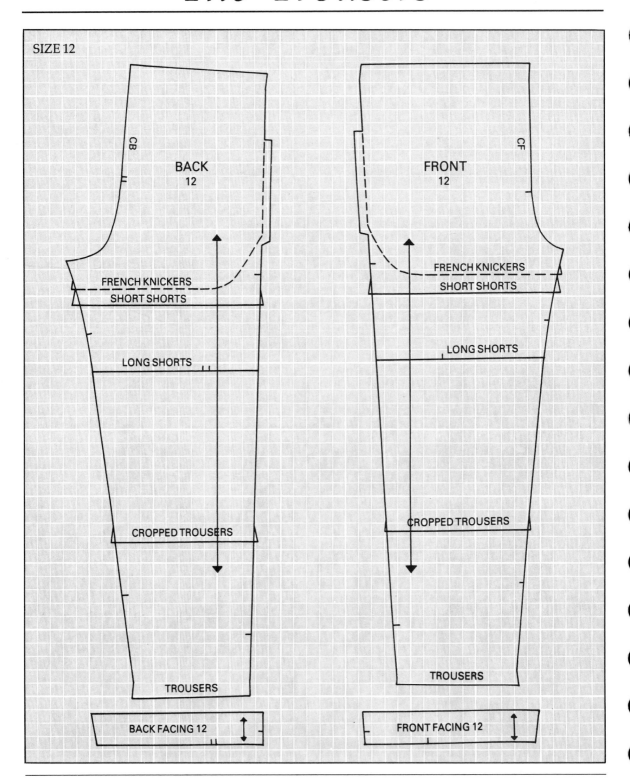

SIZE 12

CB

BACK
12

FRENCH KNICKERS
SHORT SHORTS

LONG SHORTS

CROPPED TROUSERS

TROUSERS

BACK FACING 12

CF

FRONT
12

FRENCH KNICKERS
SHORT SHORTS

LONG SHORTS

CROPPED TROUSERS

TROUSERS

FRONT FACING 12

The Trousers

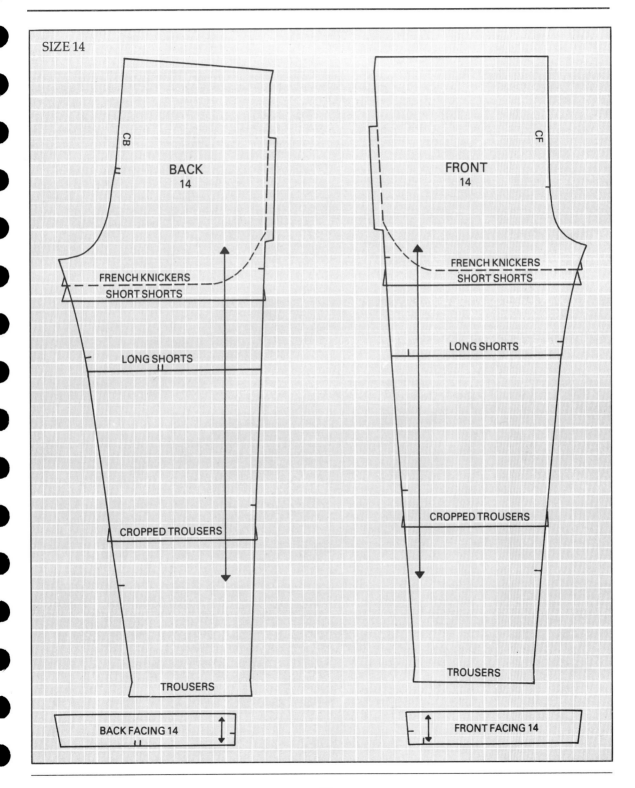

SIZE 14

CB

BACK
14

FRENCH KNICKERS
SHORT SHORTS

LONG SHORTS

CROPPED TROUSERS

TROUSERS

BACK FACING 14

CF

FRONT
14

FRENCH KNICKERS
SHORT SHORTS

LONG SHORTS

CROPPED TROUSERS

TROUSERS

FRONT FACING 14

The Trousers

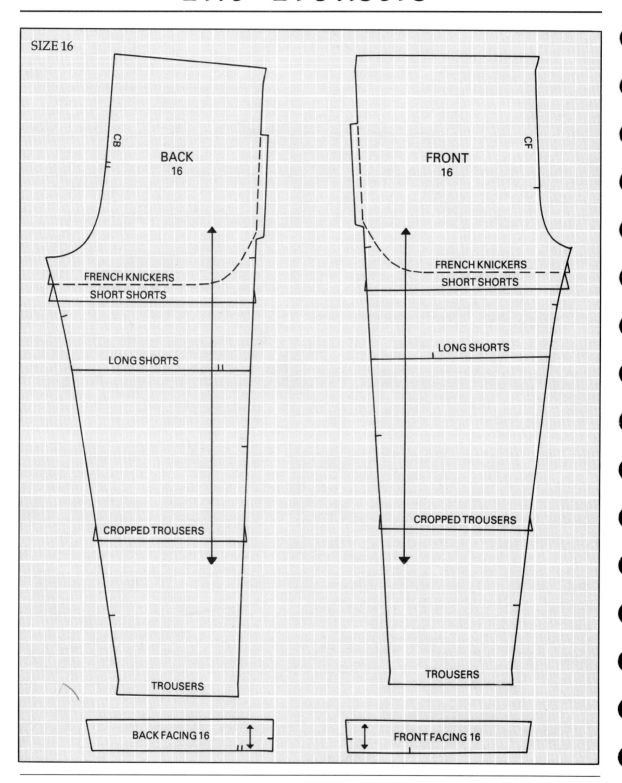

SIZE 16

CB

BACK
16

FRENCH KNICKERS

SHORT SHORTS

LONG SHORTS

CROPPED TROUSERS

TROUSERS

BACK FACING 16

CF

FRONT
16

FRENCH KNICKERS

SHORT SHORTS

LONG SHORTS

CROPPED TROUSERS

TROUSERS

FRONT FACING 16

The Trousers

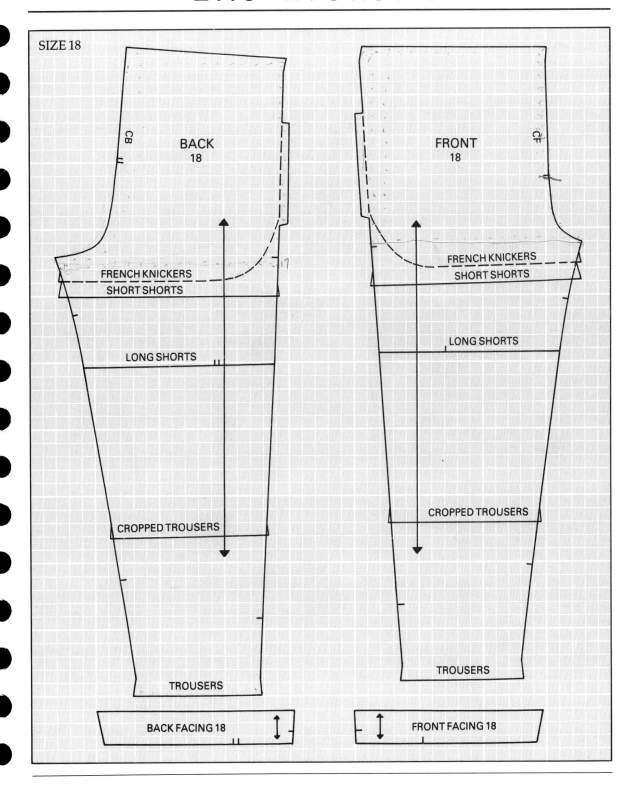

SIZE 18

CB

BACK
18

CF

FRONT
18

FRENCH KNICKERS
SHORT SHORTS

FRENCH KNICKERS
SHORT SHORTS

LONG SHORTS

LONG SHORTS

CROPPED TROUSERS

CROPPED TROUSERS

TROUSERS

TROUSERS

BACK FACING 18

FRONT FACING 18

The Trousers

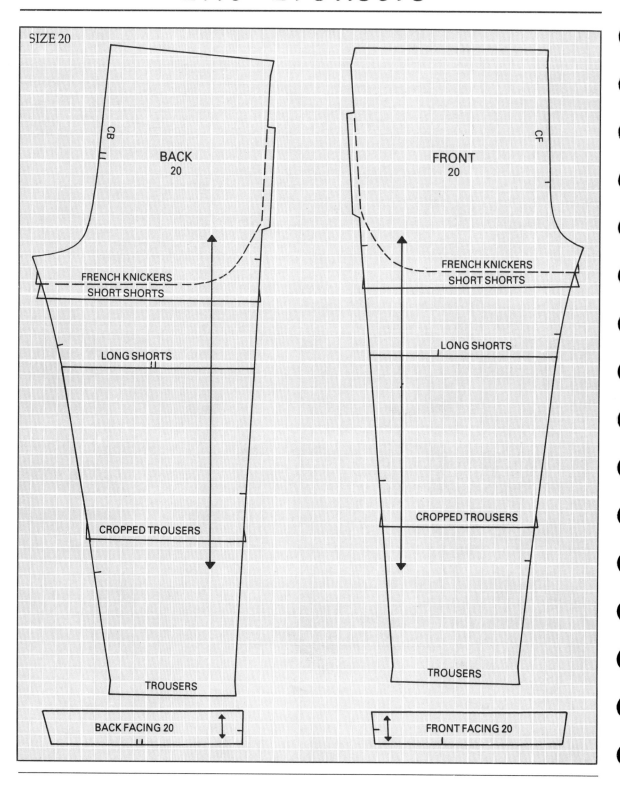

SIZE 20

CB

BACK
20

FRENCH KNICKERS
SHORT SHORTS

LONG SHORTS

CROPPED TROUSERS

TROUSERS

BACK FACING 20

CF

FRONT
20

FRENCH KNICKERS
SHORT SHORTS

LONG SHORTS

CROPPED TROUSERS

TROUSERS

FRONT FACING 20

The V-Neck Top

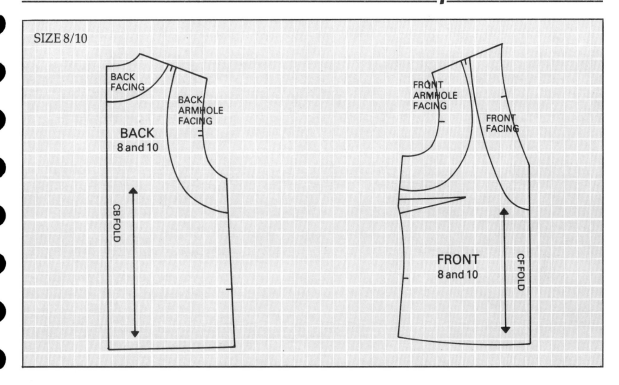

SIZE 8/10

BACK FACING

BACK ARMHOLE FACING

BACK
8 and 10

CB FOLD

FRONT ARMHOLE FACING

FRONT FACING

FRONT
8 and 10

CF FOLD

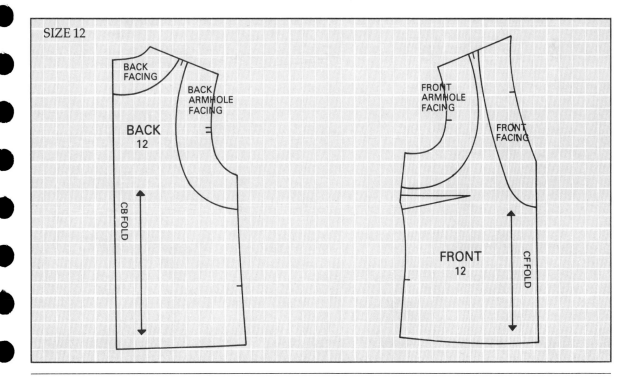

SIZE 12

BACK FACING

BACK ARMHOLE FACING

BACK
12

CB FOLD

FRONT ARMHOLE FACING

FRONT FACING

FRONT
12

CF FOLD

The V-neck Top

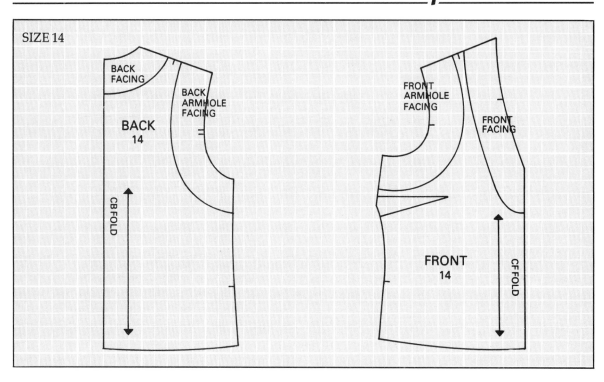

SIZE 14

BACK FACING

BACK ARMHOLE FACING

BACK 14

CB FOLD

FRONT ARMHOLE FACING

FRONT FACING

FRONT 14

CF FOLD

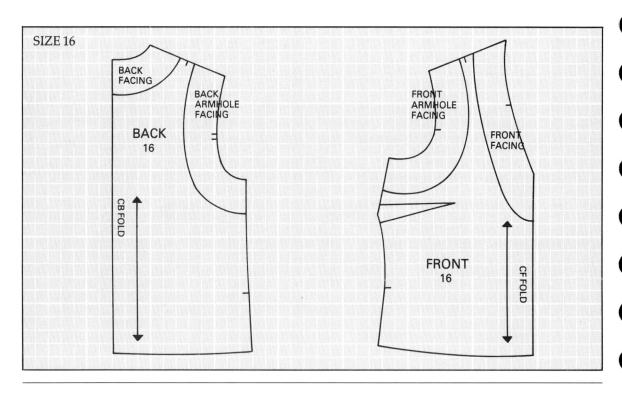

SIZE 16

BACK FACING

BACK ARMHOLE FACING

BACK 16

CB FOLD

FRONT ARMHOLE FACING

FRONT FACING

FRONT 16

CF FOLD

The V-neck Top

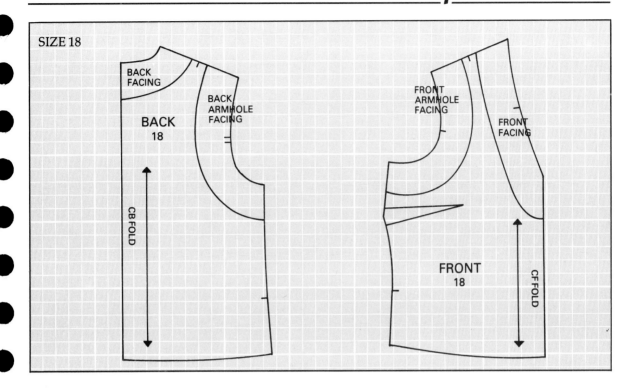

SIZE 18

BACK FACING

BACK ARMHOLE FACING

BACK 18

CB FOLD

FRONT ARMHOLE FACING

FRONT FACING

FRONT 18

CF FOLD

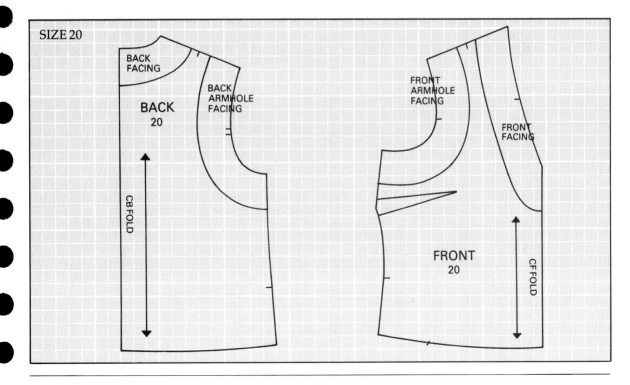

SIZE 20

BACK FACING

BACK ARMHOLE FACING

BACK 20

CB FOLD

FRONT ARMHOLE FACING

FRONT FACING

FRONT 20

CF FOLD

The Child's Dress Skirt

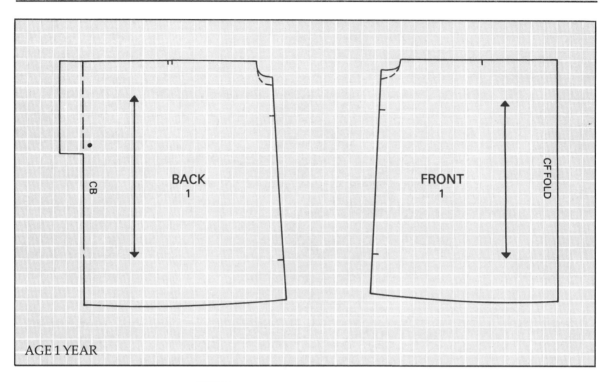

AGE 1 YEAR

(BROKEN LINES ARE CUTTING LINES FOR PINAFORE)

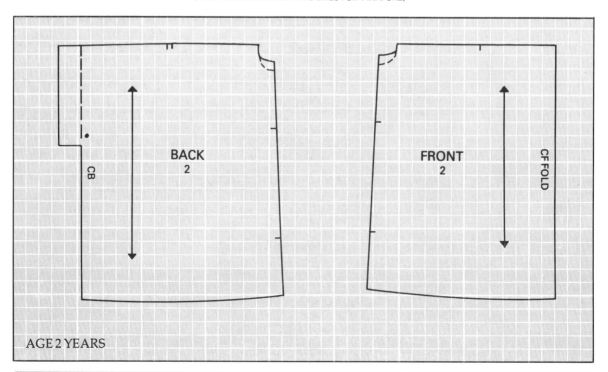

AGE 2 YEARS

The Child's Dress Skirt

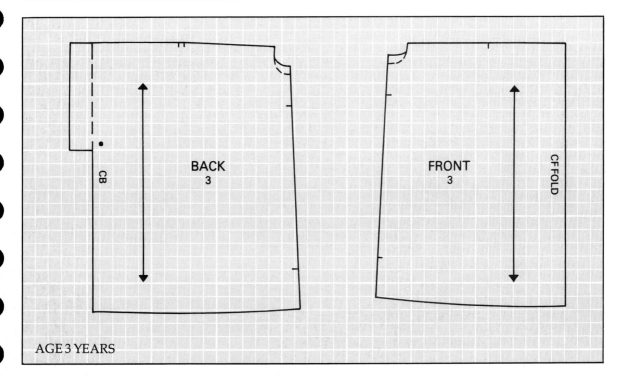

BACK
3

CB

FRONT
3

CF FOLD

AGE 3 YEARS

(BROKEN LINES ARE CUTTING LINES FOR PINAFORE)

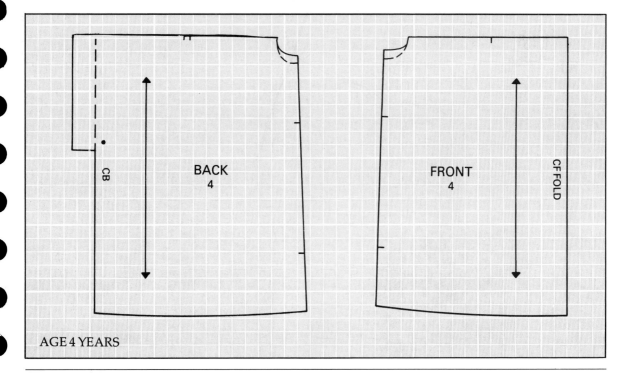

BACK
4

CB

FRONT
4

CF FOLD

AGE 4 YEARS

The Child's Dress Skirt

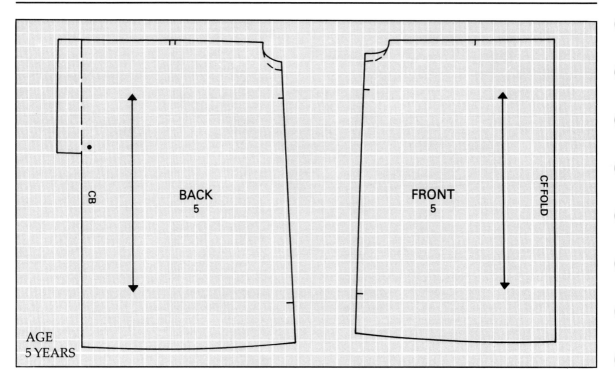

(BROKEN LINES ARE CUTTING LINES FOR PINAFORE)

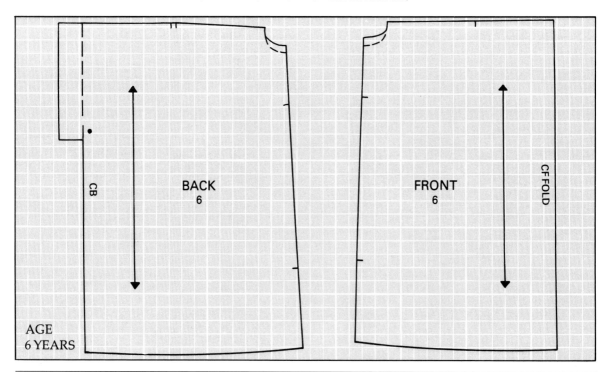

The Circular Skirt

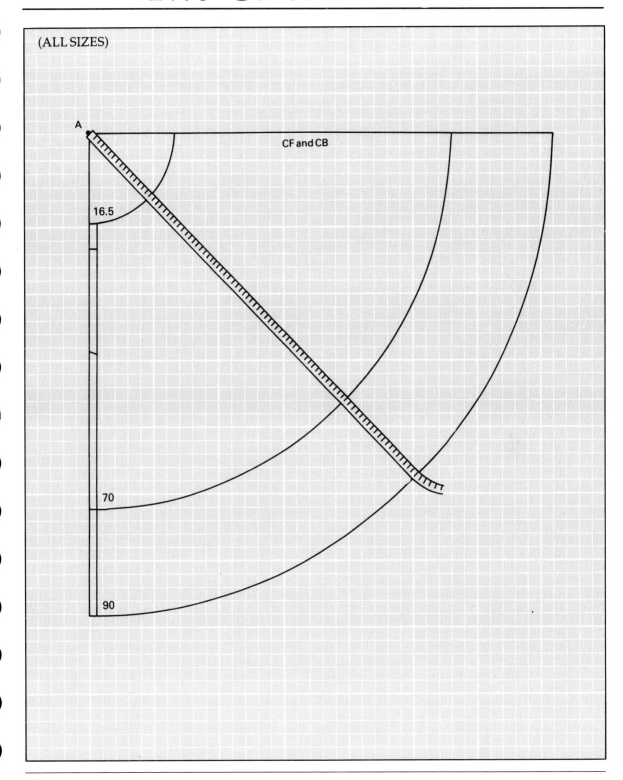

(ALL SIZES)

A

16.5

CF and CB

70

90

The Gathered Dress

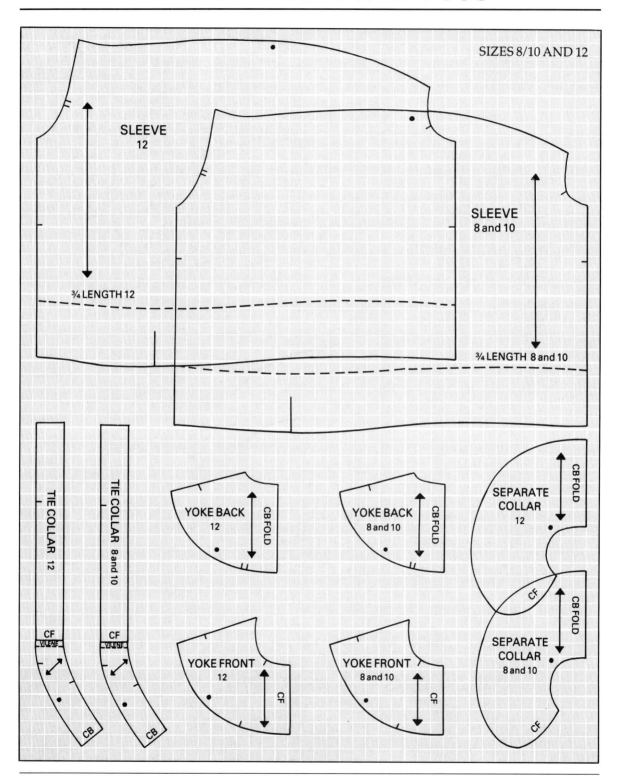

SIZES 8/10 AND 12

SLEEVE
12

¾ LENGTH 12

SLEEVE
8 and 10

¾ LENGTH 8 and 10

TIE COLLAR 12

TIE COLLAR 8 and 10

CF

VILENE

CF

VILENE

CB

CB

YOKE BACK
12

CB FOLD

YOKE BACK
8 and 10

CB FOLD

SEPARATE
COLLAR
12

CB FOLD

CF

CB FOLD

YOKE FRONT
12

CF

YOKE FRONT
8 and 10

CF

SEPARATE
COLLAR
8 and 10

CF

The Gathered Dress

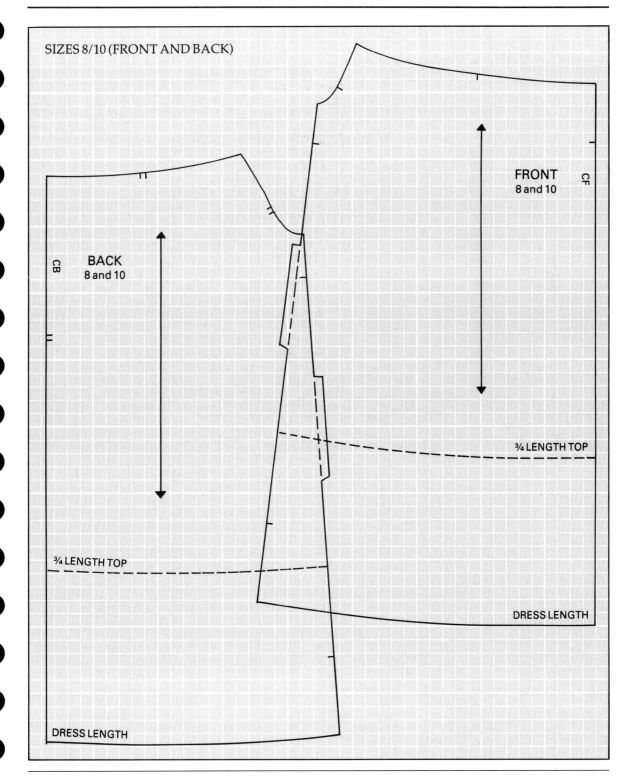

SIZES 8/10 (FRONT AND BACK)

FRONT
8 and 10

CF

BACK
8 and 10

CB

¾ LENGTH TOP

¾ LENGTH TOP

DRESS LENGTH

DRESS LENGTH

The Gathered Dress

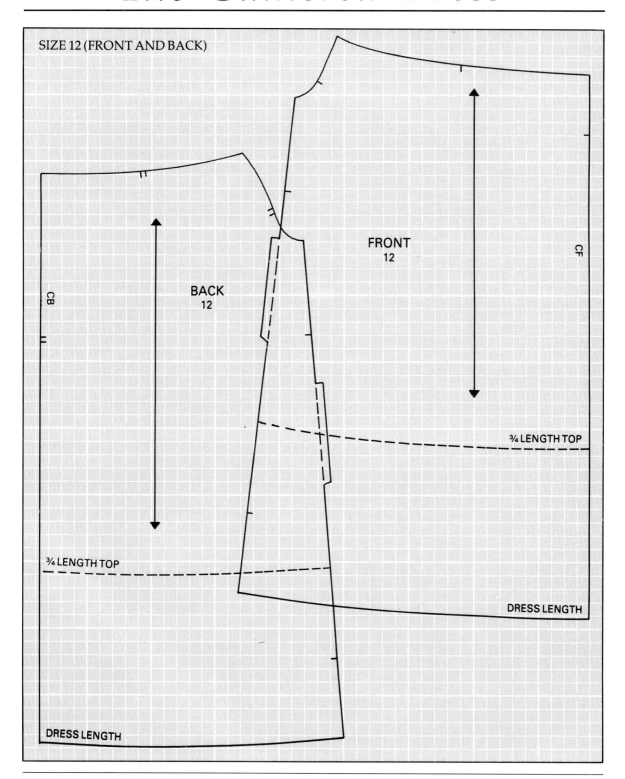

SIZE 12 (FRONT AND BACK)

FRONT
12

BACK
12

CB

CF

¾ LENGTH TOP

¾ LENGTH TOP

DRESS LENGTH

DRESS LENGTH

The Gathered Dress

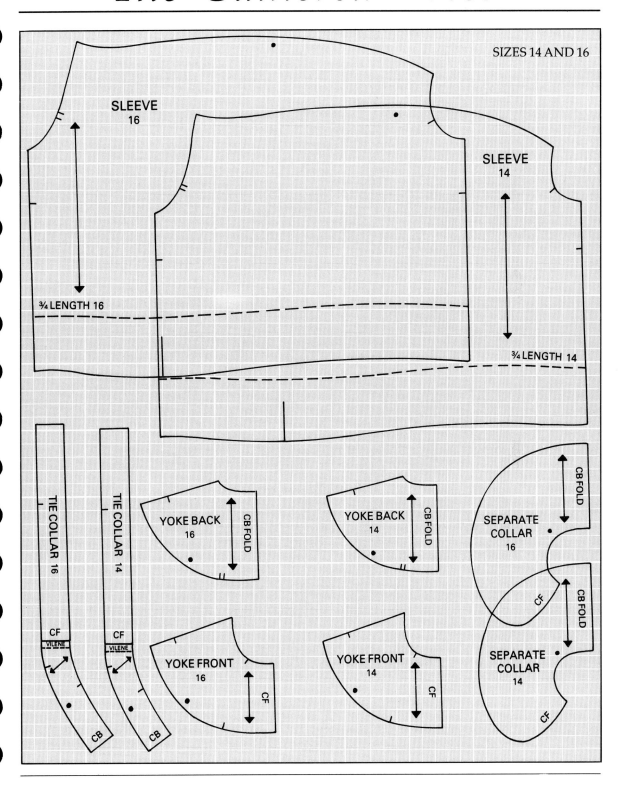

SIZES 14 AND 16

SLEEVE 16

SLEEVE 14

¾ LENGTH 16

¾ LENGTH 14

TIE COLLAR 16

TIE COLLAR 14

CF

CF

VILENE

VILENE

CB

CB

YOKE BACK 16

CB FOLD

YOKE BACK 14

CB FOLD

SEPARATE COLLAR 16

CB FOLD

CF

YOKE FRONT 16

CF

YOKE FRONT 14

CF

SEPARATE COLLAR 14

CB FOLD

CF

The Gathered Dress

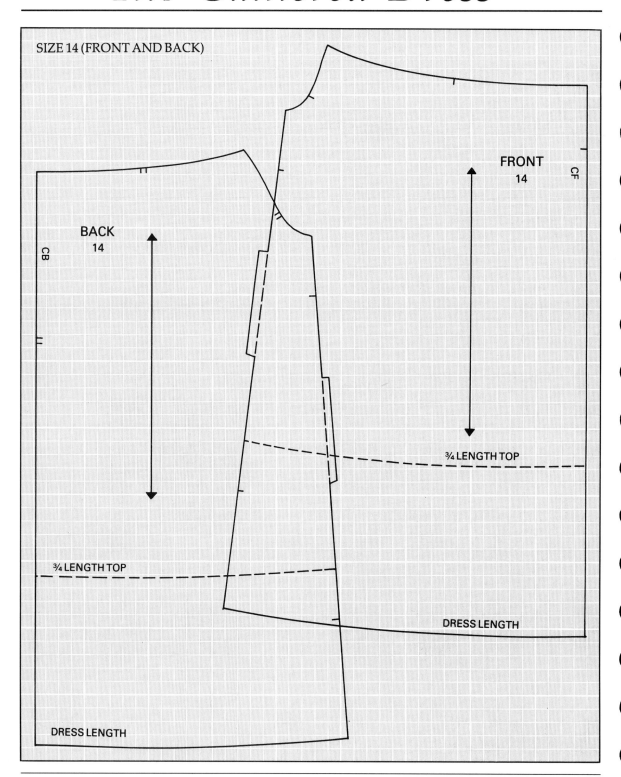

SIZE 14 (FRONT AND BACK)

FRONT
14

CF

BACK
14

CB

¾ LENGTH TOP

¾ LENGTH TOP

DRESS LENGTH

DRESS LENGTH

The Gathered Dress

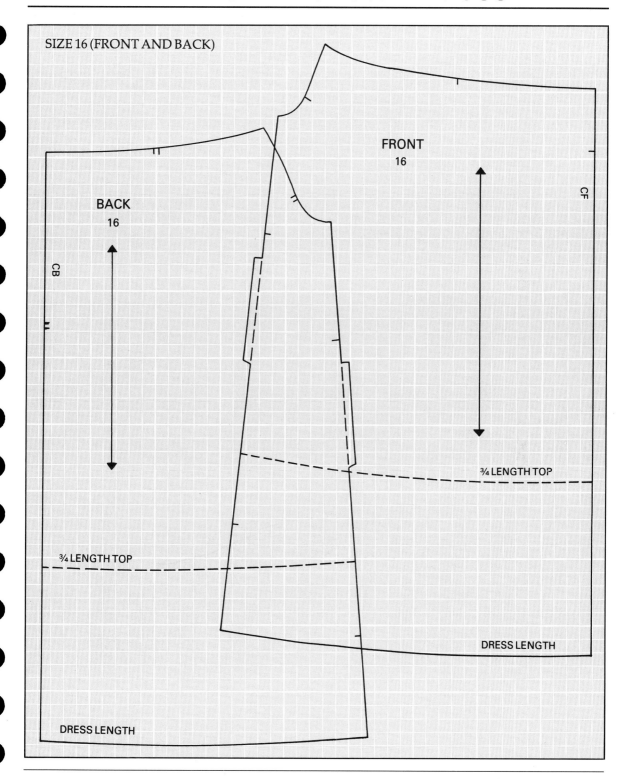

SIZE 16 (FRONT AND BACK)

FRONT
16

BACK
16

CB

CF

¾ LENGTH TOP

¾ LENGTH TOP

DRESS LENGTH

DRESS LENGTH

The Gathered Dress

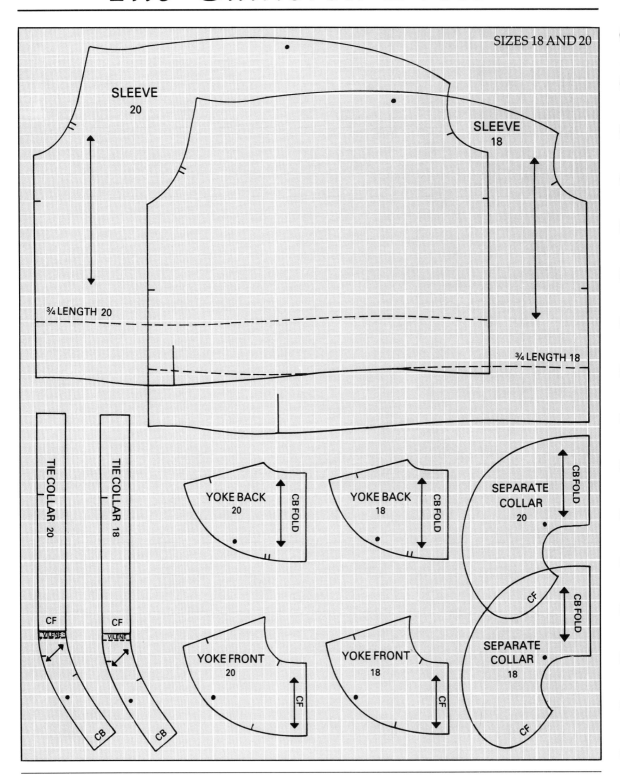

SIZES 18 AND 20

SLEEVE 20

SLEEVE 18

¾ LENGTH 20

¾ LENGTH 18

TIE COLLAR 20

TIE COLLAR 18

YOKE BACK 20

YOKE BACK 18

SEPARATE COLLAR 20

CF

CF

CF

VILENE

VILENE

CB

CB

YOKE FRONT 20

YOKE FRONT 18

SEPARATE COLLAR 18

CB FOLD

CB FOLD

CB FOLD

CB FOLD

CF

CF

CF

The Gathered Dress

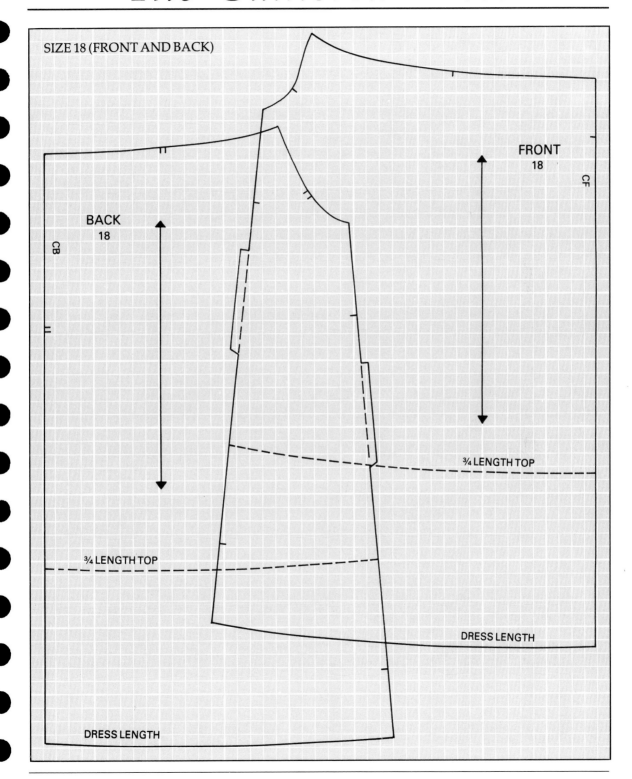

SIZE 18 (FRONT AND BACK)

FRONT
18

CF

BACK
18

CB

¾ LENGTH TOP

¾ LENGTH TOP

DRESS LENGTH

DRESS LENGTH

The Gathered Dress

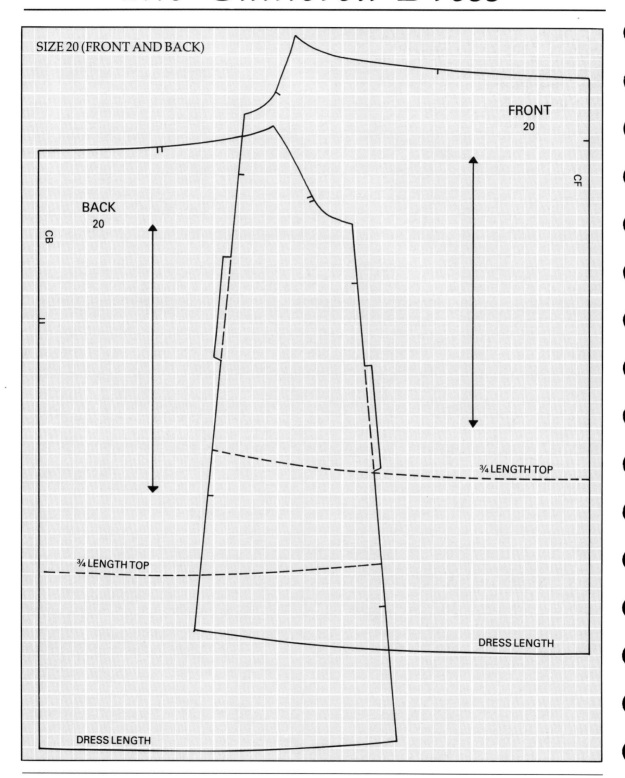

SIZE 20 (FRONT AND BACK)

FRONT
20

CF

BACK
20

CB

¾ LENGTH TOP

¾ LENGTH TOP

DRESS LENGTH

DRESS LENGTH

The Bikini

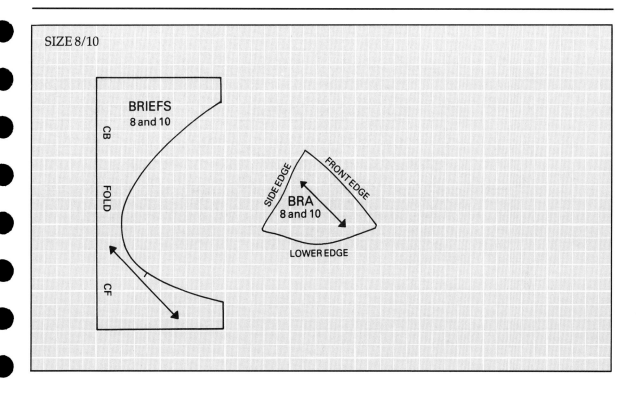

SIZE 8/10

BRIEFS
8 and 10

CB

FOLD

CF

BRA
8 and 10

SIDE EDGE

FRONT EDGE

LOWER EDGE

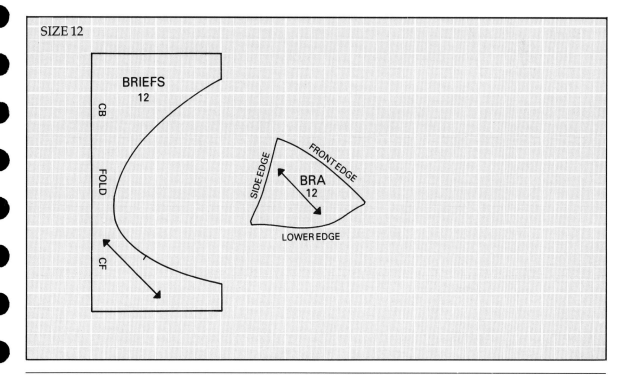

SIZE 12

BRIEFS
12

CB

FOLD

CF

BRA
12

SIDE EDGE

FRONT EDGE

LOWER EDGE

The Bikini

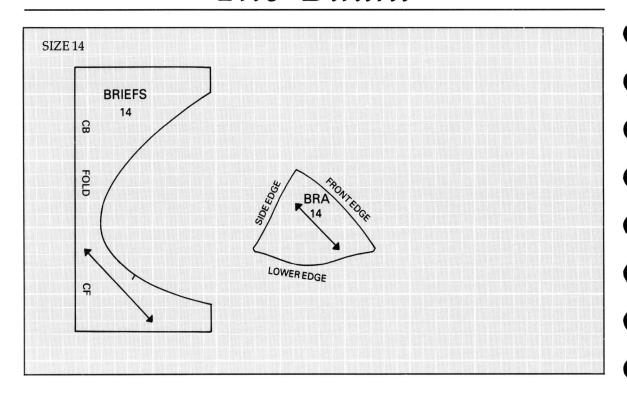

SIZE 14

BRIEFS
14

CB

FOLD

CF

SIDE EDGE

FRONT EDGE

BRA
14

LOWER EDGE

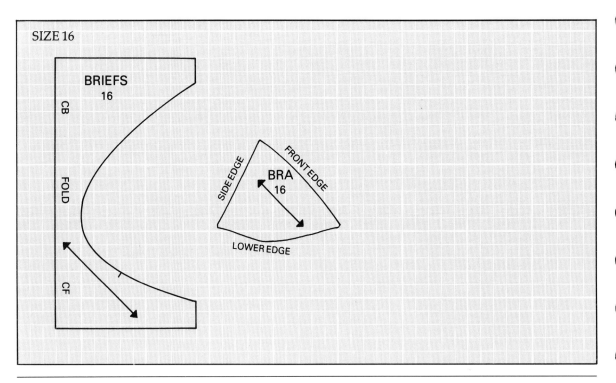

SIZE 16

BRIEFS
16

CB

FOLD

CF

SIDE EDGE

FRONT EDGE

BRA
16

LOWER EDGE

The Bikini

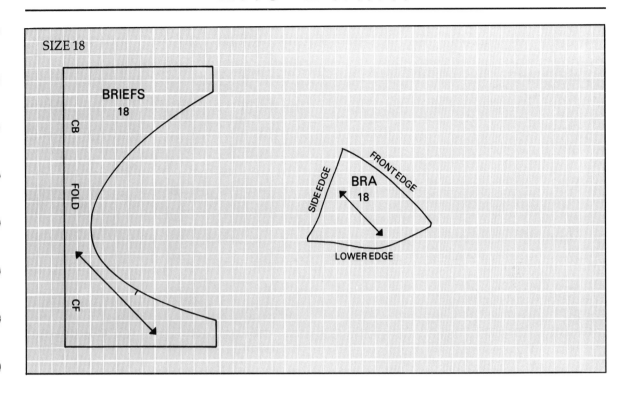

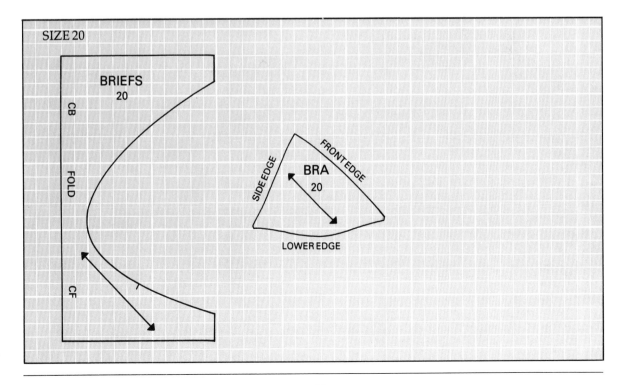

The Straight Dress

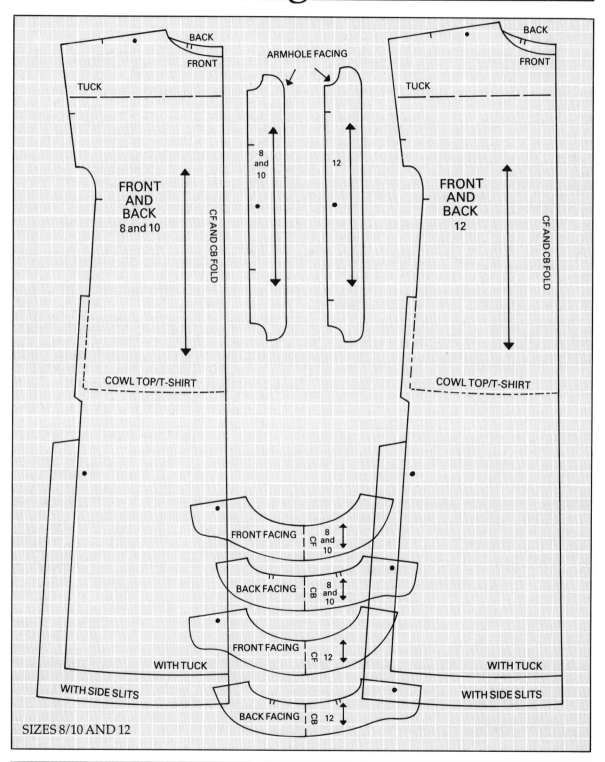

BACK
FRONT

ARMHOLE FACING

BACK
FRONT

TUCK

TUCK

8 and 10

12

FRONT AND BACK 8 and 10

FRONT AND BACK 12

CF AND CB FOLD

CF AND CB FOLD

COWL TOP/T-SHIRT

COWL TOP/T-SHIRT

FRONT FACING CF 8 and 10

BACK FACING CB 8 and 10

FRONT FACING CF 12

WITH TUCK

WITH TUCK

WITH SIDE SLITS

WITH SIDE SLITS

BACK FACING CB 12

SIZES 8/10 AND 12

The Straight Dress

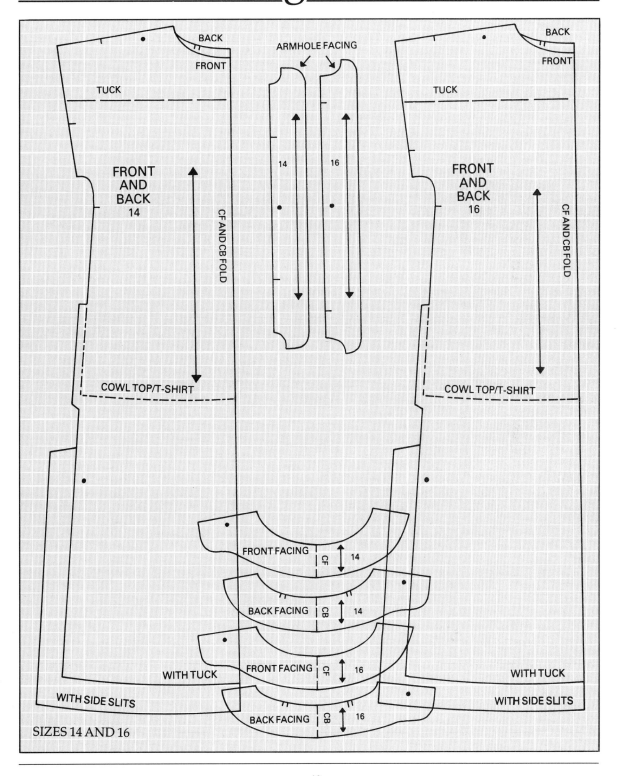

BACK
FRONT

ARMHOLE FACING

BACK
FRONT

TUCK

TUCK

FRONT
AND
BACK
14

14   16

FRONT
AND
BACK
16

CF AND CB FOLD

CF AND CB FOLD

COWL TOP/T-SHIRT

COWL TOP/T-SHIRT

FRONT FACING   CF   14

BACK FACING   CB   14

FRONT FACING   CF   16

WITH TUCK

WITH TUCK

WITH SIDE SLITS

BACK FACING   CB   16

WITH SIDE SLITS

SIZES 14 AND 16

The Straight Dress

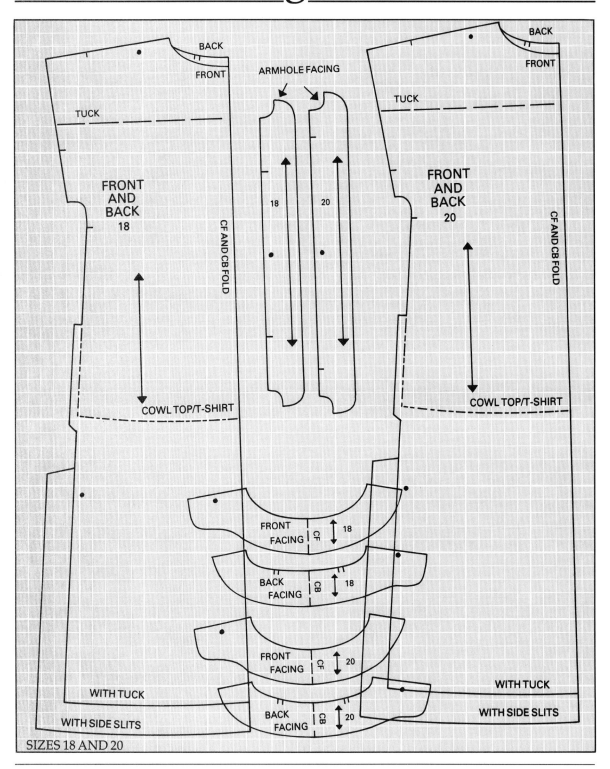

BACK

FRONT

ARMHOLE FACING

TUCK

BACK

FRONT

TUCK

FRONT
AND
BACK
18

FRONT
AND
BACK
20

CF AND CB FOLD

CF AND CB FOLD

18

20

COWL TOP/T-SHIRT

COWL TOP/T-SHIRT

FRONT
FACING

CF

18

BACK
FACING

CB

18

FRONT
FACING

CF

20

WITH TUCK

WITH TUCK

BACK
FACING

CB

20

WITH SIDE SLITS

WITH SIDE SLITS

SIZES 18 AND 20

The Cowl Top Neckline

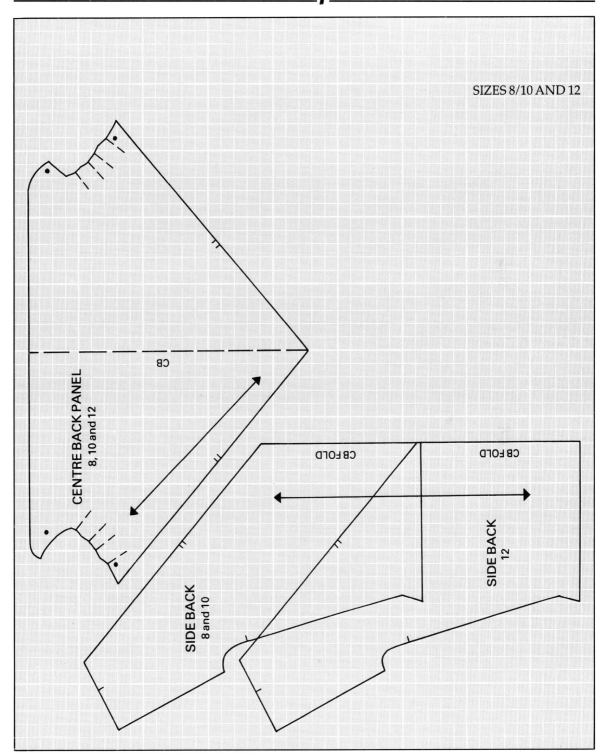

SIZES 8/10 AND 12

CENTRE BACK PANEL
8, 10 and 12

CB

SIDE BACK
8 and 10

CB FOLD

SIDE BACK
12

CB FOLD

The Cowl Top Neckline

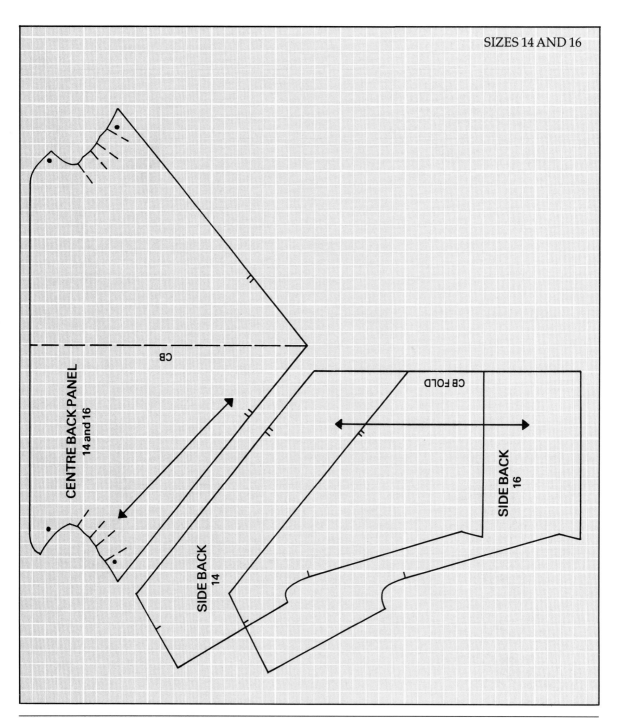

SIZES 14 AND 16

CENTRE BACK PANEL
14 and 16

CB

SIDE BACK
14

SIDE BACK
16

CB FOLD

The Cowl Top Neckline

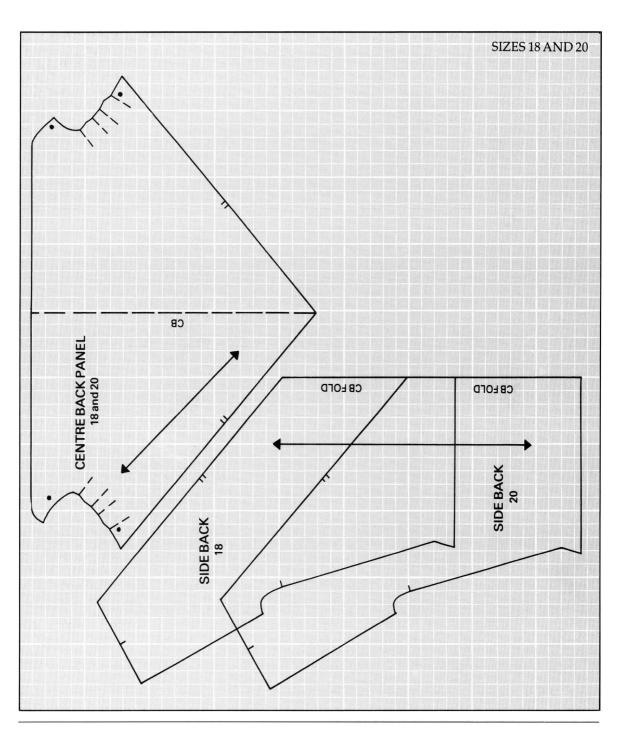

SIZES 18 AND 20

CENTRE BACK PANEL
18 and 20

CB

SIDE BACK
18

CB FOLD

CB FOLD

SIDE BACK
20

Rabbit · Bows · Cummerbund

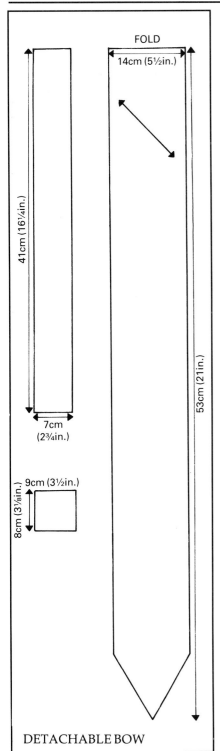

FOLD

14cm (5½in.)

41cm (16¼in.)

7cm (2¾in.)

53cm (21in.)

9cm (3½in.)

8cm (3⅛in.)

DETACHABLE BOW

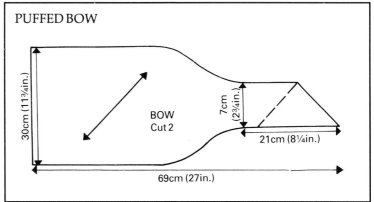

PUFFED BOW

30cm (11¾in.)

BOW
Cut 2

7cm (2¾in.)

21cm (8¼in.)

69cm (27in.)

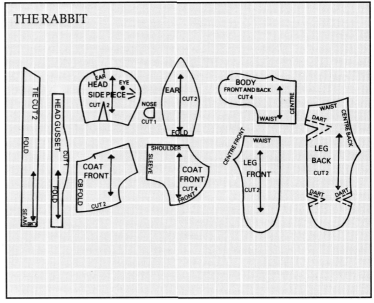

THE RABBIT

TIE CUT 2 FOLD SEAM

HEAD GUSSET CUT 1 FOLD

EAR HEAD SIDE PIECE EYE CUT 2

NOSE CUT 1

EAR CUT 2 FOLD

BODY FRONT AND BACK CUT 4 WAIST CENTRE

WAIST DART CENTRE BACK

COAT FRONT CB FOLD CUT 2

SHOULDER SLEEVE COAT FRONT CUT 4 FRONT

CENTRE FRONT WAIST LEG FRONT CUT 2

LEG BACK CUT 2 DART DART

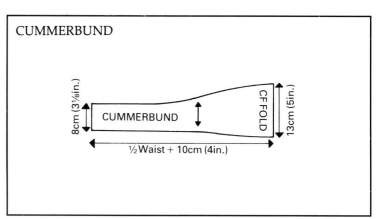

CUMMERBUND

8cm (3⅛in.)

CUMMERBUND

CF FOLD

13cm (5in.)

½ Waist + 10cm (4in.)

Caring for Pattern Pieces

PATTERN RECORD

After making up each pattern for the first time it is a good idea to make a note of any adjustments; you will find your own record very useful when you use the pattern again.

REINFORCING THE PATTERNS

In order to make the pattern pieces durable for future use, mount them on to iron-on Vilene.

Having made up a paper pattern once, whether it is a tissue from the back of the book or a diagram you have scaled yourself, make sure any alterations you made to the fit, either width or length, are clearly marked on the pattern pieces. It also helps to write on it any points you discovered that will be useful next time.

Smooth out the pieces with a cool dry iron, avoiding parts that are Sellotaped. Spread out a length of light-weight Vilene with the adhesive side uppermost, place pattern pieces on it one at a time and press the iron once in the middle of the pieces then smooth towards the outer edge of the paper but not over the edge. Cut out each piece, trimming the Vilene accurately in line with the pattern edge, then re-press to ensure the paper is firmly stuck to the Vilene. Store the pieces for each garment in a polythene bag with a label showing exactly what is inside.

As the same pockets are used on all outfits store those separately.

If you make the diagram patterns directly in light sew-in Vilene they will not need reinforcing.

Liberty Prints

All the designs we photographed were made up in beautiful Liberty fabrics. The range of Liberty prints includes new designs from current and recent seasons, as well as the famous and much-loved prints – some of which have a history dating back almost to the opening of the store itself in 1875.

Each season new designs are added to those taken from Liberty's extensive archive; these often include bold geometric and abstract designs that dictate the direction of textiles in the world of fashion. Many famous fashion designers have used Liberty fabrics in their collections, including Yves St. Laurent, Mary Quant and Cacharel.

Liberty fabrics, plain as well as print, are available in a range of different weights and fibre mixes that are comfortable for round-the-year dressing, and are ideal for the home dressmaker. They include Tana lawn, of course, named for Lake Tana in the Sudan where the fine quality long staple cotton is grown. The yarn gives the fabric its smooth silkiness, and makes it so comfortable to wear. Liberty Print Tana Lawn is woven on fast water jet looms at a rate of 1.60 metres per minute.

Liberty Varuna Wool was introduced in 1925, but in the more usual width of 36in. By the 1970s, however, wider cloths were gaining favour among home dressmakers, and the width was increased accordingly to 136cm (54in.). Varuna wool is made from finest Merino wool of the very best grade. Another popular fabric, Jubilee, is a mixture of 82% cotton and 18% wool, and it was introduced to celebrate the Silver Jubilee of Her Majesty the Queen in 1976.

The most luxurious fabric for special occasions is silk crêpe de chine. Easier to wear, and cheaper, Tyrian silk is versatile enough to be worn every day of your life. Both silks reflect the beauty of how intricate printing, by skilled craftsmen in Britain and France, can transform the raw silk, which is mostly imported from China, into exquisite dressmaking fabric.

Whichever fabric you finally select, consult the list below for needle size and suggested techniques, and, most important, for washing and pressing instructions.

The designs included in the book are, of course, perfectly adaptable to other fabric types. Consult the list overleaf for a guide for which types to choose from for which pattern.

HANDLING AND CARE OF LIBERTY FABRICS

FABRIC	WIDTH	FIBRE CONTENT	MACHINE NEEDLE	HAND NEEDLE	CARE		
Varuna wool	136-138cm (54in.)	100% wool	90 (14)	6	40°	⌂	Hand wash. Steam iron or use dry iron with damp muslin. Or dry clean.
Wandel	150-153cm (60in.)	100% cotton	90 (14)	6	40°	⌂	Hand wash. Steam iron or iron dry with hot iron. Or dry clean.
Country cotton	114-116cm (45in).	100% cotton	80 (11)	9-10, 8 for tacking	40°	⌂	Hand wash. Iron damp or steam iron. Or dry clean.
Crêpe de Chine	89-92cm (36in.)	100% silk	70 (9) Ball point	9-10, 8 for tacking	Ⓟ	⌂	Dry clean. Use warm iron for pressing
Jubilee	89-92cm (36in.)	82% cotton 18% wool	80 (11)	7, but 6 for tacking	40°	⌂	Hand wash. Dry flat. Steam iron. Or dry clean
Tana Lawn	89-92cm (36in.)	100% cotton	70 (9)	8, but 7 for tacking	40°	⌂	Hand wash. Steam iron or iron damp with hot iron. Or dry clean.

Other Suitable Fabrics

SUITABLE FABRICS

GARMENTS	FABRICS
SHIRT* T-SHIRT V-NECK TOP	Cotton lawn; Polyester cotton; Cotton shirting; Madras cotton; Voile; Poplin; Cotton jersey; Silk crêpe
STRAIGHT SKIRT; A-LINE SKIRT	Soft and crisp cotton; Lightweight wool; Wool crêpe; Flannel; Needlecord; Linen and linen weave fabrics; Poplin, Suede fabric; Wool challis, Bouclé
BUTTON-THROUGH DRESS*	Wool and cotton blends; Lightweight wool; Wool crêpe; Polyester cotton; Needlecord; Poplin; Fine silk; Shantung; Seersucker; Bouclé
SHORTS BIKINI BANDEAU	Cotton; Polyester cotton; Lawn; Seersucker; Towelling; Stretch towelling
BRA, PANTS FRENCH KNICKERS	Cotton lawn; Silk or polyester satin or crêpe; Cotton or silk jersey
ROBE	Towelling; Stretch towelling; Velour; Cotton lawn; Polyester cotton; Cotton jersey; Seersucker; Broderie anglais; Crêpe; Satin; Silk jersey
STRAIGHT SLEEVELESS DRESS GATHERED SKIRT SUNDRESS DROP-WAIST DRESS	Cotton; Polyester cotton; Seersucker; Broderie anglais; Lightweight linen-type fabrics; Poplin
STRAIGHT DRESS WITH TUCK AND SLEEVES	Wool crêpe; Wool challis; Crisp silk; Shantung; Slub silk; Polyester cotton
JACKET*	Medium-weight cotton; Lightweight wool; Firm silk; Raw silk; Shantung; Quilted fabrics; Denim; Satin; Line and line weave fabrics; Taffeta; Brocade; Slub silk
COWL TOP* AND LONG SKIRT	Silk crêpe de chine; Polyester crêpe; Satin; Synthetic or silk jersey; Georgette
TROUSERS	Cotton twill; Drill; Denim; Polyester cotton; Cotton or polyester jersey; Wool crêpe; Flannel; Worsted; Satin; Crêpe; Suede fabric; Linen
CHILD'S DRESS	Cotton lawn; Polyester cotton; Wool and cotton; Blends; Brushed cotton; Needlecord
PINAFORE	Cotton lawn; Broderie anglais; Border prints; Organdie; Voile
ROMPERS	Cotton; Wool and cotton blends; Polyester cotton

* Avoid diagonals and bold stripes

Some Preliminary Hints

Other hints, relating to specific Liberty fabrics, are included with the making-up instructions for the relevant outfit.

CUTTING OUT ONE-WAY MATCHING PRINTS AND CHECKS

The beauty of printed fabric lies in the relationship between the arrangement of that print and the body inside it. Some prints look best used in generous amounts, gathered, to create moving swirls of colour and bring closer the motifs and those areas of colour that are widely spaced. Some prints on the other hand are best viewed flat so that the intricacy of the colour and tracery is unbroken. Many prints can be made up equally effectively either flat or full.

An important point to consider is the effect of the print on your figure. It is very important, especially when planning an outfit with a lot of fabric in it, to arrange the fabric on you, gathering it up, in front of a mirror, before deciding to select it. Drape several prints in various colours before you decide; you will soon see clearly which looks most effective on you. Remember that if you are shorter than average, fewer design repeats will be visible; if you are tall, more print will show.

If you are planning accessories, contrasting plain or print fabric to team with it, or intending to match the garment up with existing plain sweaters etc., move right back from the mirror in order to be sure which colour in the print is the one that is really distinct at a distance. If you are selecting another plain or print fabric to go with it, hold that up too but only showing the amount that you will be using – sash, piping, etc.

When calculating the amount of fabric required remember to add enough to match the print. The fabric quantities given in the chart on page 00 are for one-way fabrics, but they do *not* allow for matching a particular print. The calculation should be made in the same way as for wallpaper, that is by adding one extra print depth for each main pattern piece to the basic length of the fabric given in the chart. Look at the layout diagram for the garment, count how many pattern pieces are placed end to end, and add that number of design repeats to the fabric when buying the fabric for that pattern.

If you make your own adaptations to the pattern remember to assess whether you will then require more or less fabric. For absolute accuracy lay out the pattern pieces on a cutting board and measure the quantity.

Always cut out with the right side of the fabric uppermost. Some are easier to cut out on single fabric, reversing the pattern to cut the other half of each piece. With some, such as the classic tartan Jubilee fabric, you can fold it but make sure the lines of check are matched by putting pins along the edges.

When you are cutting on the cross try always to do it on single fabric, because the grain and therefore the print can easily be distorted when folded.

Always adjust all pattern pieces for length before cutting out.

KEEPING PATTERNS MATCHED AT SEAMS

Once the careful cutting out has been done, most seams can be made by tacking the fabric and machining, especially on floral prints. However, for crucial matching lines and checks, take extra

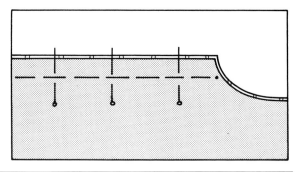

care. First pin with pins placed across the seams at main parts of the print. Tack and then machine but stitch from the hem upwards, with a stitch that is not too small in case you have to unpick it, leaving the pins in the fabric. The machine will ride over them provided the heads of the pins are not passing under the foot. If you have a dual feed on your machine you will only need to tack accurately and machine the seams. It also helps to hold checks together with short pieces of basting tape which are removed after stitching.

If you have difficulty in matching a seam, perhaps because of the interfacing, piping etc., covering the fabric design, then tack from the right side. Turn under one edge of the fabric and place it over the other edge with right sides up as for an overlaid seam. Pin and then tack by

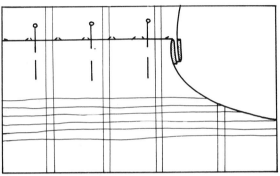

slipping the needle through the fold alternately with picking up a stitch on the lower layer. Remove pins and open out the fabric wrong side up. Insert the pins again and stitch the seam.

Laying Out Patterns and Cutting Out

SEAM AND HEM ALLOWANCES

1.5cm (⅝in.) has been allowed on all main seams. Amounts allowed for hems are indicated on the patterns.

Note that when following a cut-off line on the pattern, for making an alternative version, allowance has been made for turning up the hem. The amount allowed is given on the pattern in each case.

All diagram patterns are drawn to the nearest 5mm (¼in.).

Having prepared your pattern by scaling up a diagram or by trimming or tracing the pieces from the full size tissue in the back of the book, check that you have all the pieces you need for the version you have chosen. Some designs combine tissue and a diagram. Check the length of skirts and trousers and adjust if necessary. Paper patterns will lie flatter and adhere to the fabric if you run a cool iron over the pieces.

Next select the appropriate layout illustration from the following section, perhaps marking it with pencil when you have identified it. Press any creases from your fabric and fold it or lay it out as shown with the right side visible so that you can match designs; with printed fabrics note which way the pattern runs. If you cannot get all the fabric flat on the table or cutting board spread out what you can and roll up the rest.

Arrange the pattern pieces as shown and pin in position, remembering the following:

Line up the straight grain arrow exactly on a lengthwise thread or on a stripe or line of print, and insert one pin in the arrow to hold it in place.

Where a piece is to be cut to a fold, place the edge of the paper at the fold of the fabric.

Pin the pieces down; one pin well inside each corner inserted at an angle to keep the fabric flat.

Do not include the selvedges unless you are short of fabric.

Cut out, keeping the fabric flat. Use large cutting out shears and cut confidently beside the edge of the paper. Cut all the main pieces leaving crossway strips, frills (ruffles and flounces), belts etc., until you need them, to avoid creasing.

Where a pattern piece is shown with a dotted outline, it indicates that it has to be cut again elsewhere. Either make a copy of the piece or reserve the area of fabric and cut separately.

Where a pattern piece is shown extending beyond the fabric it indicates that the fabric is to be opened out singly. Reserve the area, cut all other pieces of pattern and then open out the remainder, right side up.

Where the layout shows pieces cut on open widths of fabric, begin by cutting the ones that need folded fabric, then open out the remainder to cut the remaining pieces.

Liberty prints are one-way designs, so all the layouts show the pattern pieces arranged in one direction. If you are using plain or striped fabric you may be able to economise a little by dovetailing the pieces.

All layouts are for the fabrics we used for the clothes. When using fabrics in other widths, consult the chart on page 10ff for the quantity required then pin and cut out following the basic rules above.

Layout Diagrams

SHIRT (all sizes)
FABRIC 90cm (36in.) wide

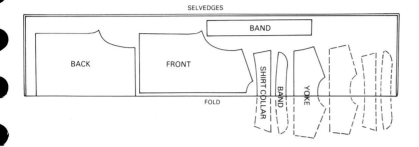

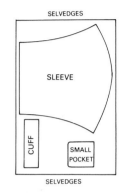

SHIRT WITH CONTRAST COLLAR AND CUFFS (all sizes)
FABRIC 90cm (36in.) wide

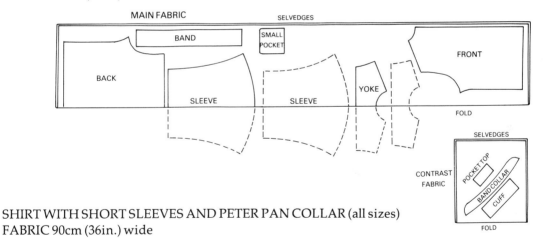

SHIRT WITH SHORT SLEEVES AND PETER PAN COLLAR (all sizes)
FABRIC 90cm (36in.) wide

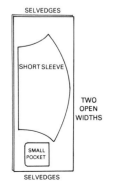

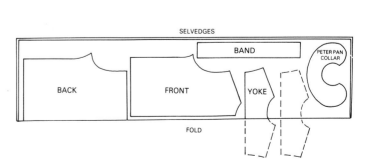

BUTTON-THROUGH DRESS (all sizes)
MAIN FABRIC 90cm (36in.) wide, lining 115cm (45in.) wide

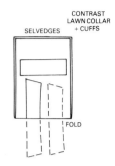

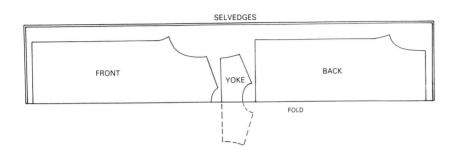

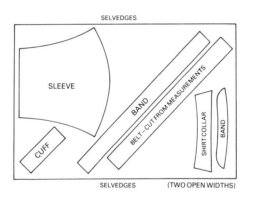

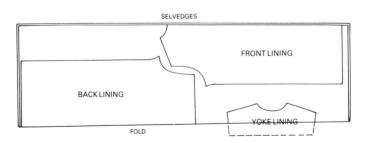

ROBE (all sizes)
FABRIC 90cm (36in.) wide

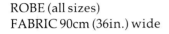

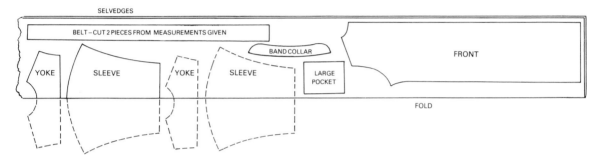

BIKINI (all sizes)
FABRIC 90cm (36in.) wide

FRENCH KNICKERS (sizes 8-16 and 18 and 20)
FABRIC 90cm (36in.) wide

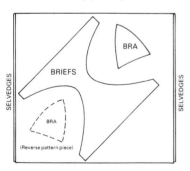

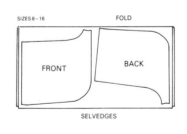

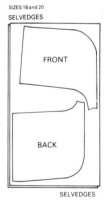

T-SHIRT TOP (all sizes)
FABRIC 90cm (36in.) wide

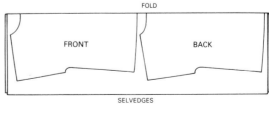

TROUSERS (sizes 8-14 and 16-20)
FABRIC 137cm (54in.) wide

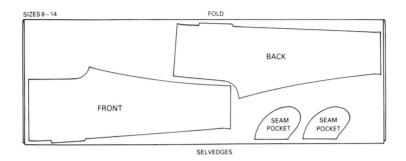

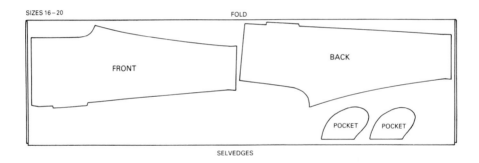

CROPPED TROUSERS (all sizes)
FABRIC 150cm (60in.) wide

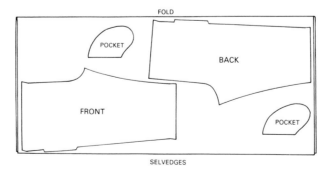

LONG SHORTS (sizes 8-16 and 18 and 20)
FABRIC 90cm (36in.) wide

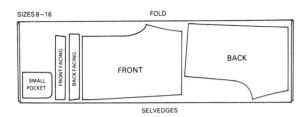

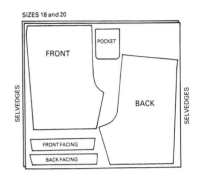

COWL TOP (all sizes)
FABRIC 90cm (36in.) wide
•SLEEVES: Cut 28.5cm (11¼in.) long and to the widths below
Size 8/10 43.8cm (17¼in.)
Size 12 45cm (17¾in.)
Size 14 46.6cm (18⅜in.)
Size 16 49cm (19¼in.)
Size 18 51cm (20in.)
Size 20 53.6cm (21⅛in.)

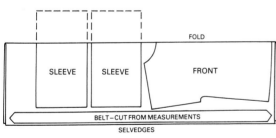

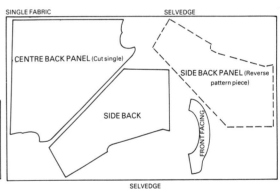

A-LINE SKIRT (sizes 8-12)
FABRIC 137cm (54in.) wide

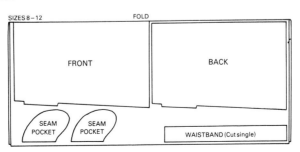

A-LINE SKIRT (sizes 14-20)
FABRIC 137cm (54in.) wide

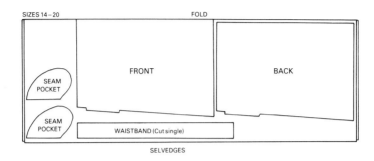

PLEATED SKIRT (all sizes)
FABRIC 137cm (54in.) wide
PANELLED SKIRT (all sizes)
FABRIC 150cm (60in.) wide

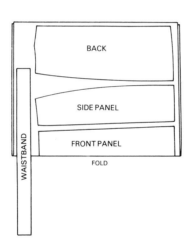

CIRCULAR SKIRT (all sizes)
FABRIC 90cm (36in.) wide

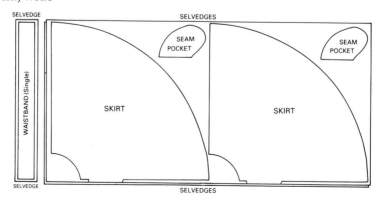

GATHERED SKIRT (all sizes)
FABRIC 90cm (36in.) wide

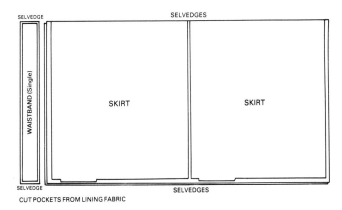

CUT POCKETS FROM LINING FABRIC

SMOCK (all sizes)
FABRIC 90cm (36in.) wide

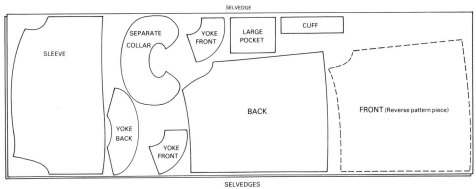

CUT BUTTON LOOPS FROM SCRAPS

GATHERED DRESS (sizes 8-14, size 16, and sizes 18 and 20)
FABRIC 137cm (54in.) wide

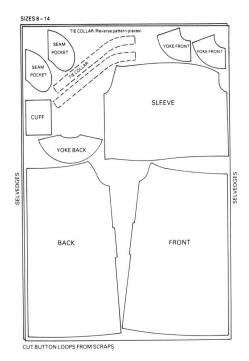

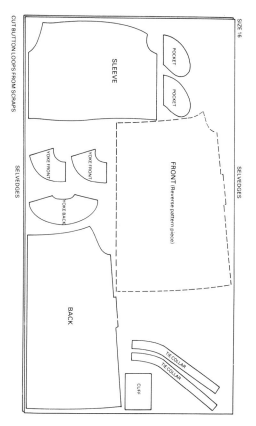

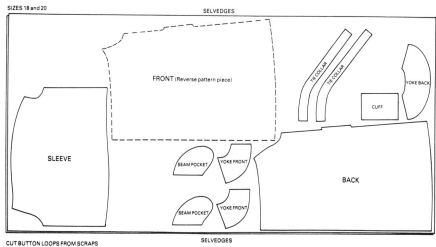

DROP-WAIST DRESS (all sizes)
FABRIC 90cm (36in.) wide

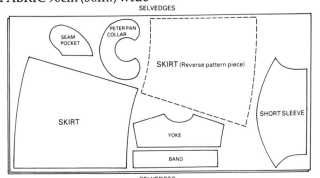

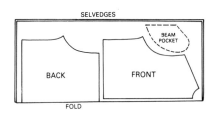

STRAIGHT DRESS (all sizes)
FABRIC 90cm (36in.) wide

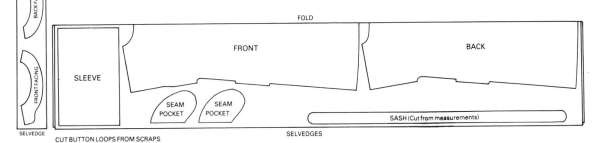

STRAIGHT DRESS WITH TUCK (all sizes)
FABRIC 137cm (54in.) wide
SLEEVES: Cut 32.5cm (12¾in.) long and to the widths below
Size 8/10 43.8cm (17¼in.)   Size 16 49cm (19¼in.)
Size 12 45cm (17¾in.)   Size 18 51cm (20in.)
Size 14 46.6cm (18⅜in.)   Size 20 53.6cm (21⅛in.)

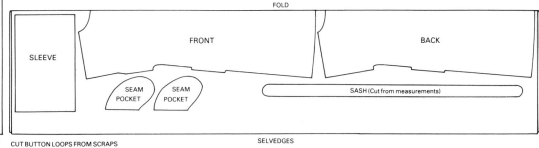

STRAIGHT DRESS WITH SIDE SLITS (sizes 8-12, 14 and 16, 18 and 20)
FABRIC 90cm (36in.) wide

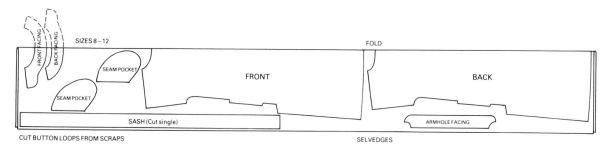

SIZES 8 – 12

FRONT FACING

BACK FACING

FOLD

SEAM POCKET

FRONT

BACK

SEAM POCKET

SASH (Cut single)

ARMHOLE FACING

CUT BUTTON LOOPS FROM SCRAPS

SELVEDGES

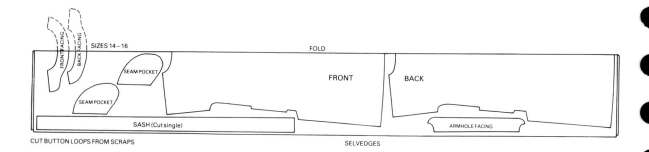

FRONT FACING

BACK FACING

SIZES 14 – 16

FOLD

SEAM POCKET

FRONT

BACK

SEAM POCKET

SASH (Cut single)

ARMHOLE FACING

CUT BUTTON LOOPS FROM SCRAPS

SELVEDGES

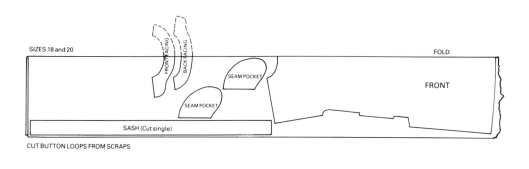

SIZES 18 and 20

FRONT FACING

BACK FACING

FOLD

SEAM POCKET

SEAM POCKET

FRONT

SASH (Cut single)

CUT BUTTON LOOPS FROM SCRAPS

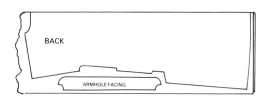

BACK

ARMHOLE FACING

SUNDRESS (all sizes)
FABRIC 115cm (45in.) wide

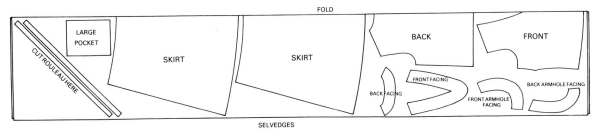

V-NECK TOP (all sizes)
FABRIC 90cm (36in.) wide

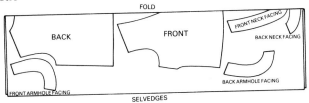

JACKET (all sizes)
FABRIC 137cm (54in.) wide

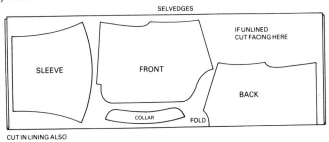

PRINT JACKET (all sizes)
FABRIC 115cm (45in.) wide

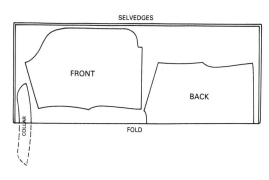

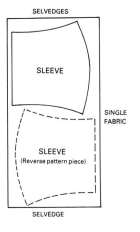

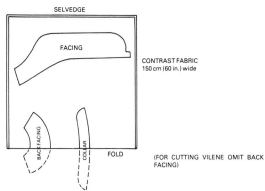

ROMPERS
FABRIC 90cm (36in.) wide

CHILD'S LONG-SLEEVED DRESS (ages 1 and 2)
FABRIC 90cm (36in.) wide

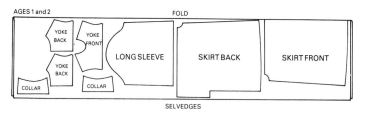

CHILD'S LONG-SLEEVED DRESS (ages 3, and 4-6)
FABRIC 90cm (36in.) wide

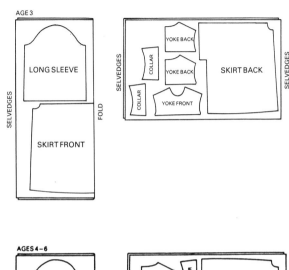

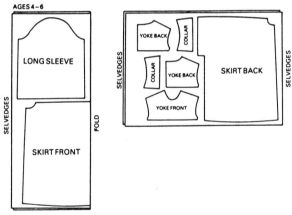

PINAFORE (ages 1 and 2)
FABRIC 90cm (36in.) wide

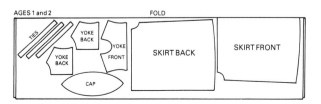

PINAFORE (ages 3-6)
FABRIC 90cm (36in.) wide

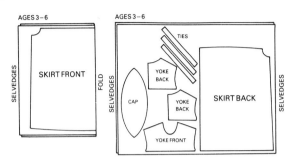

CHILD'S SHORT-SLEEVED DRESS (ages 1-3, 4-6)
FABRIC 90cm (36in.) wide

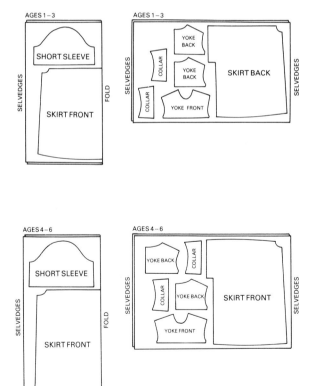

Perfect Partners

The jewel-bright blue shirt in Liberty Silk Crêpe de Chine Carousel is matched perfectly by the soft folds of the A-line skirt in plain red Varuna wool. As an alternative look, the shirt can be worn with a detachable bow at the neck. The flattering skirt has a centre back zip and seam pockets, and can be fully lined if desired.
(See page 97 for colour photograph.)

PATTERN PIECES

Shirt. Tissue pattern: Shirt back. front. yoke. front band. sleeve. band collar. shirt collar. cuff. small patch pocket. Diagram pattern: Bow. neck band.

Skirt. Tissue pattern: Seam pocket. waistband (use Fold-a-Band or light-weight Fuse 'n' Fold as guide). Diagram pattern: A-line skirt back. front.

CUTTING OUT

The silk crepe de chine is 90cm (36 in.) wide with bands of coloured stripes 10cm (4 in.) wide printed lengthwise, and narrow horizontal lines spaced 13cm (5 in.) apart, forming squares. Cutting out should be done with the fabric single, as it is slippery. Cut out the shirt fronts first with the wide band of stripes running from mid-yoke to hem. Cut out front bands from a plain area, but make sure to match the thin horizontal lines. Cut the back shirt to match the checks horizontally, and with the stripes vertical at the centre back. Cut the sleeves with the wider stripes running down the

centre, or if you wish the stripes to match when the sleeve hangs down, cut them with stripes running across. This will require additional fabric because the design repeat across the width of the fabric is 30cm (12 in.), so there are only three full patterns on the silk. The stripes are also one-way so the pattern cannot be turned around. An alternative would be to cut the

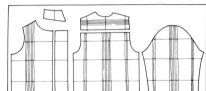

sleeves on the cross, which would be extravagant of fabric but very attractive. Cut the collar and front bands from plain areas, and cut the cuffs either plain or with stripes. The optional neck bow is made from double fabric on the cross attached to a narrow straight band that fits under the collar and fastens at the back.

THE SHIRT

Making up

1. *Cut out.* Cut out fabric, Vilene (Pellon) and Fold-a-Band (Fuse 'n' Fold). Transfer markings for back tucks, shoulder and sleeve points, neck and collar, matching points and pocket position. Mark sleeve opening.

2. *Front bands.* Attach Fold-a-Band. Stitch to right sides of shirt. Turn under and tack on inside. Hem on the inside to within 20cm (8in.) of the hem.

3. *Pocket.* Make up pocket, attach to left side of shirt by hand, matching the stripes.

4. *Yoke.* Tack tucks in position, attach back of shirt to yokes. Attach front yokes to shirt front. Turn under and hem to yoke seam on the inside.

5. *Collar.* Baste Vilene to one piece of collar and band. Make up collar and insert between bands. Attach collar to neck edge, finish inner edge by hemming.

6. *Sleeve.* Cut sleeve openings and make faced slit or bound openings using fabric cut on the cross. Attach sleeves to armholes.

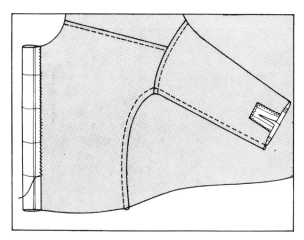

Make openings in sleeves. Attach sleeves to armholes, then sew sides and sleeve seams.

7. *Side seams and sleeve seams.* Fold shirt wrong sides together and make French seams from shirt hem to wrist, matching the stripes.

8. *Cuffs.* Insert gathering threads at wrist instead of tucks. Make and attach cuffs.

9. *Hem.* Open out front bands at hem, turn up shirt hem including bands, tack. Hand stitch hem with hemming or slip hemming. Finish bands by slip-stitching the folds together at the bottom and completing the hemming at the front edge.

Use a suitably-sized Velcro circle to fasten the detachable bow at the back neck.

10. *Buttonholes and buttons.* Work four buttonholes, preferably by hand, mid-way between the horizontal stripes at the front; make one horizontal buttonhole in the neck band or attach a press stud if you intend always to wear the bow. Attach buttons.

An alternative neck finish would be to omit the collar, cut the crossway piece for the bow a little longer, and attach it directly to the neck of the shirt as a tie.

An alternative finish for the neckline would be a detachable pussy bow, made from double fabric on the cross and attached to a narrow band that fits under the collar and fastens at the back (see page 18 for making-up instructions).

THE SKIRT

Making up

1. *Cut out.* Cut back and front skirt to fold of fabric. Cut again in lining. Cut 4 pocket pieces in lining and attach light iron-on Vilene to two if required. Transfer markings to fabric.

2. *Waistband.* Measure Fold-a-Band round waist, mark waist size and cut off allowing at least 7.5cm (3in.) extension. Press to wrong side of fabric and cut leaving turnings. Press one long edge on to wrong side. Fold-a-Band. Fold band and mark centre front, centre back and sides.

3. *Centre back.* Stitch centre back seam to base of zip. Press. Insert zip.

4. *Pockets.* Attach interfaced pockets to back skirt and the others to the front.

5. *Side seams.* Stitch skirt side seams, above and below pocket opening. Stitch across pocket opening with large stitch. Stitch around pocket bag. Press towards front.

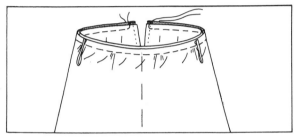

Tack lining to skirt, attach hanging loops by tacking in position at side seams, insert gathering threads.

6. *Lining.* Stitch lining seams leaving 25cm (10 in.) open at top of centre back seam. Put lining inside skirt wrong sides together. Tack together at waist. Turn in and hem lining beside the zip.

7. *Waist.* Make two hanging loops and tack to inside at seams. Insert gathering thread. Place waistband and skirt right sides together. Pin at centre front, centre back and sides. Pull up gathers to fit waistband, even out, and tack. Stitch and finish band by hemming inside.

8. *Hem.* Put on skirt and mark hemline. Turn up skirt hem. Turn up lining hem so that it is 4cm (1½in.) shorter. Make bar tacks 3cm (1¼in.) long between skirt and lining at seams.

9. *Fastening.* Work buttonhole and attach button, or attach large hooks, or hem Velcro to skirt band extension.

Print In The Pink

*This version of the crisp short jacket is in Liberty Print Country Cotton Spring,
faced with a splash of bright pink Liberty Wandel. The jacket fastens at the shoulder
front with a single loop and button, but it can also be worn with one lapel turned
back to show off the contrast facing and collar. The sleeve hems could also be
faced with the same shade and worn turned back. Cinch the jacket at the waist
with a wide belt if you have the figure for it, or leave it more gently loose over
trousers in the same bright pink, cropped below the knee for a young look. An
alternative choice for the less adventurous might be plain black trousers, cut to the
ankle-bone. (See page 98 for colour photograph.)*

PATTERN PIECES

Jacket. Tissue pattern: Jacket back.
front. sleeve. collar. front facing. back
neck facing.
Trousers. Diagram pattern: Trouser
front. back. seam pocket.

CUTTING OUT

The jacket illustrated was cut with
contrast plain fabric facing and collar,
but they could equally well be cut in a
toning or contrasting print, or in the
same fabric as the rest of the jacket. The
sleeve hems could also be faced in
toning or contrasting fabric and worn
turned back.

THE JACKET

Making up

1. *Cut out.* Cut out back, front, one collar and
sleeve in print plus one collar, back neck facing
and front facing in contrast. Cut Vilene (Pellon)
and attach to print collar and jacket facing.
Transfer pattern markings to fabric.

2. *Loop.* Make one rouleau loop for the button
and tack it to right side of jacket.

3. *Shoulders and sleeves.* Join shoulder seams.
Attach sleeves to jacket at shoulders. Press.
Neaten sleeve hem edges.

4. *Side seams.* Stitch sleeve and jacket seams in
one. Press. Neaten raw edge of jacket hem.

5. *Collar.* Stitch print and plain collars together
and turn right side out. Press. Tack to right side
of jacket neck.

6. *Facing.* Join neck facing to front facings at
shoulders. Neaten outer edge of facing. Put facing

right side down to right side of jacket. Tack round
neck and front edges. Stitch, enclosing collar and
rouleau loop. Trim and roll facing to wrong side.
Tack edge; press. Hold in place with Wundaweb.

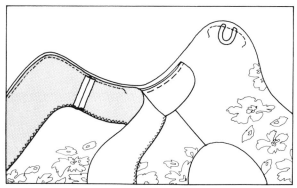

Attach collar and button loop, place facing on top, stitch
around edge of jacket.

7. *Hems.* Try on jacket. Turn up sleeve and jacket
hems. Finish with hemming, Wundaweb or
machine stitching.

8. *Button.* Pin up the jacket front. Fold a small piece of tape or fabric and pin it on the wrong side of left jacket front under the loop. Attach the button, sewing through the reinforcement.

THE TROUSERS

Making up

1. *Cut out.* Cut out 2 backs, 2 fronts and 4 pocket pieces.

2. *Leg seams.* Stitch inside leg seams with open seams.

3. *Pockets.* Stitch pocket bags to back and front legs.

4. *Side seams.* Stitch outside leg seams above and below pocket opening. Press pockets towards front. Make open seams below pocket. Stitch pocket bags together. Neaten outer edge and continue up to waist.

5. *Crotch seam.* Join crotch with machine fell seam. Make hanging loops from seam tape or from fabric and stitch on wrong side of waist at back and front.

6. *Waist.* Fold over waist casing and machine. Insert elastic and adjust to size. Join elastic.

7. *Hems.* Try on and check length. Turn up hems and catch stitch, machine or use Wundaweb.

Black, White and Quilted

Liberty Varuna Wool Ficelle, a bold black and white design, lends itself particularly well to quilting in diamond patterns. The jacket quilting is backed with plain black silk, and the edges are bound with black satin as a luxurious final touch. The jacket fastens with three loops and buttons (try jet ones if you can find them), and can be worn with the cuffs turned back to show a band of silky black lining. The straight and simple black Varuna wool trousers are easy to make, with an elasticated waist and seam pockets. (See page 99 for colour photograph.)

PATTERN PIECES
Jacket. Tissue pattern: Jacket back. front. sleeve. collar.
Trousers. Diagram pattern: Trouser front. back. trouser front and back also in lining (if required). seam pocket (cut 4 in lining).

CUTTING OUT
The jacket illustrated was cut from specially quilted Liberty Varuna Wool, but it could equally well be made from any of the attractive ready-quilted fabrics now available. In this case omit the lining, use welt seams in making the jacket, binding the outer edges as described.

THE JACKET

Making up

1. *Cut out.* Cut out back, front and sleeve in quilting and in lining. Cut collar twice in quilting.

2. *Loops.* Make a length of rouleau tubing from the binding. Either stitch as three loops to right jacket front on the right side so that the ends are caught when the edge is bound, or sew to the inside of the jacket after completing the binding.

3. *Shoulders and side seams.* Stitch shoulders and attach sleeves with open (plain) seams on quilting and lining. Stitch underarm and sleeve seams in both. With jacket wrong side out, slip lining over it right side out. Hold seam allowances of both together by machining or back stitch worked from 7 cm (2¾ in.) above the hem up to the underarm. Push remainder of lining into position in jacket. Tack edges of lining and quilting together all around jacket inside the edges.

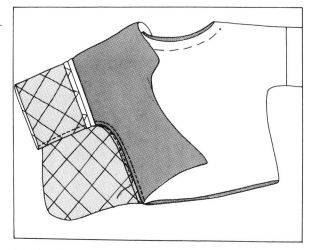

Hold jacket inside out, slip lining over it and stitch seam edges together. Fold remainder of lining into position and tack to jacket around edges.

4. *Collar.* Place collar pieces wrong sides together and baste. Bind outer edge. Place to

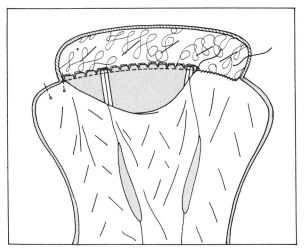

Bind outer edge of collar and attach to neckline. Baste lining to inside of jacket, hem lining over neck join.

neckline and machine, keeping lining out of the seam. Trim and press seam allowances into neckline. Bring lining over the seam and hem round neck, snipping lining at end of collar so that it lies flat.

5. *Binding.* Attach binding to outer edge of jacket, turning in the ends at a neat right angle below collar ends. Try on jacket and adjust sleeve length if necessary. Bind the sleeves, attaching it to the outside and finishing on the inside if they are to be turned back.

6. *Fastening.* Sew buttons in position under rouleau loops. Sew a small piece of Velcro or a Velcro circle inside the jacket to hold the left side in place.

THE TROUSERS

Making up

1. *Cut out.* Check inside leg seam length before cutting out. Adjust if necessary. Cut out back and front in fabric and in lining, if used. Cut 4 pieces of pocket in lining and press soft iron-on Vilene (Pellon) to two of them if a stiffer pocket bag is appropriate.

2. *Seams.* Stitch inside leg seams in fabric and linings, placing back and front legs together. Use open (plain) seams on inside legs and either open or welt seams on outside leg.

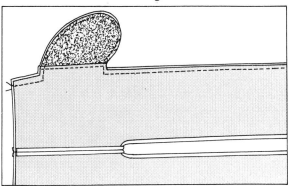

Attach pocket bag pieces, stitch side seams. Snip seam allowances above and below pocket; press seams open.

3. *Pockets.* Stitch interfaced pocket bags to back trousers, matching balance marks. Stitch the second pair to the front trousers.

4. *Side seams.* Stitch side seams above and below pocket opening. Stitch across pocket opening with a large machine stitch. Press pockets towards front. Stitch round pocket bag.

5. *Crotch seam.* Join trouser crotch seam.

6. *Lining,* if used. Join lining seams, stitch outside leg seams leaving an opening where the pocket comes. Put lining inside trousers with wrong sides together. Pin lining turnings (seam allowances) of crotch seam to trouser crotch seam and back stitch together. Baste lining to trousers around pocket. Turn in lining edges and hem to seams on each side of pocket.

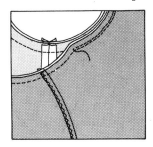
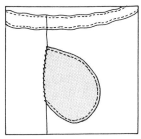

Left: stitch together the seam allowances of lining and trousers. Right: pull trouser pocket through gap in lining and hem round.

7. *Loops*. Make two hanging loops from lining or from narrow petersham ribbon. Place at centre front and centre back and machine through loop, lining and trousers 2 cm (¾ in.) below waist.

8. *Waist*. Turn in fabric and lining together to form waist casing. Edge stitch. Trim lining away below stitching. Turn under raw edge of trousers so that casing is 3mm (⅛ in.) wider than elastic. Either stitch casing and thread elastic through, or slip elastic webbing under the casing and stitch with two rows of stretch stitch. Check the fit of the elastic before stitching.

9. *Hems*. Turn up trouser hems with Wundaweb (Stitch Witchery) or catch stitch. Turn up lining hems so that they are 2.5 cm (1 in.) shorter and hem or machine. Press.

Press creases in trousers if you wish, using a medium hot iron and damp muslin and keeping the lining out of the way.

Print One, Plain One

The gathered skirt is given double emphasis in two layers of Liberty Tana Lawn. In the version we photographed the split-fronted overskirt and waistband is in a warm flower print, and the underskirt is a plain lawn, dark green to pick up the leafy background of the print. The skirt might also have added frills at the hem and even to edge the split, and it could be worn with the simplest T-shirt top in plain lawn, as photographed, or with the V-neck top, or any version of the shirt. (See page 100 for colour photograph.)

PATTERN PIECES

Skirt. Tissue pattern: Waistband. Diagram pattern: Gathered skirt back. skirt front.

T-shirt top. Diagram pattern: Straight dress front (to hip level). back (to hip level). neck facings.

V-neck top. (not illustrated, but the top with front tucks would team attractively with the skirt). Diagram pattern: V-neck top front. back. neck facings. armhole facing.

CUTTING OUT

For the skirt, cut the plain fabric to fold at centre back and front. Cut the print fabric with seam at front, and allow for waistband in print. For the V-neck top, allocate fabric piece for front but do not cut until the tucks have been worked.

THE SKIRT

Making up

1. *Cut out* skirt and overskirt. Cut waistband to match overskirt fabric.

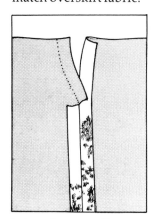

Left: snip seam allowance at base of opening on back skirt. Right: finish hems, put skirts together, gather waist.

2. *Seams.* Stitch seams in plain and print fabric leaving left seam open at the waist for 18cm (7in.). Snip seam allowance 2cm (¾in.) below slit and press front edge back but edge on back skirt should extend making a placket overlap.

3. *Hems.* Turn up hem on plain fabric with Wundaweb (Stitch Witchery). On print skirt turn in centre front edges 1.5cm (⅝in.) and hold back with Wundaweb. Turn up 4cm (1½in.) hem in the same way.

4. *Waist.* Put skirts with right sides out, tack at waist edge and insert gathering thread. Make two

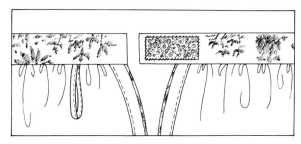

Attach Velcro to waistband overlap; side opening overlaps without fastenings.

hanging loops and stitch to inside at seams. Make waistband with at least 6cm (2½in.) overlap. Attach to skirt, pulling up gathers to fit. Attach Velcro to fasten.

THE T-SHIRT TOP

See page 133 for making-up instructions.

THE V-NECK TOP

Making up

1. *Cut out.* Cut out back to fold and cut facings. Fold remaining fabric intended for front and press a crease on the straight grain at least 8cm (3in.) longer than the pattern piece.

2. *Tucks.* Work a group of pin tucks starting each side of the centre crease. Press. Replace pattern and cut out. Transfer dart and centre front marking.

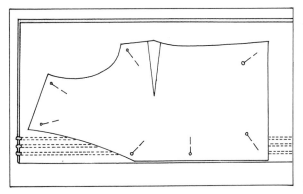

Work the rows of pin tucks on fabric first, fold fabric evenly, pin pattern in place and then cut out front.

3. *Darts.* Stitch darts, press downwards.

4. *Seams.* Stitch and press shoulders and side seams with French seams. Press.

5. *Facings.* Join neck and shoulder facings and attach to wrong side of neckline. Finish on right side. Press. If using pale lawn you may have to make the facings from double fabric to prevent seams etc., from showing through.

The colour photograph (page 100) shows the skirt matched up with a plain T-shirt top, but another choice might be a soft, sleeveless V-necked top with rows of tucks down the centre front.

6. *Hem.* Turn narrow hem and finish.

7. *Buttons.* Space 3 or 4 buttons down the centre front and attach.

Evenings in Silk

Evening dressing like this looks impressive, but the glamour is really all in the fabric. Liberty Silk Crêpe de Chine Market is a soft, abstract print in pastel colours, and the design allows it to speak for itself, emphasising it gently with the drapes of the cowl back. The top is made from the front of the straight dress pattern with the cowl added, and the A-line skirt is lengthened with a hemline split in the left side seam. With care in cutting out the silk crêpe, and attention to the angled seam of the cowl back, there should be no difficulty in creating the most luxurious of evening looks. (See page 101 for colour photograph.)

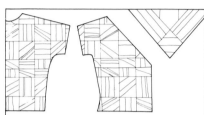

PATTERN PIECES
Cowl back top. Diagram pattern: Straight dress front (to hip). front neck facing. sleeve (short). lower side back. cowl back.
Long skirt. Tissue pattern: seam pocket. waistband (or use stiffening as guide). Diagram pattern: A-line skirt back (full length). skirt front (full length).

CUTTING OUT
This silk crêpe de chine is printed with rectangles forming horizontal stripes that must be matched. Cut out with the fabric folded carefully. Cut the front pattern first with the hemline on a line of print. Cut the side back section on the same line of print so that checks match at the side seams. The cowl part is cut singly and on the cross, so place the lower centre back corner so that it matches the edge of the small square in the print, excluding the seam allowance.

THE COWL BACK TOP

Making up

1. *Cut out.* Cut front, sleeve, front neck facing and lower back. Cut cowl back. Mark centre back. Attach interfacing to front neck facing.

2. *Rouleau loops.* Make a length of rouleau and make 3 loops to fit buttons, machine to left front shoulder between dot on pattern and end of shoulder. Attach front neck facing stitching between neck points and on left shoulder to end of facing, enclosing loops. Trim edges; do not press facing to inside.

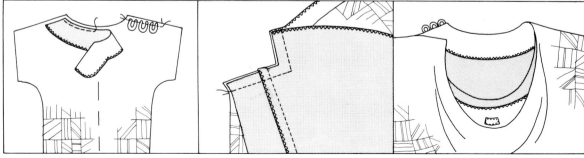

Left: place loops in position at shoulders and attach front neck facing. Centre: join back to front by stitching along shoulders and across facing.

Right: turn neck facing to the inside, letting the loops extend. Sew a small weight to the edge of the facing at the back.

3. *Back.* Join centre back seam, insert cowl back using an angled seam. Neaten neck edge of cowl.

4. *Shoulders.* Stitch right shoulder seam from shoulder to end of front facing. Stitch left seam as far as end of facing stitching. Press. Lift front neck facing and end of cowl facing, join, press open. Catch to shoulder seam on inside. Fold back cowl facing on left shoulder and stitch from neck edge to end of seam stitching, catching in a small piece of folded Vilene to reinforce the buttons. Make two hanging loops and stitch to shoulder seams of front near neck facing.

5. *Sleeves.* Join sleeves to armholes. Stitch sleeve seam and underarm seam. Press. Turn back sleeve hems and finish.

6. *Hem.* Turn up hem and finish.

7. *Buttons.* Stitch buttons through loops and Vilene reinforcement. Sew buttons in place on top of loops so that they remain fastened; they do not need to be undone.

Crystal buttons are sewn into place in the rouleau loops at the shoulder – they do not need to be undone.

8. *Weight.* Insert a small weight in the lowest point of the cowl. Cut a piece of fabric 5cm (2in.) square and wrap it round the weight like a parcel. Stitch through the central holes and sew to the edge of the facing inside cowl back.

THE LONG SKIRT

Making up

1. *Cut out.* Open out fabric to full width and cut two fronts and two backs along the length singly and one way, making sure to match the print before you cut. Cut the same pieces again in lining. Cut four pocket pieces and the waistband from the remaining fabric.

2. *Waistband.* Measure waistbanding round waist, mark size and cut off, allowing overlap of at least 6cm (2½in.). Cut a straight piece of fabric twice the width of the waistbanding plus 3cm (1¼in.). Attach waistbanding by stitching along each edge. Fold and mark seam and centre positions.

3. *Centre back.* Stitch seam to base of zip and press open.
Insert zip above seam.

4. *Pockets.* Stitch fabric pockets to back skirt and lining pockets to front.

5. *Side seams.* Tack skirt seams. Stitch above and below pocket. Stitch right side seam to hem, leaving left seam unstitched but still tacked for

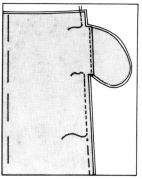 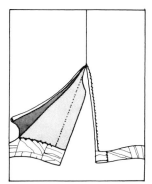

Left: tack the side seams to prevent the silk from slipping while machining. Right: at the hemline slit, fold back the edges of the skirt first, then turn under the lining and hem in place near the edge.

the lower 39cm (15⅜in.). Press seam open. Stitch round pockets. Press pockets towards front. Cut narrow strips of Wundaweb to slip under the side slit turnings to hold them back. Press.

6. *Lining.* Stitch back seam to within 25cm (10in.) of top. Press seam open and press edges back above seam. Put front and back linings together, stitch left seam right up but on right seam leave 39cm (15⅜in.) open at hemline. Press seams open. Press back edges of slit.

7. *Waist.* Put lining inside skirt wrong sides together. Tack together down seams. Tack pressed edges of lining to sides of slit for 10-15cm (4-6in.). Tack lining to skirt at waist. Make two hanging loops and sew to wrong side. Insert gathering threads. Tack waistband to skirt, pull up gathers, even out and tack. Complete the waistband. Hem lining to zip tape.

8. *Hem.* Try on skirt and mark hemline. Turn up as deep a hem as possible, with edges of slit opened out. Turn up lining hem so that it is 3cm (1¼in.) shorter. Fold slit edges into position and press. Tack lining down and hem in place round slit. Press.

9. *Fastenings.* Attach Velcro or large hooks to waistband.

The tie belt (see page 18 for making-up instructions) is trimmed with rouleau loops, each one weighted with a pearl button.

Paisley Set Straight

The simple lines of this three-quarter-sleeved straight dress allow the richly coloured Varuna wool paisley print to speak for itself. Darlington, with its bold pine cone central motif, is one of several classic paisley designs (so called after Paisley, in Scotland, where skilled but cheap manufacturing labour was available) in the Liberty print range. The earliest designs were derived from intricately woven shawls from Kashmir, and were widely copied as they became fashionable. (See page 102 for colour photograph.)

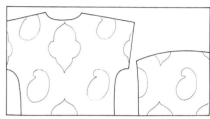

PATTERN PIECES
Tissue pattern: Seam pocket. Diagram pattern: Straight dress front. straight dress back. neck facings. sleeve.

CUTTING OUT
The paisley fabric design shows a symmetrical outline repeating at only 30cm (12in.) intervals, with paisley swirls on each side. Arrange the dark points of the print just below the neckline at the centre front but make sure the paisley part does not fall unflatteringly on the bust line. The large motif should run centrally down the front and back of the dress. Cut the front first, and match the pattern horizontally when cutting the back. To cut the sleeves match the pattern horizontally when the arm is down.

STRAIGHT DRESS WITH FRONT TUCK AND SLEEVES

Making up

1. *Cut out.* Cut across front pattern on tuck line, spread the pieces and insert 10cm (4in.). Pin to paper to make a new pattern, or pin directly to the fabric with front edge to fold. Cut back to fold. Cut sleeves and neck facings. Attach light iron-on Vilene to neckline. Cut 4 pocket pieces and attach Vilene to two of them if desired. Mark tuck on front.

2. *Tuck.* Fold front wrong sides together, tack and machine tuck. Press downwards. Make 10cm (2.5in.) length of rouleau and stitch as 3 loops to left front shoulder on right side.

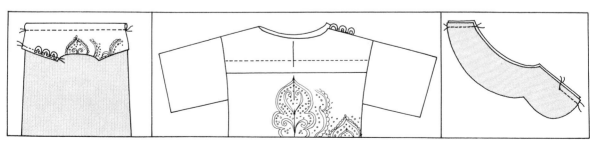

Left: stitch rouleau tubing loops to shoulder; stitch and press tuck. Centre: attach sleeves and stitch side seams.

Right: join neck facing at shoulders making sure to leave space for the loops on the left shoulder.

3. *Pockets and seams.* Attach interfaced pockets to back dress. Attach the other pockets to the front. Stitch and press shoulder seams, stitching left shoulder as far as dot on pattern.

4. *Sleeves.* Attach sleeves to armholes and press. Stitch side and sleeve seams above and below the pockets. Snip seam at underarm. Press open.

Press pockets to front. Stitch around pocket bag.

5. *Facings.* Join shoulders of facings and press. Neaten outer edge of facing. Attach to neckline. Attach buttons. Remove pocket stitching.

6. *Hems.* Try on dress and mark hemline. Turn up hem and sleeve hems.

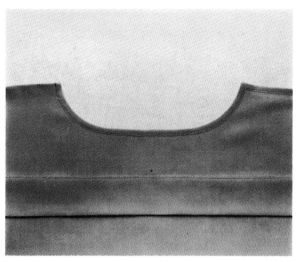

Extra interest might be added to the dress made up in a plain fabric by stitching the tuck in contrast thread. The contrast thread colour could also be picked up again with top-stitching around the neckline.

Darlington paisley print covers an emphatically shaped cummerbund (see page 20 for making instructions) and the print is further emphasised with hand embroidery and tiny beads.

Gathered Together

Layers of Tana lawn in a full smock (using the gathered dress pattern) over a gathered skirt offer plenty of opportunity for decorative tucks and trimmings. In the version we photographed, the smock yoke and patch pockets are bound with plain lawn and trimmed with ribbon. The elastic-waisted skirt has hem tucks with matching rows of narrow ribbon stitched between them. A frill could be added to the skirt hem if desired, perhaps to lengthen it, and a detachable wide collar (see the cover photograph) with yet more ribbon trimming is an optional finishing touch to the smock. (See page 103 for colour photograph.)

PATTERN PIECES
Smock. Tissue pattern: Large patch pocket. Diagram pattern: Gathered dress back to short line. front to short line. sleeve to ¾-length. yoke back. yoke front. cuff (see below).
Skirt. Tissue pattern: Elastic waist (see below). Diagram pattern: Gathered skirt front. skirt back.
Skirt with frill. For a different look, the skirt could be cut shorter and a frill could be added. Tissue pattern: Large patch pocket. waistband. Diagram

pattern: Gathered skirt front. skirt back. frill.
Collar. Diagram pattern.

CUTTING OUT
Tana Lawn Joe is a one-way print, but it is an all-over multicoloured design and therefore rather easier to cut out. When cutting the skirt to be worn under the smock, add a further 10cm (4in.) to the length shown for the tucked skirt if you would prefer a mid-calf length hemline.

THE SMOCK

Making up

1. *Cut out.* Cut back, front and sleeves. Cut 2 back yokes and 4 fronts. Attach light iron-on Vilene (Pellon) to wrong side of one set of yoke pieces. Mark dots and balance marks. Cut a length of contrast fabric on the cross 130cm (51in.) long and 1.5cm (⅝in.) wide.

2. *Seams.* Stitch centre back seam. Stitch centre front seam to dot. Press open. Hold back turnings at opening with Wundaweb. Insert gathering threads across top of back and fronts.

3. *Pockets.* Make three 5mm (¼in.) tucks on the straight grain across a piece of fabric 41cm (16in.) wide. Stitch narrow ribbon between the tucks. Fold a bias piece of contrast fabric in half, press and machine on the right side, with the fold towards tucks 2.5cm (1in.) above top tuck. Fold fabric in half with tucks level and cut two pockets. Cut two more pockets in fabric. Attach light iron-

on Vilene to wrong side of tucked pockets if required. Place pockets and linings right sides together and stitch round outer edge, enclosing the piping and leaving a gap in one side. Turn right side out. Press. Stitch the gap. Press. Place pocket on smock front mid-way between centre and side edge 7cm (2¾in.) above the hem. Machine in place.

4. *Seams.* Stitch side seams with French seams. Turn up 1cm (⅜in.) hem and machine or slip-hem. Stitch sleeve seams. Insert gathering threads across top and bottom of sleeves.

5. *Cuffs.* Cut two lengths of Fold-a-Band for cuffs as follows:

size 10, 29 cm (11½in.)
size 12, 30.5cm (12in.)
size 14, 32cm (12½in.)
size 16, 33.5cm (13in.)
size 18, 35cm (13½in.)
size 20, 36cm (14in.)

Press Fold-a-Band for cuffs to wrong side of fabric, matching perforations to straight grain, and cut out cuffs leaving turnings all round. Stitch 2 rows of narrow ribbon along one side of cuff.

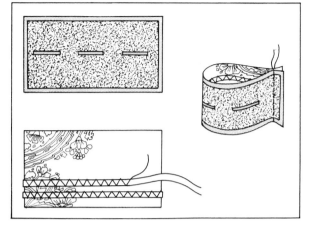

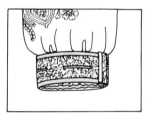 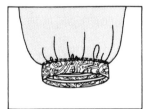

Press Fold-a-Band to cuffs and cut out, leaving turnings all round. Stitch ribbon along one side of cuff and join cuff ends.

Left: slip cuff over sleeve and pull up gathers to fit. Stitch. Right: fold cuff along centre, turn under the raw edge and hem on the inside.

For an extra decorative finish to the cuffs, or perhaps the sleeve at the shoulder, a deep band of smocking could be worked in shades to echo the flowers in the print.

Join the ends. Pin cuff to sleeve, pull up gathers to fit. Attach and finish cuff. Join sleeve to armholes along raglan edges with French seams.

6. *Button loops.* Make 30cm (12in.) of rouleau and machine to right side of right yoke as 5 button loops.

7. *Yoke.* Join shoulder seams of yoke and lining yoke. Machine a length of contrast piping to right side of yoke edge. Fold edge of yoke under so that piping extends, and press. Attach a row of contrast ribbon to yoke 5mm (¼in.) above the edge.

Attach contrast piping to outer edge of yoke. With yoke wrong side down to right side of dress, attach yoke to dress, stitching from the outside.

Place yoke edge wrong side down to right side of dress, carefully match centre front seams, shoulders and centre backs, pin and tack in place. Machine yoke to dress. Place lining yoke to yoke right sides together and tack. Machine along centre front edges catching in loops and round neck. Trim and turn right side out. Tack neck edge, baste layers together round yoke. Press. Turn under edge of yoke lining and hem to back of yoke seam. Press.

8. *Buttons.* Attach buttons to yoke. Sew small hook and thread loop to base of yoke below buttons.

THE SKIRT

Making up

1. *Cut out.* Cut skirt front and skirt back. Cut waistband 1½ times waist size and 10cm (4in.) wide.

2. *Seams.* Stitch side seams and press.

3. *Tucks.* Fold skirt wrong sides together 15cm (6in.) above hem, press and stitch to make a tuck 1.5cm (⅝in.) wide. Make 3 tucks in all with 1cm (⅜in.) between them. Press downwards. Stitch 3mm (⅛in.) wide ribbon between them.

4. *Hem.* Measure required length, turn up hem and finish with Wundaweb.

5. *Waist.* Make two hanging loops and attach to inside of waist at seams. Insert gathering thread in waist. Join ends of waistband. Attach to skirt, pull up gathers to fit. Finish band 3mm (⅛in.) wider than elastic. Insert elastic.

THE SKIRT WITH ADDED FRILL (FLOUNCE)

Making up

1. *Cut out.* Cut front and back skirt to fold. Cut 4 pieces of frill. Cut out two patch pockets.

2. *Frill.* Cut out to measurements on page 19. Join all seams on frill with narrow or French seams. Turn up narrow hem. Fold fabric wrong sides together. Make three 7mm (¼in.) tucks above the hem. Insert gathering threads in upper edge.

3. *Seams.* Stitch skirt seams leaving left seam open for 18cm (7in.) at waist. Snip seam allowance just below this. Press the seam allowance on the back to extend and press back the seam allowance on the front.

4. *Pockets.* Make up large patch pockets and attach to front skirt with top edge 8cm (3in.) below the waist.

5. *Waist.* Insert gathering threads. Make waistband with at least 6cm (2½in.) overlap. Attach to skirt. Attach Velcro or hooks to fasten.

6. *Frill.* Divide skirt hem into 4 sections and pin to frill right sides together matching marks to frill seams. Pull up gathers. Tack and machine. Neaten.

Make sure that the frill gathers are evenly distributed around the skirt edge. The version we photographed has rows of tucks and narrow ribbon.

Sweet Smocking and Stitching

The simplicity of the grown-up dress, made by attaching the drop-waist skirt to the cut-off line on the shirt pattern, offers the best opportunity for further decoration according to taste and ability. The version photographed has rows of feather stitching, in a shade picked out from the tiny flower print, around the sleeves and down the front bands beside rows of pin tucks. Other ideas might include ribbon, lace or a sprinkling of French knots. A puffed bow in a different, toning print goes under the flat collar. The little girl's dress, in perfect and traditional style, has puffed sleeves, a Peter Pan collar, smocking in the darker colours of the sweet Tana Lawn print, and trimmings of the narrowest ribbon. (See page 104 for colour photograph.)

PATTERN PIECES

Adult dress. Tissue pattern: Shirt back (to cut-off line). front (to cut-off line). front band (to cut-off line). yoke. Peter Pan collar. sleeve (short). drop-waist skirt. seam pocket or patch pocket.
Child's dress. Tissue pattern: Yoke front. yoke back. sleeve. collar (cut 4). Diagram pattern: Skirt to size required.

CUTTING OUT

The adult dress is made in Belle, a delicate print that can be cut both ways. Cut out the skirt with a front and back seam except in small sizes, or if you wish you can economise in fabric and cut the skirt without centre seams across the width of the fabric.

THE ADULT DRESS

Making up

1. *Cut out.* Cut shirt back, yoke, sleeve and collar. Cut out the front but leave at least 2.5 cm (1in.) extra at the front edge and neckline. Cut out front bands and attach Fold-a-Band.

2. *Tucks and feather stitching.* Make two pin tucks 2cm (¾in.) apart, parallel with the blouse front edges, with the first tuck 2cm (¾in.) from the raw

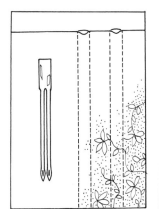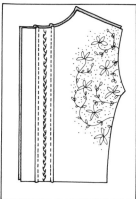

Left: pin tucks can be made using a twin needle and two reels of thread. Right: put shirt fronts wrong sides together and re-cut to size.

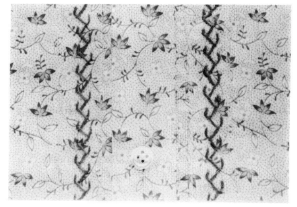

Tiny pin tucks parallel with the front bands of the dress are spaced with feather stitching in a shade to match the deepest colour in the print flowers.

edge. Make tucks on the sleeves too with the first one 5cm (2in.) above the hem edge. Use two or three strands of embroidery thread and work feather stitch between the tucks. Press shirt fronts and put them wrong sides together, replace the pattern and re-cut the edges accurately.

3. *Front bands.* Attach bands to shirt fronts. If you decide on bound buttonholes, work the first stage now. At neck edge fold band right sides together and stitch from fold to centre of band. Snip and trim and turn right side out. On inside turn in and hem bands.

4. *Yoke.* Attach and press back and front yoke seams.

5. *Collar.* Attach interfacing to one piece of Peter Pan collar. Make collar, press and attach to shirt neckline with bias strip of fabric.

6. *Buttonholes.* Whether you have decided on machine or hand worked buttonholes, make them now. Make the top buttonhole 1cm (⅜in.) below neck edge and the bottom one 8cm (3in.) above the waist. Do not cut them yet if they are machine made. Wrap right front over left and machine with a large stitch through both bands 1cm (⅜in.) above waist and again above the bottom buttonhole.

7. *Fitting.* Tack up side seams and try on; for a closer fit, take in the sides.

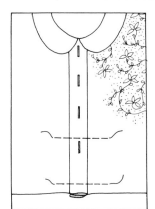
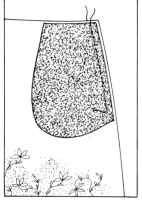

Left: wrap right side over left and hold together with two short rows of stitching. Right: position pocket pieces level with top edge of drop-waist skirt.

8. *Side seams.* This is a loose, swinging smock but it may feel too loose if you have not worn this style before. Try it on and make sure that it is comfortable before completing the side seams. Work open seams. Press.

9. *Skirt and pockets.* Make open seams at centre back and front. Place interfaced pocket pieces on back skirt side seams with top edges level with top of skirt. Stitch and press seams open. Attach the other pockets to the front skirt, press seams open. Put skirt back and front right sides together and stitch side seams from hem to pocket. Stitch across pocket opening with large machine stitch. Press pockets towards front and stitch around bags.

10. *Waist join.* Insert gathering threads in top of skirt. Pin bodice to skirt, pull up gathers. Tack. Try on the dress. Check that the waist join is suitably placed for you. If you are shorter than average you may wish to shorten the bodice. Complete the waist seam. Press.

11. *Sleeves.* Fold sleeves right sides together and stitch seams. Turn up 3cm (1¼in.) hem, turn under and hem to the upper tuck. Stitch sleeves to armholes, matching the centre of the sleeve head to the shoulder point. Press.

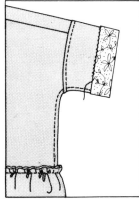

Turn up sleeve hem, turn under and hem to the upper tuck. With the centre of the sleeve head matched to the shoulder point, stitch sleeves to armholes.

12. *Buttons.* Complete the buttonholes and sew on the buttons. Attach a press stud at the neckline under the collar.

13. *Hem.* Put on the dress and mark the hem length. Complete the hem.

Instructions for puffed bow appear on page 19.

For a completely different look, the collar of the dress might be edged with fine lace and sprinkled with a cluster of French knots.

CHILD'S DRESS

Making up

1. *Cut out* rectangles for skirt back and front. Do not cut armholes. Do not cut remainder of dress until you are ready to sew.

2. *Smocking.* Insert gathering threads or use a smocking machine to gather the top edge of front and back to a depth of 8cm (3¼in.). Work the smocking. If you decide on a distinctive design like the one shown, find the centre pleat and count to the edge to make sure that the centre of a chevron comes exactly in the middle. On the back of the dress work smocking to the edge of the opening exactly on the seam line and make sure

that when the two edges meet the embroidery matches exactly.

3. *Back opening.* Pin pattern in place and cut armholes. Stitch centre back seam to base of opening. On right side fold back extension level with seam and edge of smocking. Turn under edge and hem. On under side allow half the extension to extend, fold under the remainder, turn under and hem. At base of opening, stitch across seam to hold flat.

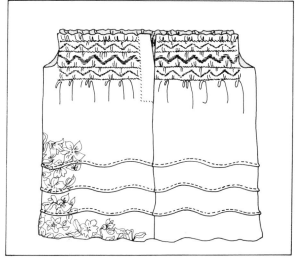

Work the smocking, join side and back seams, make back opening ready to attach yoke.

Stitch side seams. Make three 13 mm (½in.) tucks 5 mm (¼in.) apart and about 15cm (6in.) above the hem.

4. *Cut out* remainder of dress. Attach light iron-on Vilene to one pair of collars. Tack lace edging to outer edge of collars, place under collar pieces on top and stitch round outer edge. Trim and turn collar right side out. Press. Sew narrow ribbon to collar 13mm (½in.) from edge. Join collars at centre front by stitching together 13mm (½in.) from edge.

5. *Yoke.* Join shoulders of yoke and yoke lining. Press. Tack collar to neckline of yoke, place yoke lining on top right sides down, machine along back edges and round neck. Trim and turn right side out. Tack round neckline and along back edge. Attach yoke to skirt stitching an even distance from the smocking. On the back of the

Lace edges the collar and hem of the traditional smocked dress, with the narrowest white ribbon as a finishing touch. Bands of the same narrow ribbon are also stitched above the lace-edged hem.

dress, the edge of the skirt opening on the right side should be level with the centre back line on the yoke. On the under side the edge of the extension in the opening falls level with the yoke edge. Machine yoke to skirt. Trim and press turnings towards yoke. Smooth yoke lining over yoke and tack. Turn under and hem lining edge to yoke seams. Slip stitch lower yoke edges together beyond buttonholes.

6. *Lace and trimming.* Stitch sleeve seams. Turn up hems and attach lace underneath or attach with flat bias if you want to enclose the edge of the lace. Sew a row of narrow ribbon 1cm (⅜in.) above the hem. 4cm (1½in.) above the hem attach a piece of bias fabric flat, 1cm (⅜in.) wide, machined along each edge inside sleeve. Measure narrow elastic round child's arm, and insert in the casing. Join ends.

7. *Buttons and buttonholes.* Make 3 buttonholes on centre back line of yoke. Sew on buttons. Attach press studs on top and bottom corners of yoke.

8. *Hem.* Turn up the dress hem. Attach lace edging.

This version of the classic shirt is in lavish silk crêpe de chine, and can be worn with a detachable pussy bow at the neck. The softness of plain red Varuna wool is a good choice for showing off the folds of the A-line skirt. See page 75 for making-up instructions.

Choose a strong print for the short jacket and pick up the splash of colour in a turned-back lapel and cropped trousers, or aim for something completely different in softer shades with full-length trousers and the jacket left unbelted. See page 78 for making-up instructions.

Bold black and white printed Varuna wool is quilted and bound with black satin to make a striking cropped jacket, and matched up with simple, straight black wool trousers that would fit happily into any wardrobe. For making-up instructions see page 80.

Print and toning plain Tana lawn are used to good effect for a gathered skirt with a split-fronted overskirt and a quick-to-make T-shirt top. The turban is a simple length of fabric. For making-up instructions see pages 83 and 133

The most glamorous of evening dresses is really a tunic top softened with a draped cowl back, and an ankle-length A-line skirt made in silk crêpe de chine and trimmed with crystal. See page 85 for making-up instructions.

An eye-catching paisley print is a clever choice for the simplest straight dress, where the strength of the design is allowed to speak for itself and then emphasised with a shawl in the same fabric and a chunky brooch. For making-up instructions see page 88.

A full smock with a detachable wide collar is worn over a gathered skirt with an elasticated waist, and both layers are liberally tucked and trimmed with narrow satin ribbon. See the jacket photograph for the smock worn with the collar, and page 90 for making-up instructions.

Tiny-flowered traditional Tana lawn is the best choice for a little girl's dress smocked and lace-trimmed, and for an adult's loose, comfortable dress swinging from a low waist and decorated with tucks and feather-stitching. For making-up instructions see page 93.

Bright, abstract geometric prints give a simple drop-waisted sundress and long shorts and a bandeau top a completely different look for days out in the sun. The bandeau top is a simple strip of fabric, twisted and tied. See page 113 for making-up instructions.

City dressing is exemplified in a crisp pink shirt in cool and comfortable Tana lawn, trimmed with white and with a band collar, matched up with a flattering knife-pleated version of the straight skirt in yarn-dyed Varuna wool. See page 115 for making-up instructions.

A trim straight skirt with a front panel is set off by a classically cut shirt in the equally classic Liberty print Ianthe. The origin of the print design is not known but it has a long history – it dates from about 1890. For making-up instructions see page 118.

Traditional-style blue-checked baby's rompers in yarn-dyed Jubilee, easily washable and comfortable to wear, have a rounded collar with soft points, short sleeves, and darker piping for definition at the yoke and collar edge. For making-up instructions see page 121.

Hera, or Peacock Feather, is one of the most famous of all Liberty prints and it shows to its best advantage in the luxurious fullness of this dress, gathered to a deep, round yoke and with sleeves falling to a tight, wide cuff. For making-up instructions see page 124.

Pretty French knickers and a piped bra pick up the same blue-and-white striped Tana lawn as the easy robe, made from the shirt pattern and extended to the required length, patch-pocketed and lined in plain white lawn. Making-up instructions are on page 127.

The prettiest summer dressing is a simple, ankle-length dress, or a T-shirt top and circular skirt, both in the gentle flower prints of Tana lawn. Sweet Pea dates from about 1900, and Convolvulus is a fresh floral pattern from Liberty's textile archive. For making-up instructions see page 131.

The grown-up tartan dress has a double collar with the touch of white of the under collar picked up at the cuff. Over a simple dress in toning tartan, the little girl wears an apron with frilled armholes, smocking, and tucks at the hem. For making-up instructions see page 135, rabbit page 122.

Gone On Holiday

The sundress is an easy, go-anywhere look for shopping, sightseeing, or just the trip down to the beach, made by combining the drop-waist skirt pattern with the V-neck top. The long shorts have leg facings finished on the right side, and neat patch pockets on the back. For a shorter, sportier version simply turn up the hems to the required length and omit the facings. The bandeau top is simplicity itself, no more than a length of matching fabric, self- or contrast-lined, worn twisted at the front and tied in a knot at the back. (See page 105 for colour photograph.)

PATTERN PIECES

Sundress. Tissue pattern: Drop-waist skirt front. back. large patch pocket. Diagram pattern: V-neck top front. back. neck facings. armhole facings.

Shorts and bandeau: Tissue pattern: small patch pocket. Diagram pattern: Trouser front. back. back facing. front facing. bandeau piece (cut 2). also cut sufficient bias strip 2.5cm (1 in.) wide to bind outer edge of bandeau.

CUTTING OUT

For the sundress, cut the small size skirt back and front with the fabric folded in the centre of a stripe. Cut larger sizes with centre seams, carefully matching the stripes. All sizes need seams when using narrower fabric. For the shorts, the pockets and leg facings should be cut either so that the print will match perfectly, or so that the stripes alternate and emphasise the print. You could economise on fabric for the bandeau by making it from double fabric instead of lining it as shown here.

THE SUNDRESS

Making up

1. *Cut out.* Cut the skirt back and front. Cut top back front and armhole facings. Reserve fabric for pockets. Cut neck facings on single fabric.

2. *Darts.* Stitch and press darts.

3. *Seams and facings.* Stitch shoulder seams and side seams with open seams. Press. Attach neck and armhole facings to right side and finish on wrong side. Hold in place with pieces of Wundaweb.

4. *Pockets.* Make 3 tucks 6mm (¼ in.) wide or of a width to fit in with the stripe of the print. Make the tucks at least 18cm (14 in.) long. Press. Fold fabric and cut two pockets. Make pockets and attach to front skirt.

5. *Waist join.* Insert gathering threads and join skirt to top. Tack and fit. Adjust if necessary. Also, you may prefer to arrange the gathers in groups, leaving the skirt smooth over the hips.

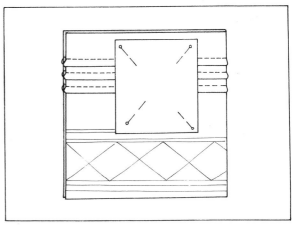

Make tucks before cutting out, then fold carefully and cut out pockets.

6. *Hem.* Put on dress and mark hemline. Turn up and finish hem.

7. *Rouleau.* Make a 1m (39 in.) length of rouleau tubing as a belt or head band.

THE BANDEAU

Making up

1. *Cut out.* See page 19 for measurements.

2. *Stitch.* Place fabric wrong sides together and machine around outer edge 1cm (⅜ in.) from raw edges.

3. *Binding.* Join the bias strips. Begin 20 cm (8 in.) from one end and attach to right side, stitching 1.5cm (⅝ in.) from edge. Trim. Join the binding. Finish on wrong side by hemming into machining. Press.

THE LONG SHORTS

Making up

1. *Cut out.* Cut out back and front shorts. Cut pockets and leg facings either so that the print will match perfectly or so that the stripes alternate and emphasise the print.

2. *Pockets.* Make and attach patch pockets 14cm (5 in.) below waist.

3. *Leg seams.* Join inside leg seams with open seams. Join outside leg seams with machine fell seams. Join crotch seam.

4. *Facings.* Join facing seams and press. Turn in and press upper edge of facings. Attach facings to legs with right side facing to wrong side of shorts. Turn facing to right side, turn in raw edge, tack to shorts and top-stitch close to the fold and again near the hem.

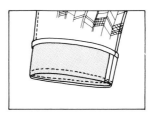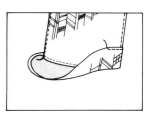

Left: join seams of shorts, join seams in leg facing. Attach facings to wrong side. Right: turn facings to outside, turn in and press. Top-stitch near the hem and near facing edge.

5. *Loops.* Make two hanging loops and attach to centre front and centre back.

6. *Waist.* Turn in top edge of shorts and press. Measure and join waist length of elastic webbing. Attach to wrong side of waist with two rows of zigzag stitch. Fold elastic and fabric over again and stitch again from right side twice. Alternatively, make a casing and insert elastic.

Short shorts can be made in the same way as long shorts, but omit the leg facings and turn up hems to the required length.

Executive Suite

The most citified of the shirt and skirt outfits we chose is achieved by matching yarn-dyed Liberty Tana Lawn in a faint pink stripe with plain white lawn band collar, cuffs and pocket tops, the perfect business shirt, with a skirt in yarn-dyed Varuna wool, also with a faint stripe. This version of the straight skirt pattern has knife pleats in the panel seams for easier movement, and side pockets.
(See page 106 for colour photograph.)

PATTERN PIECES

Shirt. Tissue pattern: Shirt back. front. yoke. front band. sleeve. band collar. cuff. small patch pocket.
Skirt. Tissue pattern: Straight skirt back. front panel. side front. seam pocket. waistband to fit.

CUTTING OUT

Cut the shirt front, back and sleeves with vertical stripes, but place the stripes horizontally on the yoke. The Varuna wool used for the skirt is woven in lengthwise striped bands 13cm (5in.) wide. Cut the skirt so that the stripes are balanced.

THE SHIRT

Top-stitch the front bands, collar band, pockets and cuffs, using thread to match the main fabric so that it shows as a contrast on the white trimming. Make the top-stitching the same width as the stripe in the fabric, repeated on all edges. Use pearl shirt buttons, spacing 6 on the front band and one in the collar band, the last with a horizontal buttonhole. Attach the cuff without an extension, work a buttonhole in each end and fasten with cuff links.

Interface the collar band with soft iron-on Vilene attached to both pieces. This is to stiffen it so that it remains crisp, and also to ensure that seam allowances of the darker main fabric do not show through to the right side.

Making up

1. *Cut out.* Cut shirt back, front, yoke, sleeves and front bands from striped Tana lawn. Cut band collar and cuffs from white lawn. Transfer pattern markings to fabric. Fold back 6cm (2½in.) on top edge of pocket pattern. Cut one or two pockets in striped fabric, adding a seam allowance along the top. Cut a length of Fold-a-Band the width of the pocket, press to the wrong side of the white lawn and cut out, adding a seam allowance all round.

2. *Front bands.* Attach Fold-a-Band. Stitch bands to wrong side of shirt fronts, bring to right side, turn under and top-stitch.

3. *Pockets.* Attach contrast bands, top-stitch. Attach to shirt by machine.

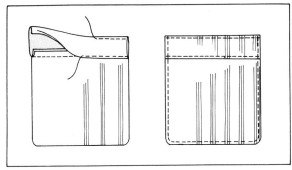

Attach pocket band, fold over to right side and top-stitch. Turn in edges; attach to shirt.

4. *Yoke.* Insert tucks. Stitch back and front shirt to yokes, turn to right side and press.

5. *Collar.* Interface both collar pieces. Make collar and attach to right side of shirt neck, turn to inside and hem. Top-stitch. Press.

The white collar is contrast top-stitched in the same shade as the shirt, and the same stitching is picked up on the pocket band.

6. *Sleeves.* Make faced slit openings. Attach sleeves to shirt armholes with narrow or machine fell seams.

7. *Side seams and sleeve seams.* Stitch from shirt hem to wrist with French or machine fell (flat felled) seams. Press.

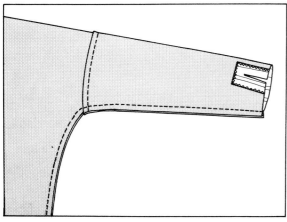

Make faced slit opening in sleeves, holding the fabric down with Wundaweb.

8. *Cuffs.* Put 4 tucks in wrist. Attach cuffs for links without extensions. Top-stitch. Press.

9. *Hem.*

10. *Buttonholes and buttons* in shirt front and cuffs.

THE SKIRT

Making up

1. *Cut out.* Cut out in fabric, and again in lining, but pin lining front panel and lining side front together without the pleats, in order to cut in one piece to a fold at the centre front. Cut two pockets in fabric and two in lining. Mark darts and pleat lines. Attach Vilene to lining pockets if required.

2. *Pleats.* Stitch front seams on pleat line and press well. Top-stitch from top of pleat to waist.

3. *Pockets and zip.* Attach lining pockets to front skirt. Attach interfaced pockets to back skirt. Join centre back seam to base of zip. Insert zip.

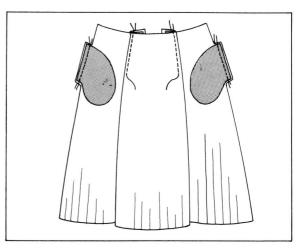

Join side panels to centre panel, press and top-stitch pleats from top of pleat to waist. Attach pocket bags.

4. *Seams.* Join side seams above and below pockets. Stitch across pocket opening. Press seams. Snip turnings and press pockets to front. Stitch round pocket bags.

5. *Lining.* Stitch lining seams. Stitch darts, fold tucks in front lining to correspond with the shaping between the front and side panels. Put lining in skirt with wrong sides together. Tack round waist. Turn in lining edges beside zip and hem. Remove pocket stitching.

6. *Waistband.* Make two hanging loops and attach to skirt waist at side seams. Make and attach waistband. Attach fastening.

7. *Hem.* Put on skirt and mark hemline. Press light Fold-a-Band to wrong side of pleats, locating perforations over the pressed crease. Turn up hem with pleat seam open. Complete hem and re-press. Turn up lining hem so that it is 2.5cm (1in.) shorter than skirt. Work loose bar tacks at side seams.

The Classic Choice

The straight skirt is a basic in every wardrobe, and matched up with an equally classic shirt it can, according to the fabrics chosen, go easily from season to season and from work to play. Choose a gaberdine, a light wool worsted or even plain cotton for the skirt, the flowery prettiness of a Tana lawn or a stricter white poplin for the shirt, dress them up or down, and the variations are almost endless. Our own choice for the shirt was Ianthe, here in a smaller-scale version of one of the best-loved Liberty prints, with plain blue Wandel for the skirt. (See page 107 for colour photograph.)

PATTERN PIECES

Shirt. Tissue pattern: Shirt back. front. yoke. front band. sleeve. band collar. shirt collar. cuff. small patch pocket.
Skirt. Tissue pattern: Straight skirt back. centre front panel. front side panel. seam pocket. waistband.

CUTTING OUT

Ianthe is a one-way print 90cm (36in.) wide with a horizontal band effect. The design repeats every 13cm (5in.). For the best placing of the pattern elements, cut out as follows. Cut out the yoke to the fold of the fabric with the main print motif at the fold and the dark band of colour with its base on the seam line. Cut out the shirt back to the fold on the print motif but also make sure the pattern will continue uninterrupted down the shirt back. To do this accurately, fold back the seam allowances on the pattern to pin it to the fabric, then open them out flat to cut out.

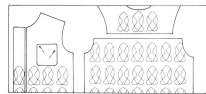

To cut out the shirt front, fold the fabric with the print matched and have the shirt back beside it while you pin the front pattern in position to ensure that the print matches at the side seam.
Cut the front band of the shirt in the same way.
To match the pocket, pin the pattern to the shirt front and trace the fabric design on to the paper. Remove the pattern and find an area of spare fabric where you can match the pocket design exactly.

THE SHIRT

Making up
Use thread to match the ground colour of the print.

1. *Cut out.* Cut out fabric, Vilene and Fold-a-Band. Transfer markings for all tucks, shoulder and sleeve points, neck and collar matching points and pocket position. Cut fabric at sleeve opening.

2. *Front bands.* Attach Fold-a-Band. Stitch to right sides of shirt fronts and hem on the wrong side. Top-stitch both edges.

3. *Pocket.* Make up and attach to left shirt front. Machine in place.

4. *Yoke.* Pin tucks in position. Attach back shirt to yoke and yoke lining. Top-stitch. Attach front yokes to shirt; top-stitch. Turn under and hem raw edge of yoke lining.

5. *Collar.* Interface collar and neck band to required degree of stiffness. If you want a really stiff collar and neck band allow twice the quantity of Vilene and attach it to both outer and inner pieces of fabric. Make collar and top-stitch insert between bands, trim and top-stitch. Attach to shirt neck edge. Top-stitch.

In gneral, when top-stitching at different stages, ensure that the stitch length is always the same.

THE SKIRT

Making up

1. *Cut out.* Fold back pleat extension on pattern pieces and cut. Transfer markings. Cut two pocket pieces and attach light iron-on Vilene if required. Cut back skirt in lining. Pin front panel pattern to side front and cut out front lining in one piece to a fold. A small dart will be made at the waist between pattern edges. Cut two pockets in lining.

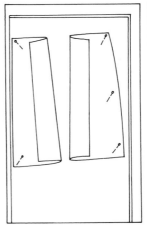 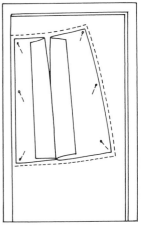

Left: Using straight skirt pattern fold back pleat sections then cut out around each piece. Right: to cut the lining front in one piece use the same pattern pieces put together and against the fold.

2. *Panel.* Stitch side fronts to front panel. Press seams towards centre, trim underneath seam allowance. Top-stitch beside seam.

3. *Pockets.* Attach lining pockets to front skirt. Attach interfaced pockets to back. Join side seams above and below pockets. Press seams open. Lift back and pocket out of the way and top-stitch front seam beside pocket to match panel seam. Stitch round pocket.

4. *Back.* Stitch centre back seam and darts. Press. Insert zip above seam.

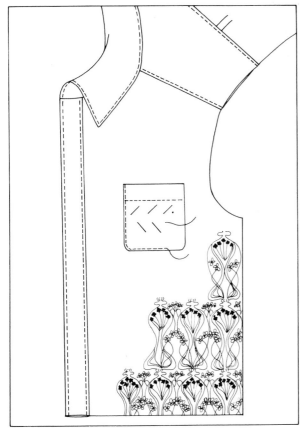

Make up shirt collar to required degree of stiffness and attach to shirt. Top-stitch collar to match yoke and front. Attach pocket to shirt front.

6. *Sleeves.* Make continuous strip openings in sleeves. Attach sleeve head to shirt matching shoulder point and sleeve head point.

7. *Side seams and sleeve seams.* Fold shirt wrong sides together and make French seam from shirt hem to underarm and down to wrist.

8. *Cuffs.* Insert tucks. Attach cuffs.

9. *Hem.* Finish by hand or machine.

10. *Buttonholes and buttons.* Work one horizontal buttonhole by hand or machine in the neck band, work the first buttonhole vertically in the front band 7cm (2¾in.) down. Make the bottom buttonhole 13cm (5in.) above the hem and space out five more buttons in between.

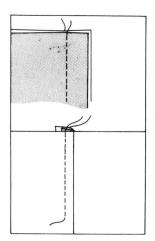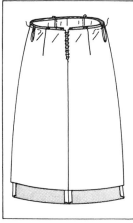

Left: before top-stitching the panel seams, trim one seam allowance to reduce bulk. Right: tack skirt and lining with wrong sides together. Attach loops and hem lining around zip before attaching waistband.

5. *Lining.* Stitch darts in front and back lining. Stitch side seams and back seams. Put lining inside skirt with wrong sides together. Tack together round waist and turn in lining edges beside zip. Tack and hem to zip tape. Make two hanging loops and stitch to each side of waist at side seams.

6. *Waistband.* Make waistband and tack to skirt. Try on the skirt and check the fit of the waist. Attach and finish the band, top-stitching around it to match the panel and making sure that the stitch length is the same.

7. *Hem.* Put on skirt and mark hemline. Turn up and stitch or use Wundaweb. Turn up lining hem 2.5cm (1in.) shorter than skirt. Work a 2.5cm (1in.) long bar tack between lining and skirt at side seams.

8. *Fastening.* Attach waist fastening using either button and buttonhole or Velcro, according to choice.

Checking The Baby

Best-dressed babies have rompers in yarn-dyed Liberty Jubilee with a restrained small check. The design features a neat collar and short sleeves, and plain lawn piping for definition at the yoke and collar edges. The romper legs are elasticated for comfort, and there are three buttons at the back yoke. The essential accessory is a lop-eared rabbit to match in leftover fabric, or any suitable scraps of Jubilee or Tana lawn, with his own reversible jacket. (See page 108 for colour photograph.)

PATTERN PIECES

Rompers. Tissue pattern: Back. front. yoke back (cut 2). yoke front (cut 4). sleeve. collar (cut 4).

Rabbit. Diagram pattern: Body front and back. leg front. leg back. nose. head side piece. head gusset. ears (in fabric and Vilene). coat front (and lining). coat back (and lining). tie.

CUTTING OUT

For the rompers, cut all the pieces on the straight grain and take care to match the checks at the seams. The rabbit can be made in left-over fabric to match the rompers, or in Tana lawn or Jubilee scraps from any of the other patterns, or in any mixture of patterns. The pattern makes a rabbit 30cm (12in.) high.

THE ROMPERS

Making up

1. *Cut out,* transfer markings. Cut two pieces of fabric on the bias 18cm (7in.) long and 2.5cm (1in.)

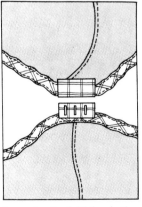

Left: snip the French seam in order to fold back the edges for back opening. Right: After making leg hems attach two pieces of fabric for nappy opening.

wide for sleeves. Cut 82cm (32in.) of contrast fabric on the bias 1.5cm (⅝in.) wide.

2. *Stitch* centre front seam on the body and centre back seam to base of opening with French seams. Snip seam at base of opening. Fold back extension on to right side on fold line and stitch across the bottom. Trim and turn right side out. Lay right side of opening over left, slip-stitch base to rompers.

3. *Seams and hems.* Stitch side seams. Turn 1.5cm (⅝in.) hems on legs, machine twice to form a casing leaving a gap to thread elastic. Cut two pieces of fabric 10cm (4in.) long and 6.5cm (2½in.) wide. Stitch to right side of each under leg. Turn in ends and press. On front of romper fold in half to form a binding, turn under again and hem all around.

4. *Buttons and buttonholes.* Make three buttonholes in flap. On back of romper fold fabric right back, turn under and machine stitch all around. Sew three buttons in place to correspond with buttonholes. Insert elastic in hems, join ends. Insert gathering threads along top edges of rompers for drawing up to fit yoke.

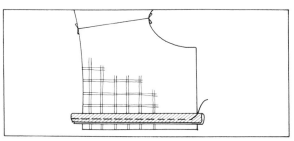

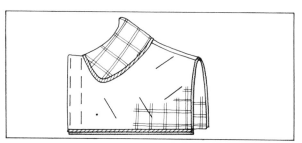

Join shoulders of yoke and yoke lining and press open. Attach piping.

5. *Yoke*. Join shoulders of yoke and yoke lining. Stitch bias contrast piping to yoke edges.

6. *Collar*. Attach light iron-on interfacing to two collars. Stitch contrast piping to outer edge of both. Place second collar pieces right side down on top of piping and stitch together. Trim and turn right side out. Press. Join collars at centre front by stitching together 13mm (½in.) from the edge.

7. *Attach collar*. Place collar to neckline of yoke matching centre fronts and centre backs. Tack to yoke. Tack lining yoke right side down on top of collar. Stitch round neck to corners of yoke at back and down to yoke edge. Trim and turn yoke lining to inside. Tack yokes together round neck and armholes.

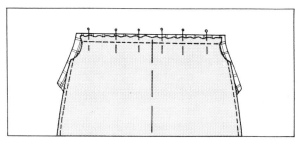

Top: baste yoke and lining together, leaving edges free. Bottom: hold the lining out of the way and attach the yoke to the body section. Pin, pull up gathers, tack.

edge with bias strip joining it at under arm. Insert sleeves into armholes.

10. *Button and buttonholes*. Make 3 hand or machine buttonholes in yoke and attach buttons. Sew press stud to yoke edge below buttons.

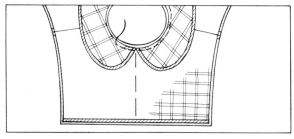

Tack collar to right side of yoke then place lining yoke on top and stitch.

8. *Attach yoke*. Matching centre of yoke to front seam, and matching end of back yoke to opening, pin yoke to rompers pulling up gathers to fit. Even out gathers. Stitch from piping side holding lining aside. Trim and press turnings towards yoke. Turn under edges of yoke lining and hem.

9. *Sleeves*. Stitch sleeve seams. Insert gathering threads in top and bottom of sleeve. Bind lower

THE RABBIT (*Colour photograph page* 112)

Making up

1. *Cut out*. Cut 4 body sections; 2 front legs; 2 back legs; 2 head side pieces; 1 head gusset to fold; 4 ears; 1 back coat to fold and 1 in lining; 2 front coats and 2 in lining; 2 tie pieces cut to fold. Attach iron-on Vilene to one pair of ears. Note that 1cm (⅜in.) turnings are allowed on pattern.

2. *Ears*. Place pairs of ears right sides together, stitch outer edge, trim and turn right side out. Stitch darts in head pieces. Fold ears at lower edge and stitch to right side of head piece with fold of ear to back of head. Join side head pieces to gusset.

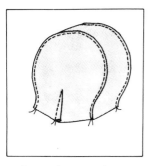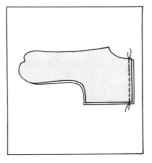

Left: stitch gusset between head sections. Right: stitch body sections together at front and back.

3. *Darts.* Stitch all darts in back legs. Stitch the centre front and back crotch seams.

4. *Seams.* Stitch pairs of body sections together at centre front and centre back. Stitch waist seams joining front body to front legs and back body to back legs, matching centre seams. With front and back bodies right sides together, stitch all round outer edge matching seams, leaving neckline open. Snip turnings at intervals all round.

5. *Attach body* to head, stitching front of neck only and leaving back neck open. Turn body right side out, easing out all seams. Stuff the body until firm. Slip-stitch back neck opening.

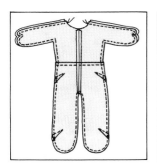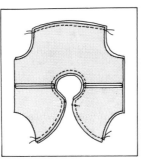

Left: join front to back all round. Right: stitch jacket lining to jacket.

6. *Coat.* Stitch shoulder seams of coat and coat lining. Put coat and lining right sides together,

Any leftover scraps of fabric and odd lengths of ribbon make a loveable rabbit with big ears and embroidered features.

stitch across ends of sleeves. Stitch round front, neck and across bottom of coat. Snip and turn right side out. Join coat side seams. Join lining side seams by folding in edges and slip stitching together. Press. Join ends of tie, then fold tie in half and stitch across ends and down long edge leaving a gap for turning through. Trim and turn right side out. Press. Slip-stitch the gap. Attach tie to back neck of coat with a few oversewing stitches.

7. *Features.* Stitch felt nose in position, embroider eyes and whiskers. To make the ears stand up, join them near the tips with a bar tack.

The Full Treatment

A luxuriously full dress with a deep round yoke, gathered raglan sleeves and wide cuffs, is set off by contrasting plain piping and a flattering tie neck. The perfect eye-catching print for the dress is Liberty Varuna Wool Hera, one of the most famous of all the Liberty prints, sometimes called Peacock Feather. It dates from the turn of the century, when it was designed by Rex Silver as a furnishing fabric, and – recently revived – it now appears on the complete range of fabrics; even, in a delicate reduced scale version, on Tana lawn. (See page 109 for colour photograph.)

PATTERN PIECES
Tissue pattern: Seam pocket. Diagram pattern: Gathered dress back. front. sleeve. yoke front. yoke back. tie. seam pocket. cuff (see below).

CUTTING OUT
The peacock's feather eyes of the one-way print design, which has a 30cm (11¾in.) repeat, are arranged in fan shapes. Cut all the pattern pieces singly, starting with the front yoke. Fold back the centre front seam allowances and place the pattern with the centre front in the centre of the eye. Pin and cut out. Make another copy of the yoke pattern and reverse it to cut a matching half of yoke, or reverse the yoke and the pattern still pinned together and carefully re-locate it on the print to cut it again.

Spread out more fabric below the yoke with the peacock eye in line. Fold back seam allowance on the skirt front pattern and place it in position 30cm (11¾in.) lower excluding seam allowance. This will ensure the print arrangement is uninterrupted down the length of the dress. Cut out. Cut out the other front to match.
Cut out the sleeves with the centre of the print down the middle and with the horizontal fan shapes matching those on the dress. Cut the cuffs with one peacock eye in the middle.
Cut the back yoke with the eye in the centre. Cut the back dress with the centre back seam in the middle of an eye and with the first one 30cm (11¾in.) below the one on the yoke, excluding seam allowances.

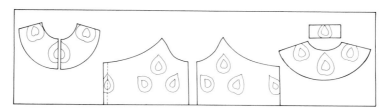

THE DRESS

Making up
1. *Cut out.* Cut back, front and sleeve. Cut one yoke back and two yoke fronts in fabric and repeat in lining or again in fabric. Cut tie and 4 pockets or 2 pockets in fabric and 2 in lining. Cut cuffs 17cm (6¾in.) wide and to the following length:

size 8, 21cm (8in.)
size 10, 21.5cm (8½in.)
size 12, 22cm (8¾in.)
size 14, 22.5cm (8⅞in.)
size 16, 23cm (9in.)
size 18, 23.5cm (9¼in.)
size 20, 24cm (9½in.)

Attach light iron-on Vilene to 2 pockets, cuffs and yoke. Transfer pattern markings to fabric on sleeves, yoke and gathered edge of dress.

2. *Contrast piping and rouleau.* Cut a strip of contrast fabric on the bias 84cm (33in.) long and

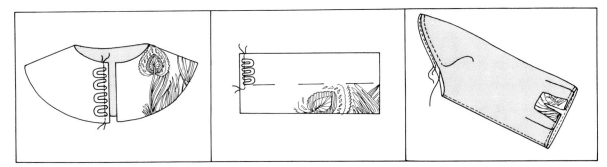

Left: join shoulders of yoke, make button loops and stitch to right side. If you are working with Varuna wool or similar weight fabric, piping cord can be enclosed within the rouleau loops to give them extra definition. Centre: attach interfacing to cuff. Make button loops and stitch to one end on right side. Right: join sleeve seams, make wrist openings and insert gathers.

13mm (½in.) wide. Fold right side out and press. Make 50cm (19¾in.) of rouleau for button loops.

3. *Seams and gathering.* Stitch centre back seam matching pattern. Press open. Stitch centre front seam up to dot marking base of opening. Press open. Hold edges flat with Wundaweb. Insert gathering threads in top edges of back and front.

4. *Sleeves and yoke.* Make 4 or 5 rouleau loops to take the buttons, spaced out and machined to the right side of the right yoke. Stitch three rouleau loops to the right side of each cuff. Make faced slit openings in the sleeves where marked. Stitch sleeve seams, insert gathering threads at wrist. Stitch yoke seam and press open. Stitch on contrast piping to outer edge. Stitch yoke lining seams. Place yoke to yoke lining, stitch centre front seams and along neck to dot, enclosing loops on right yoke. Trim and turn yoke right side out. Baste together round neck and along shoulders.

5. *Pockets.* Stitch interfaced pockets to back of dress at sides. Stitch lining pockets to front of dress.
Stitch dress side seams above and below pocket. Press pockets to front. Stitch round pocket bags. Press.

6. *Join sleeves* to dress along raglan edges. Press. Insert gathering threads round top of dress and sleeves. Place yoke to dress right sides together starting at centre back to match fabric print and pinning at sleeve seams and at centre front. Pull up gathers to fit. Even out carefully and pin. Tack with small stitches. Machine round from yoke side in order to follow piping stitching. Trim and press. Bring yoke lining down to cover join. Baste along centre front edges and round yoke. Trim raw edge and turn in and tack and hem to yoke join. Press.

7. *Neck bands.* Place neck bands right sides

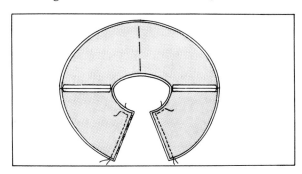

Stitch round neck and along front edges to join yoke to yoke lining and enclose button loops.

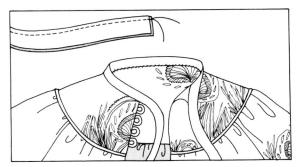

Join neckband pieces. Attach band to dress, stitch across tie ends and turn right side out.

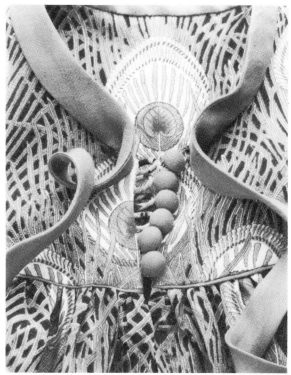

The yoke is piped in the same contrast shade as the neck ties, rouleau loops and self-covered buttons.

together and stitch along top edge. Trim, turn right side out and press. Stitch one edge to dress neck edge, snip edges. Fold the ends right side together and stitch, fastening off at neck edge. Trim and turn ends right side out. Press. Finish by turning under raw edge of neck band and hemming.

8. *Cuffs.* Stitch contrast piping to right side of one long edge of cuff. Turn in and press the other long edge. Attach cuffs to sleeves so that ends are level with edges of opening. Pull up gathers to fit. Tack and stitch from piping side.

Fold cuffs in half and stitch across ends, enclosing loops. Trim and turn right side out. Press. Baste layers of cuff together. Finish by hemming folded edge to sleeve.

9. *Hem and buttons.* Try dress on and mark and turn up hem. Sew buttons to yoke and cuffs. Sew small hook and thread loop to yoke below bottom button loop.

Quilting makes an effective extra finish for the dress yoke, and could also be picked up on the deep cuffs if required.

Undercover Story Told

*Blue and white striped Tana lawn, with a white lawn lining and navy piping, adds
up to a fresh and pretty full-length robe, simply made by lengthening the basic
shirt pattern. The bra and French knickers are made up in the same striped lawn,
but would work equally well in any suitable lingerie fabric. An alternative pattern
for bikini pants is included, and in a bright print or plain fabric would happily
team up with the bra for beachwear. (See page 110 for colour photograph.)*

PATTERN PIECES

Bra. Diagram pattern: Bra (cut 4).
French knickers. Diagram pattern:
Trouser back. trouser front (both
traced to French knickers hem line).
Pants. Diagram pattern: Pants (cut 2).
Robe. Tissue pattern: Shirt back
(lengthened). shirt front (lengthened).
yoke. band collar. front bands
(lengthened). sleeves. large patch
pockets. Follow instructions for tie
belt.

CUTTING OUT

Cut out the robe with the stripes
running lengthwise, except on the
yoke and collar where they run
horizontally. As an alternative to
French knickers, bikini pants for either
lingerie or beach wear may be cut on
the cross using the pattern given.

THE BRA

Bra cups can be inserted if you wish, but make
sure when you cut out the fabric that there is at
least 1cm (⅜in.) surplus all round. Insert the cups
before the final join is made. The straps can be
tied as a halter or looped round the back tie.

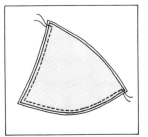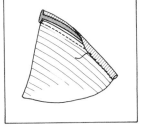

Making up

1. *Cut out.* Cut 4 pieces in fabric or 2 in fabric and
2 in contrast. Cut 3.60m (4¼ yd) of bias fabric
2.5cm (1in.) wide.

2. *Lining.* Place lining and bra pieces right sides
together. Stitch along side and lower edges. Turn
right side out and press. Insert cups at this point.

3. *Bind* remaining edges with contrast fabric.
Binding should be 6mm (¼in.) wide when
finished.

4. *Elasticated rouleau.* To keep the bias edges
neat and yet allow elastic to be threaded, make
rouleau and attach it to the finished edges. Make

Left: put bra sections and linings right sides together,
stitch side and lower edge. Trim edges and turn right
side out. Right: bind remaining raw edge with
crossway strips of contrast fabric.

two lengths of rouleau 70cm (27in.) long. Cut two
pieces of elastic 12cm (4¾in.) long and thread into
the rouleau, stitching it firmly across the end. Pull
up the elastic slightly, place the rouleau flat on the
side of bra with edges level and machine with a
decorative stretch stitch set to full width. Anchor
the stitching firmly at the top corner of the bra and
stretch the elastic as you stitch, finishing with the
end of the rouleau at the lower corner of the bra.

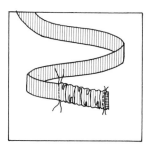 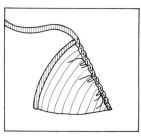

Left: make rouleau pieces for the sides and straps, insert elastic and stitch. Right: stitch rouleau to side edges, stretching the elastic.

5. Make remaining crossway fabric into a length of rouleau. Cut a piece of elastic 25cm (10in.) long and thread it into the middle of the rouleau. Anchor one end of elastic by stitching across it, stretch the elastic out to 4.7cm (16in.) or the distance across the lower edge of both sections of bra. Put bra sections together and machine across to join the corners. Place the rouleau on the edge and stitch, starting with end of elastic level with side of bra and stretching it as you stitch with a decorative stretch stitch. Finish with end of elastic at the other corner.

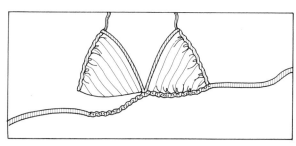

With elastic anchored in a long piece of rouleau tubing, stretch it and stitch across lower edges.

FRENCH KNICKERS

The knickers can be made with straight or curved hems, plain, bound or lace-edged.

Making up

1. *Cut out.* Cut out the back and front. Cut sufficient contrast crossway strips to bind hems.

2. *Seams.* Join centre front and centre back crotch edges with French seams. Stitch side seams in the same way. With crotch seams together make a seam across the two inside leg seams.

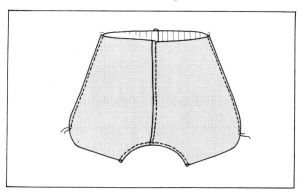

Join fronts, back, and sides with French seams; join leg seam under crotch.

3. *Hems.* Turn up hems with slip-hemming or bind edges.

4. *Waist.* Neaten top edge, turn down 1.5cm (⅝in.) and machine. Measure narrow elastic round waist. Thread through casing and join.

THE PANTS

Making up

1. *Cut out.* Reduce bulk by making the pattern in one without a seam under the leg.

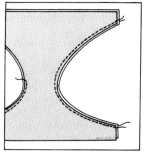 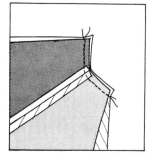

Left: put pants section to lining right sides together and stitch leg curves. Right: press seams and join the sides stitching across lining and fabric.

The bikini pants have casings for elastic top-stitched in contrast thread, and navy lawn rouleau bows at the hip. The bra is also bound in navy and finished with a bow to match.

2. *Lining*. Place the fabric and lining right sides together and stitch round leg curves. Trim, turn right side out.

3. *Seams and elastic*. Open out pants and stitch side seam through fabric and lining matching the leg joins. Trim and press. Top-stitch legs to form casing by working one row of stitching on the edge and a second about 6mm (¼in.) from the first or 2mm (¹⁄₁₆ in.) wider than the width of the

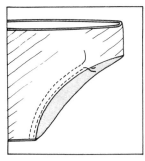 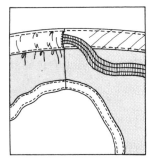

Left: tuck lining inside pants and press. Make casing for elastic. Right: stitch waist edge to make elastic casing.

elastic. Fold over top edge of pants, 1.5cm (⅝in.), press, turn under and stitch twice to form casing. Thread waist length of elastic through waist.
To thread the elastic either snip the lining on the

wrong side and work a buttonhole, or undo the seam in the lining, stitching up the gap after inserting the elastic.

THE ROBE

Making up

1. *Cut out*. Allocate fabric for pockets but do not cut. Cut facings for sleeve hems 6cm (2½in.) wide. Cut and join sufficient contrast crossway strips for all edges where you want it. Attach interfacing to one collar piece. Cut Fold-a-Band and press to fabric for front bands.

2. *Pockets*. Cut a piece of Fold-a-Band for both pockets and press to a piece of fabric on the straight grain. Add any decoration you wish on right side 2.5cm (1in.) below the line of perforations. The robe illustrated has a crossway strip of fabric 4cm (1½in.) wide turned in and machined along each edge with plain piping under the edge. Make one long strip and attach.

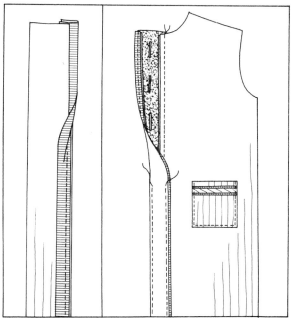

Left: attach piping to right side of front bands along one edge. Right: attach band to wrong side of robe and finish on the right side with top-stitching.

Fold fabric, pin on pocket pattern and cut out. Make and attach pockets to robe fronts 25cm (10in.) below armhole and 6cm (2½in.) from side seam.

3. *Bands.* Stitch plain bias piping to right side of one edge of each band over edge of Fold-a-Band. Roll piping to wrong side and press. Attach bands to wrong side of robe fronts. Turn to right side and stitch down. Press.

4. *Yoke.* Stitch plain bias piping to right side of yoke edges. Insert back tucks, join yoke and yoke lining to back and front robe. Finish front yoke edges by hemming into machining. Press.

5. *Collar.* Stitch plain bias piping to right side of interfaced collar. Stitch collar pieces together,

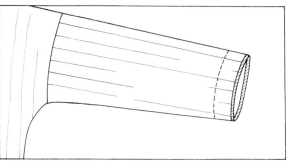

Join facing to sleeve, turn facing to inside and hem or machine in place.

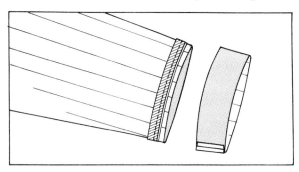

Join piping to fit sleeve, fold and attach. Join seam in sleeve facing.

trim and turn right side out. Press. Attach collar to neckline, hem on inside to finish.

6. *Sleeves.* Stitch sleeves to armholes matching sleeve point to shoulder with French seams. Stitch sleeve and side seams with French seams. Stitch plain bias piping to right side of sleeve hem, join at seam. Join ends of sleeve facing, neaten outer edge. Attach facings to sleeve on top of piping, stitch, turn to wrong side. Hold in place with machining or Wundaweb. Press.

7. *Hem.* Try on robe and decide on length. Turn up hem and machine or slip-hem.

8. *Belt.* Make belt if required following instructions on page 19.

Flowers in the Sun

A straight and simple summer dress in Tana lawn is the ideal first project for the novice dressmaker. The one we photographed is in a sophisticated longer length, although it could, of course, be shortened to below the knee, with hemline slits and buttons on the left shoulder. The second outfit is not a dress but a T-shirt top and a circular skirt, worn with a soft sash of a toning Tana lawn print. An alternative, slightly more dressy, partner for the circular skirt might be a short-sleeved version of the shirt pattern, with a Peter Pan collar and a narrow satin ribbon trimming. (See page 111 for colour photograph.)

PATTERN PIECES

T-shirt dress. Tissue pattern: Seam pocket. Diagram pattern: Straight dress back. front. neck facings. sleeve facings. sash (optional).

T-shirt top. Diagram pattern: Straight dress front (to hip level). back (to hip level). neck facings.

Circular skirt. Tissue pattern: Waistband. seam pocket. Diagram pattern: Circular skirt.

Short-sleeved shirt. Tissue pattern: Shirt back. front. yoke. front band. sleeve (traced to short hemline). Peter Pan collar. small patch pocket.

CUTTING OUT

Convolvulus, the print used for the dress, is an all-over print, one way, with a lengthwise bar of slightly darker flowers, so cut the dress with this bar at the centre front and centre back. Sweet Pea, used for the T-shirt top and circular skirt, is a one-way print with sprays of flowers arranged in vertical lines, so the skirt must be cut with seams at centre front and back with the sprays matching. The design repeats every 20cm (8in.). Cut each quarter of the circle on single fabric with the waistline at the top of the spray of sweet peas. Make one pattern piece or mark the shape directly on to the fabric. Cut one quarter of the skirt and use that as the outline for the other three, reversing it for two of them and matching the rows of sweet peas each time.

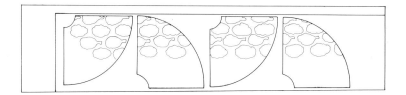

THE DRESS

Making up

1. *Cut out.* Cut front and back dress to fold. Cut neck and sleeve facings. Cut 4 pocket pieces and attach soft iron-on Vilene to two if required. Cut interfacing for neckline.

2. *Rouleau loops.* Make a length of rouleau and arrange 3 loops close together, to fit buttons on right side of left front shoulder. Machine in place.

3. *Shoulders.* Stitch left seam to dot shown on diagram pattern. Stitch right shoulder seam. Press seams open.

4. *Facings.* Attach Vilene to neckline. Join right shoulder seam of facings. Join left seam as far as dot on diagram pattern. Neaten outer edge. Tack facing to right side of neck, stitching along left shoulder from end of seam stitching on back and front. Finish facing on inside by stitching to shoulder seams.

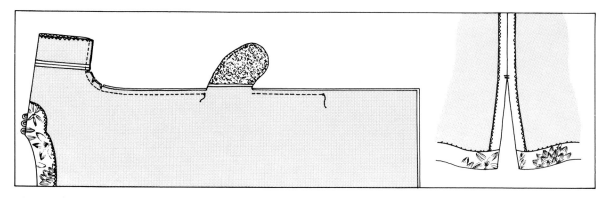

Left: attach loops for fastening and neck facing, attach sleeves and pockets. Stitch side seams from top of hemline slit. Right: measure skirt for desired length, turn up and complete hem. Finish off by working a bar

tack at top of slit for extra strength. The hemline slit can be made on either or both sides of the dress, and it can of course be made deeper if preferred, for greater ease of movement.

Neaten outer edge of sleeve facing. Attach to armhole, press so that it extends.

5. *Pockets and side seams.* Stitch interfaced pockets to extensions on back of dress. Attach the other two pocket bags to the front. Stitch side seams from top of hemline slit to base of pocket and from top of pocket to armhole and through sleeve facing. Snip turnings at underarm. Press seams open. Turn sleeve facings to inside and catch. Press pockets towards front. Stitch round pocket bags. Neaten seam edges.

6. *Hem.* Try on dress. Turn up hem and slip hem. Turn back seam allowances at slits, hold down with Wundaweb. Work bar tacks at top of slits on wrong side.

7. *Buttons.* Sew buttons to correspond with loops.

THE SHORT-SLEEVED SHIRT

Making up

1. *Cut out front, back, yoke, front bands, collar.* Also cut out sufficient crossway strips 2.5cm (1in.) wide. Cut out pockets to fold line only. Cut short sleeves. Transfer pattern markings to fabric.

2. *Front bands.* Attach Fold-a-Band, press bias strip in half wrong side inside, attach to right side of one edge of each band. Place bands to fronts with bias strip to shirt edge and right sides

together. Tack, turn fabric over and machine on first row of stitching to attach band to shirt. At neck edge fold bands right sides together, stitch from fold to middle of band – centre front – trim and turn corner right side out, snipping the turnings to the end of the stitching. Press. Finish inner edge of bands by turning under and hemming.

The collar, front bands and pocket of this version of the shirt are bound with narrow bias strips, and the yoke and pocket tops are decorated with narrow ribbon.

3. *Pocket.* Bind top edge with crossway strip. Attach narrow ribbon 1cm (⅜in.) below. Turn in edges and attach pocket to left shirt front.

4. *Yoke.* Place bias strip, folded and pressed, to right side of one yoke piece on yoke seam edges. Machine on seam line with 5mm (¼in.) of bias fold extending into yoke. Insert tucks in blouse back. Attach blouse back and fronts to yoke using the previous line of stitching as a guide. Attach ribbon 1cm (⅜in.) above yoke edge. Attach lining of yoke to back, tack flat and complete front edges of yoke by hemming in place. Press.

5. *Collar.* Attach light sew-in Vilene to under collar. Make collar by tacking both pieces wrong sides together. Bind outer edge of collar with a 2.5cm (1in.) bias strip. Position it so that you stitch 2cm (¾in.) from the collar edge. Place collar to blouse neck edge and attach with bias strip. Press.

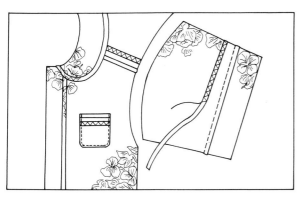

Attach collar and bands to shirt. Complete decoration of sleeve before attaching sleeve to armhole.

6. *Sleeves.* Press a crease in each sleeve 6cm (2⅜in.) above the hem with the fabric right side out. Work a row of stitching 5mm (¼in.) from the fold and press it to one side to form a tuck. Attach narrow ribbon 1cm (⅜in.) above it, using the same stitch as on the yoke. Join sleeve to blouse with French or narrow seam. Press.

7. *Side and sleeve seams.* Fold shirt wrong sides together and make French seams from shirt hem to sleeve hem.

8. *Sleeve hems.* Turn up 3.5cm (1⅜in.) to wrong side, turn in raw edge and hem over tuck. Press.

9. *Hem.* Turn up a narrow hem, and either machine stitch or slip-hem to finish.

10. *Buttons and buttonholes.* Make buttonholes by hand or machine or bound. Attach press stud to top corner of front band under the collar.

THE T-SHIRT TOP

Making up

1. *Cut out.* Cut back and front to fold. Cut facings. Interface neckline with light iron-on or sew-in Vilene.

2. *Seams.* Stitch shoulders and side seams and press open.

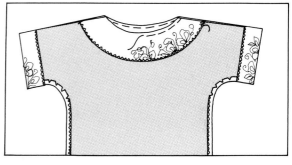

Join shoulders and side seams. Snip curves and press seams open. Turn up hems, attach neck facings to neckline.

3. *Facings.* Join facing shoulder seams. Neaten outer edge of facing. Attach to neckline.

4. *Hems.* Turn up narrow hem and stitch. Neaten sleeve edges, turn back 1.5cm (⅝in.) and catch at seams.

THE CIRCULAR SKIRT

Making up

1. *Cut out.* Cut 4 skirt sections as described above with flowers growing upwards. Cut 4 pocket sections and attach light iron-on Vilene to two of them if required. Cut a waist length of waistbanding plus an overlap. Cut a length of fabric for it and attach the waistbanding.

2. *Seams.* Join centre front seam and back seam to base of zip. Insert zip. Attach interfaced pockets to back of skirt and attach the other two

A wide, shaped belt might be worn with the circular skirt, covered in matching or toning fabric and finished with a rouleau bow. For making-up instructions for this belt or a simple sash as photographed see page 19.

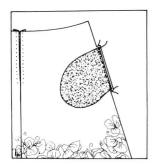 

Left: insert zip in centre back seam; attach pockets. Right: make waistband to fit waist neatly, gather the skirt and attach waistband.

to the front skirt extensions. Join side seams above and below pockets. Press pockets towards front. Stitch round pocket bags.

3. Make two hanging loops and machine to waist at side seams. Insert gathering thread in waist. Attach waistband, draw gathers up to fit.

4. *Hem.* Put on skirt and mark hemline. Turn up narrow hem and machine. Attach narrow ribbon 3cm (1¼in.) above hem.

5. *Fastening.* Attach a large hook or Velcro to the waistband.

In The Tartan Tradition

The button-through dress in classic tartan yarn-dyed Jubilee is cut from the lengthened shirt pattern. The lower part of the double collar is a crisp touch of white that can be picked up at the cuffs or the top of optional added patch pockets. The fabric-covered belt is fastened with a bold buckle. The child's dress in a complimentary tartan has elasticated wrists, a small collar, and buttons at the back yoke. The lawn pinafore, made from the skirt and yoke of the child's dress pattern, has frilled armholes and hemline tucks. The yoke smocking can be a deep, bold design and the version photographed is composed of an outline of cable stitch top and bottom with rows of surface honeycomb and a band of trellis. (See page 112 for colour photograph.)

PATTERN PIECES

Adult's dress. Tissue pattern: Shirt back (lengthened to below knee). front (lengthened to below knee). front band (lengthened to below knee). yoke. shirt collar. band collar. sleeve. cuff. Follow instructions for belt.

Child's dress. Tissue pattern: Dress yoke front. back. collar (cut 4). sleeve. Diagram pattern: Skirt to size required.

Child's pinafore. Tissue pattern: Back and front yokes (double). frill. Diagram pattern: Skirt back and front.

CUTTING OUT

For the adult dress, cut the front bands and cuffs on the cross. Cut a second collar and cuffs in white lawn a little wider than the pattern pieces to extend beneath the tartan ones.

THE ADULT DRESS

Instructions are included for lining the body of this dress, but it is optional. Patch pockets or seam pockets may be added if required. The fabric-covered belt is made using belt backing and fastened with a bought clasp.

Making up

1. *Cut out.* Lengthen back, front and front band patterns either by adding paper or by pinning the shirt pattern to the fabric and extending front and side edges using tailor's chalk and a long ruler. Cut out matching checks at side seams on back and front. Cut out sleeves, collar and collar band. Cut the yoke on single fabric with the centre back matching the dress back. Cut the cuffs and front bands in Fold-a-Band and press it to the wrong side of the fabric on the cross. Cut out collar and cuffs again in white lawn. Cut out the yoke singly in lining and also the back and front, lengthening to match the tartan.

2. *Front bands.* Attach bands to right side, press join open, insert a strip of Wundaweb to reduce fraying of buttonholes. If making bound buttonholes, work the first stage now. Turn bands to inside and tack flat. Machine or hand prick-stitch in the seam join from the right side but stop at least 15cm (6in.) from the hem.

3. *Yoke.* Join back dress to back yoke and fronts to front yoke edges. Press turnings towards yoke. Tack dress side seams.

4. *Lining.* Join yoke seams, press turnings towards yoke. Tack side seams. Place back yoke lining turnings against dress yoke turnings and stitch together with machine or hand back stitch. Press. Arrange remainder of lining over dress fronts, tack lining and dress together round neck and armholes and down front edges. Turn under raw edges of lining at centre front and tack on top of band. Hem from neck to within 15cm (6in.) of the hem.

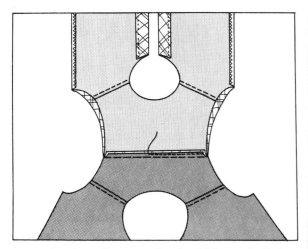

Attach bands to dress, attach yoke. Make up the lining and, to prevent it slipping in wear, stitch the back yoke seam allowances together.

5. *Collar.* Interface tartan under collar and outer collar band. Make tartan collar and white lawn collar, insert together in top edge of collar band, stitch trim and turn right side out. Attach collar to neck edge of dress.

6. *Fitting.* Try on dress. Check width at underarm, waist and hips and retack if you want a closer fit. Make open seams in dress and in lining. Press. Baste lining and dress together from underarm to hem.

7. *Make faced slit* openings in sleeves, stitch seams, attach cuffs and insert sleeves in armholes.

8. *Hem.* Put on dress with belt, mark the hem length. Open out the front bands, turn up the hem. Fold band into position and complete the stitching. Slip-stitch the folds together. Turn up the hem on the lining so that it is 4cm (1½in.) shorter than the dress. Finish hemming the lining to the front bands.

9. *Buttonholes and buttons.* The dress fastens with 10 buttons spaced down the length of the band. Make one horizontal buttonhole in the collar band. Make the bottom buttonhole at least 20cm (8in.) above the hem. Space the others evenly between these, making sure that a button does not fall under the belt. Attach buttons. Make buttonholes through both cuffs and attach buttons, or as an alternative to working through so many fabric thicknesses, attach Velcro and sew

a button on the outside. Stitch a small press stud on the front band just below the neck join.

The under collar in white lawn is cut a little wider than the pattern pieces, so that the edges just extend under those of the tartan top collar.

THE CHILD'S DRESS

Making up

1. *Cut out.* Cut front and back skirt. Cut front and back yokes and lining yokes, sleeves and 4 collars. Attach light iron-on Vilene to one pair of collars. Press a narrow piece of Vilene or half-width Fold-a-Band to buttonhole edge of yoke.

2. *Skirt.* Stitch back skirt seam to base of opening. Snip seam, fold back extension to right side on fold line, stitch across base. Trim and turn right side out. Press, pin right over left and hem base of opening extension to dress. Insert a double row of gathering threads along the top edges of the skirt.

3. *Collars.* Place a pair of collars right side together, stitch and turn through. Press. Join at centre front by stitching together 1cm (⅜in.) from edge. Join shoulders of yoke and yoke lining. Tack collar to neckline bringing ends to centre back. Place yoke lining on top and tack. Stitch along centre back edges and round neck. Trim and snip, turn yoke lining to wrong side, tack around the neck and back edges. Press.

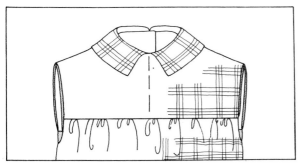

Attach collar to yoke, make back opening, attach skirt to yoke.

4. *Yoke.* Join yoke to dress right sides together, holding the yoke lining out of the way and matching centres and pulling up gathers to fit. Machine. Trim turnings. Press towards yoke. Baste yoke lining to yoke all round edges. Turn in yoke seam edges and hem to back of the waist seam.

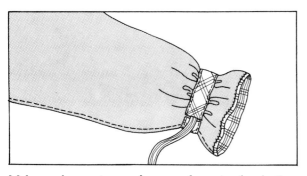

Make up sleeves, turn up hems, make casing for elastic.

5. *Sleeves.* Stitch sleeve seams. Turn narrow hems and stitch. Attach elastic 3cm (1¼in.) above hem. Either attach a bias casing and thread it through to fit wrist or use narrow elastic, and zigzag it to the wrong side, stretching it as you stitch. Set sleeves into armholes.

6. *Buttons and buttonholes.* Make 3 machine or hand buttonholes in back yoke. Attach press studs on yoke under collar and below buttons.

7. *Hem.*

THE CHILD'S PINAFORE

Making up

1. *Cut out.* Cut out rectangles for back and front skirt. Do not cut armholes. Do not even pin the rest of the pattern in place until the smocking is complete. Mark width to be smocked as shown on pattern.

2. *Smocking.* Insert gathering threads or use a smocking machine to gather top edge of front and backs to a depth of 8cm (3in.). Pull up, anchor ends. Work smocking. Replace pattern and cut armholes.

The deep band of smocking is worked on rectangles of fabric for the front and back of the pinafore before the pattern pieces are cut out.

3. *Seams.* Join centre back and side seams. Press open back seam above opening and turn a narrow hem level with the smocking. Hem the edges.

4. *Tucks.* Make 3 13mm (½in.) wide tucks 7.5cm (3in.) above the hem and 6mm (¼in.) apart. Press downwards. Turn up hem.

5. *Ties.* Make 6 ties 20cm (8in.) long and 6mm (¼in.) wide finished width. Stitch two to each side of yoke opening.

Cut remainder of pinafore pieces.

6. *Frills.* Fold armhole frills in half wrong sides inside and run gathering threads along curved edges. Join shoulders of yoke and lining. Put yoke and lining yoke together and stitch round neck and down centre back edges enclosing ends of ties. Trim, turn yoke right side out. Tack neck edges. Press.

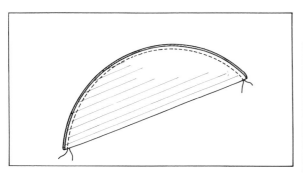

Fold the armhole frills in half and insert a gathering thread round the outer edge.

7. *Yoke.* Attach yoke backs and front to skirt taking care to stitch an even distance from the smocking. You may need to remove the gathering threads to allow skirt to fit yoke. Trim. Press turnings into yoke.

8. *Attach frills.* Pin frills to yoke over shoulders with ends of frills extending a little below the yoke seam. Pull up gathers, tack and machine to yoke. Machine crossway strip to underarm on right side overlapping it on to yoke by 1cm (⅜in.) Fold to wrong side and hem. Tack yoke lining in

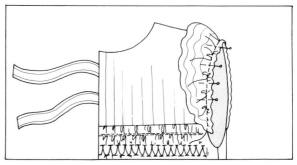

Pin frill to armhole with ends of frills extending a little below the yoke seam. Pull up gathers, tack, and then stitch through outer fabric only.

position and turn in and hem all lining edges to yoke seams, over shoulders and around armholes.

9. *Ties.* Sew remaining pair of ties under the edge in the centre of the band of smocking.

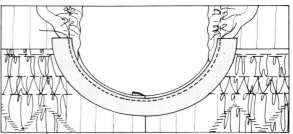

Stitch a crossway strip to the right side at the underarm.

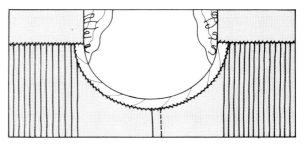

Turn under and hem crossway strip edge and edges of the lining.

Techniques and Terms

This section sets out, in alphabetical order, detailed explanations of all the techniques included in the making-up instructions in the front half of the book and also some alternative suggestions. A number of sewing terms and expressions are also used in the instructions to describe particular methods of working, and some equipment is specified. Consult this list if you are uncertain as to their meanings.

ANGLED SEAMS

The top with the cowl back is not difficult to make but the angled seam must be handled with care.

With any angled seam at least one edge will be on the cross or bias, and so will be liable to stretch while being sewn. In addition, if the seam is stitched in one operation along both sides the top layer of fabric will probably move out of position. Both problems can be eliminated by stitching as follows.

Mark the seam allowances on all edges. Mark the centre back point on all three pieces of fabric. Stitch the centre back seam from the hem up to the centre back point. Fasten off the stitching. Neaten (finish) edges. Press seam open. Place the cowl section to the lower section

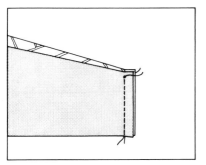

with right sides together, matching the centre back point. Tack (baste) together. Machine stitch, starting exactly on the centre back point. Remove tacking, press the stitching, press the seam allowances down into the lower section.

Lift the centre back seam edges and stitch the other section of angled seam, tacking and machining from the centre back

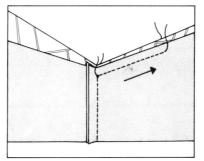

point. Make sure the two rows of stitching meet exactly and do not overlap. If there is a gap when you have finished you will get a neater finish if you stitch it up by hand. Remove tackings. Press seam edges

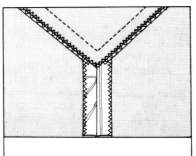

downwards. Trim the raw edges and neaten them separately to lessen the chance of a ridge showing on the right side.

BACK STITCH

A strong stitch used for starting and ending thread when hand sewing to prevent the stitching coming undone. Make 2 or 3 small stitches on top of each other. When working a row of continuous stitching, create a back stitch by taking the

needle halfway back to the previous stitch to insert it, bringing it up the same distance beyond.

BALANCE MARKS

Also called notches, these are shown on the pattern pieces either as triangles set against pattern edges or as a circle or dot. Balance marks are put on corresponding edges to enable you to join the seams accurately, match collars to necklines, gather long pieces to shorter ones, etc. It is not necessary to transfer all notches to the fabric, although beginners often find it helpful once they realise that they are a guide to correct assembly. But it is essential to transfer those which indicate something other than a straightforward seam – for example the position of gathers, or points of attachment for collars etc.

Mark the fabric before removing the pattern, using either single tailor tacks, a fabric marking pen, or dressmaker's carbon paper on the wrong side of the fabric only (do not use carbon on crêpe de chine or any white fabric).

BAR TACK

A strong, neat and very useful way of strengthening a point of strain such as the base of an opening in a seam, a slot for elastic, the top of hemline slits or a pleat. Make three stitches 3mm (⅛in.) long on top of each other then work loopstitch over them. Longer bar tacks can be made between two pieces of fabric that need holding together loosely, for example attaching a shoulder pad to a shoulder seam or armhole or holding a lining seam in place against a garment seam.

BASTING TAPE

A narrow adhesive tape that is useful for holding fabric edges in place or zips in position instead of tacking. It can be used on top of layers of fabric, in which case it must be removed after stitching, or peel off the backing so that both sides are adhesive and use it between layers of fabric. There is no need in this case to remove it after stitching.

BELT CARRIERS

Fabric loops for belts and sashes and for hanging skirts and trousers can be made as follows. Make a length of narrow bias tubing or rouleau long enough for two loops. Hangers should be 16cm (6¼in.) long, carriers should be equal to 3 times the belt width, including seam allowances at ends.

Cut the tubing in half, fold each piece and crease the middle. Attach hangers by tacking (basting) to wrong side of garment before completing waist finish. For belt carriers measure the width of the belt from the crease plus 5mm (¼in.), ease and insert a pin.

Put on the dress, belt it and mark the waist point at each side seam. Take off the dress and snip the side seam stitching at the waist mark for 2cm (¾in.). Push the ends of the carrier through from the right side

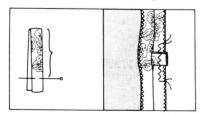

until the pin is level with the seam stitching. Hold the loop ends against one seam allowance and zigzag stitch across the ends. Hold

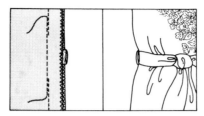

the seam allowances together and re-stitch the dress seam, overlapping the stitching by at least 2.5cm (1in.) each end.

BIAS BINDING TOOL

A very useful little tool, also known as a tape maker, available in two sizes for making binding 6mm (¼in.) and 1cm (⅜in.) wide. Cut bias strips the correct width for the tool as stated on the instruction card. Pass the fabric through the tool, pressing it as it emerges folded.

BINDING

Used on frills, sleeves, necklines or hems, a narrow binding adds decoration, outlines a style feature and, in the case of hems, adds extra weight. Use either matching or contrast fabric and texture. Apply the binding to collar or pocket edges before attaching the feature to the garment but make it the final process on hems, frills, belts, cuffs, etc.

Cut and join crossway strips of fabric 2.5cm (1in.) wide or the width stated in the garment instructions. Stretch them under the iron or pass through a bias binding tool and press and stretch. Fold the binding in half and press the crease.

Tack and stitch to the right side of the garment remembering that 1.5cm (⅝in.) seam allowance is to be taken off the garment but only 6mm (¼in.) from the binding.

Press by pushing the toe of the iron along the seam on the right side so that the binding extends. Trim the raw edge. Fold the binding over twice until the edge rests on

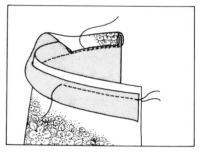

the stitching. Tack in place and hem. Remove tacks and press on the right side.

An alternative method is to attach the binding initially to the wrong side, fold it over on to the right side of the garment and finish it by machining on the fold with a straight or zigzag stitch.

To bind the outer edge of double fabric such as collars, etc., attach interfacing to the collar, tack both

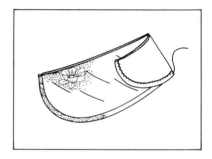

pieces of fabric together right side out. Bind the outer edge. Attach to the garment in the usual way.

To bind a cuff, stitch the sleeve seam, cut the sleeve opening, attach interfacing to one cuff piece and machine it to the sleeve. Turn in one

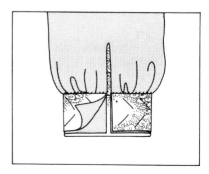

edge of the other cuff piece, place it against the outer one and baste together. Hem the fold to the stitching. Cut a crossway strip and bind the outer edge of the cuff and the opening. It will be easier to handle if the cuff corners are rounded.

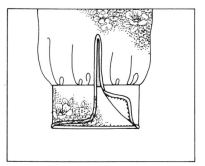

BOUND EDGE WITH FRILL

A bound finish with the frill lying over the garment. This could be used on the neckline of the child's dress in place of the collar or on the neckline of the gathered dress as a decorative extra.

Make the frill, complete the outer edge, insert a gathering thread in the raw edge. Divide frill into 4 equal sections. Divide garment edge into 4 sections. Pin frill to right side of garment pulling up gathers to fit. Even out the gathers. Tack and machine 1.5cm (⅝in.) from the edge. Remove the gathering thread.

Cut a crossway strip 2.5cm (1in.) wide, stretch it, pass it through a binding tool or turn under one edge 6mm (¼in.) and press. Place binding right side down on top of

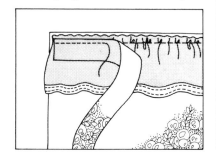

frill with the crease over the machine stitching but slightly further to the left. Machine the binding, stitching in the crease. Trim raw edges to less than 6mm (¼in.). Roll binding to the wrong

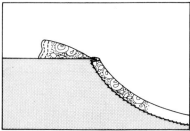

side, fold under the raw edge, tack down on to machine stitching and hem stitch to finish off neatly.

BOUND NECKLINE WITH TIE ENDS

A finish that can be used on the neckline of the child's dress or shirt neckline instead of the collar. Use either matching or contrasting fabric. A tie neck with a similar effect is shown on the neckline of the gathered dress. The differences in construction are that the fabric is cut slightly shaped and that there is a seam to be made in the upper edge of the neck band.

Prepare the centre front corners of the neckline by folding facing on front band to right side and

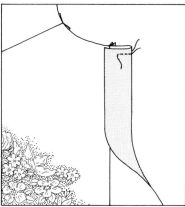

stitching from the edge to the centre front point. Snip and turn the corner right side out, snipping the turnings right to the end of the stitching.

Cut a length of crossway fabric the length of the neckline plus 60cm (24in.) for the ties. The width should be from 2.5cm (1in.) for a narrow finish up to 8cm (3¼in.) for a wide, soft effect. Match the middle of the strip to the centre back of the neckline, place it to the right side, tack and stitch round the neck on

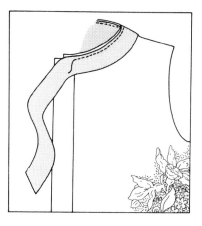

the seam line and taking 5mm (¼in.) from the neck band. From the edge of the garment fold strip right side together and stitch. Sew across

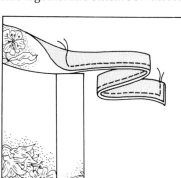

the end. The stitching on neckline and strip must be level but for a neat finish leave a gap of about 1cm (⅜in.). Trim the raw edges and turn the ties right side out. Round the neck trim the turnings, turn under the raw edge of the binding and tack, taking care to keep it smooth and unwrinkled. Hem into the machine stitches, slip stitch the gap.

BOUND OPENING

This technique makes a neat opening for sleeves in Tana lawn or crêpe de chine, but it would be too bulky on heavier fabrics. For an added decorative effect use fabric of another colour or texture, eg. satin.

Cut the opening in the sleeve as marked on the pattern. Tana lawn does not fray so this can be done when cutting out. Cut crêpe de chine when ready to work the opening. Cut a strip of fabric on the cross four times the length of the opening and 1.5cm (⅝in.) wide. Fold it wrong side inside, and press the crease. Turn in both side edges and press, or pass the fabric through a bias binding tool and press. Cut strip into two.

Place strip right side down on to right side of garment with ends level and strip open. Begin tacking, taking 5mm (¼in.) seam.

Open out the slit, continue taking the same amount off the strip, but as you reach the centre of the slit it will reduce to almost nothing. To be

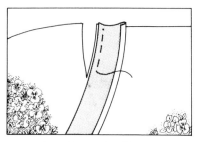

sure of catching the fabric in the tacking and to make certain the slit is lying evenly on the strip, turn it over so that the garment is wrong side uppermost.

Stitch strip to garment using a small stitch, sewing with strip uppermost. Remove tacking, turn it over so that garment is uppermost and stitch again at the centre for a distance of 2.5cm (1in.). This will reinforce the weak point.

Trim raw edges. Press strip to extend, press raw edges towards strip. Fold strip over so that the crease is on the machine stitching. Tack. Finish by hemming, taking the needle into each machine stitch

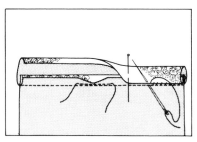

or machine along the edge. Press it so that one side folds under and the other extends, and stitch across the fold at the top. Fastenings such as press studs (snaps) may be attached

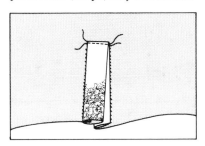

on a long opening but usually the cuffs, yoke, etc. attached afterwards will keep the edges overlapped.

BUTTONHOLES

All types of buttonhole should be neat, accurately placed and identical in size. Space them and mark the length using an adjustable marker. Use tailor's chalk, tacking stitch or fabric pen to mark the fabric. Make sure you have two layers of fabric and a layer of interfacing. Try to make them all at one sewing session so that they look alike. It may not be a good idea to leave them until last, especially if you are inexperienced: it is often a relief to make buttonholes as soon as the opening of the garment is complete.

Make the buttonholes vertical in the front band of the shirt and horizontal on cuffs to take the pull of the button; on the child's dress they can run in either direction. If they are to be vertical make them on the centre front or centre back line; if horizontal the buttonhole starts on the centre line and extends into the main area of the garment. If you have no centre line start the buttonhole the diameter of the button from the garment edge.

Hand-worked, machine-made or bound buttonholes are suitable on all the fabrics used for the designs in the book.

1. BOUND BUTTONHOLES

These can be used if you wish on all the clothes in the book and on any of the fabrics.

They are made using a small piece of extra fabric and they are easy to make in fine fabrics like Tana lawn and crêpe de chine. However the proportions can look wrong in other fabrics such as Varuna wool if the buttonholes are less than about 1cm (⅜in.) in length, so take extra care to make them narrow.

It is easier to keep them narrow if the piece of fabric is on the cross. Work the first stage as follows and early in the construction of the garment if you can.

Begin by attaching interfacing to the wrong side of the fabric. Cut a strip of fabric on the cross 8cm (3in.) longer than the total length of all

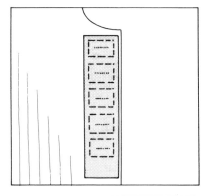

buttonholes and 2.5cm (1in.) wide. Place this evenly over the buttonhole markings on the right side. Tack in position or anchor with pieces of basting tape. Mark the exact length and position of each buttonhole and tack round each through the bias strip, the fabric and the interfacing.

Set the machine to a small stitch and work a rectangle of stitching the exact length marked and no more than 3mm (⅛in.) wide. Count the stitches of the first one and repeat that number on all the other buttonholes. Overlap the start and finish of the machine stitches and cut off all thread ends close to the fabric. Remove tacking.

Cut the buttonhole by snipping through strip and garment at the centre in the middle of the rectangle

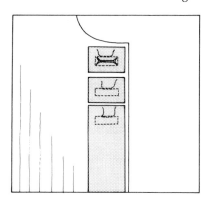

then snip into each corner. Cut through the bias strip between the buttonholes. Push the toe of the iron under each strip and run it against the stitching round each buttonhole.

Push each piece of fabric through its buttonhole then, with right side up, manipulate it so that it forms two equal folds of fabric that meet in the centre of the buttonhole slot.

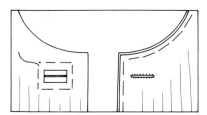

Crease the fabric with your fingers then press with the toe of the iron. Tack round each buttonhole with small stitches.

Complete the buttonholes after attaching and turning back the facing. Baste the facing to the garment. Insert a pin at each end of each buttonhole, mark the end of each slit with chalk or fabric pen. Carefully snip the facing between the marks and turn under the raw edge. The easiest way to do this is to use the point of the needle to tuck it under, hemming immediately with very small stitches. Remove pins. Press the buttonholes.

2. HAND-SEWN BUTTONHOLES

If you enjoy hand sewing, and especially embroidery, you will find it easy to work neat buttonholes. They can be made on all fabrics on the shirts, dresses, child's dress and rompers. Use one of the other types of buttonhole when using buttons larger than about 6mm (¼in.) as it is difficult to keep bigger hand-sewn buttonholes looking neat.

Insert light sew-in or iron-on Vilene (Pellon) interfacing between the layers of fabric making sure it extends well beyond the end of the buttonhole. In addition a strip of Wundaweb (Stitch Witchery or Save-a-Stitch) pressed between the layers will make the buttonhole easier to sew and prevent fraying. Wundaweb stiffens the fabric slightly so do not use it on crêpe de chine or lawn, or if you want a soft effect generally. If you do not use Wundaweb, baste round the area of each buttonhole to keep the layers together.

Mark the size and position carefully using tailor's chalk or fabric pen. Place a button on the fabric and put a mark at each side. Hand-sewn buttonholes stretch in use so no extra ease is necessary.

Thread a small size Between needle and knot the end. Take a back stitch on the under side of the garment near the buttonhole position. Insert a pin at one end of the buttonhole, bring it out at the other,

fold the fabric and snip at the fold. Remove pin, open out fabric and snip to the mark at each end. Bring the needle up 2mm (1/16in.) from the cut edge at one end.

Arrange fabric so that the first side of stitching is on your left and you are stitching towards yourself. The stitches should be 2mm (1/16in.) or less in depth. Wind the thread round the point of the needle towards you, pull needle through and settle the knot on the cut edge and slightly on top. The stitches should be fairly close but the knots should touch so that they form a close beaded edge that will wear well and prevent fraying.

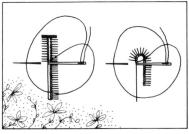

On reaching the end of the buttonhole take four straight stitches across the width, pulling the thread tight so that it shows as little as possible, then bring the needle up near the cut edge and work buttonhole stitch along the second side. Stitch across the end, again making a bar of stitches in the same way as before, but to fasten off pass the needle to the wrong side and fasten off by working loopstitch over the threads that show. Cut off the thread and cut off the knot.

Making end bars in this way produces an effect similar to machine-made buttonholes and is the neatest and least visible finish for the ends. For this reason it is the best method of working both ends of the vertical shirt buttonholes because both ends can show even when the buttons are fastened. An alternative finish for one end of horizontal buttonholes in cuffs, collar band etc., is to make a semicircle of buttonhole stitches at the end nearest the garment edge. If this method is chosen the sewing must be very neat as it shows more.

BUTTONS

Use small neat buttons for all openings, to match or compliment the fabric, or cover button moulds with fabric. Buttons with two holes should be sewn on with the holes in line with the buttonhole. Those with four holes should have the threads worked as a cross and all neatly in line on the garment. Always make a thread shank to raise the button above the surface of the fabric, with the exception of dome buttons or self-covered buttons which are sewn through the metal loop and do not require a thread shank.

Sew buttons to settle in the top of vertical buttonholes and at the end nearest the edge of the garment in horizontal ones.

SEWING ON BUTTONS

Pin the side of the garment that has the loops or buttonholes on to the under side. Mark the exact position of the top button with the point of a pin or fabric pen. The button fits in the top of a vertical buttonhole or in the far end of a rouleau loop.

Thread a needle with a long length of sewing thread, double it and knot the end. If you have more than two buttons to attach thread several needles before starting so that you maintain the rhythm of the stitching. You will also find that the task will seem quicker and less laborious.

Run each thread over beeswax twice and twist the thread between the palms to form a strong waxed cord.

Make a back stitch on the fabric

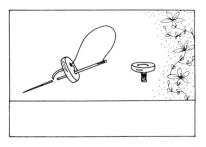

on the marked point; cut off the knot and make another stitch. Slip the button on to the needle and sew it on from the right side taking the needle in and out of the fabric before pulling the thread through. Keep the button almost vertical to ensure that there is surplus thread to form a shank. Make 4 stitches then wind the thread tightly round under the button to cover the shank. Pass the needle to the under side and loopstitch over the visible threads to fasten off.

Dome or ball buttons and covered buttons have a shank on the back so attach by making 6 stitches then

wind the thread round firmly between the button and the fabric. If you use beads as buttons sew them close to the fabric without a shank.

Press by carefully pushing no more than the toe of the iron round and between all the buttons.

CHANNEL SEAM

A decorative seam for plain or patterned fabric which could be used on the panel seams of the panelled straight skirt (see page 107). No adjustment need be made to the pattern when cutting out but fabric allowance must be made for cutting 2.5cm (1in.) strips of bias fabric in contrast or matching fabric.

Turn in and press back the seam allowance on both edges of the seam. Cut a bias strip slightly longer than the seam, place one pressed fold along the centre of the bias strip on the right side, and tack. Place the second fold against it and hold the folds together at intervals with basting tape. Tack

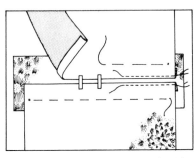

the second side. Machine each side the width of the foot from the fold, removing the tape as you come to it.

CONTRAST BANDS

Use contrasting plain or print fabric to insert contrast bands in skirts, sleeves, pockets etc. Decide on the width and position of the bands and cut the pattern into sections. Cut out the pieces to be in the main fabric allowing 1cm (⅜in.) seam allowance on the cut edge. Cut out contrast bands with the straight grain running in the same direction as on the main section. Cut out the other pieces of garment. Allow 1cm (⅜in.) seam allowance for joins on each edge. Join any seams on the garment and in contrast fabric, but leave one seam open.

Join contrast to garment with right sides together. Press open and

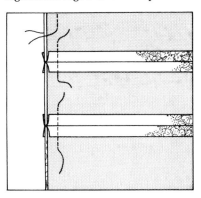

neaten. Decorate with ribbon, stitching, etc. Join the final seam, inserting pins at the joins to ensure that they match. Stitch across each join first to avoid slippage, keeping the pins in position and seams open. Remove pins and stitch seam.

CONTRAST HEM

This finish can be used on straight edges of sleeves or necklines, as well as on skirt hems.

A contrast band, whatever the position, is best made from double fabric because it adds weight and looks crisp. Decide on a width of band that will look balanced on the garment. Reduce the length of the garment when you cut out, leaving 1cm (⅜in.) seam allowance. Cut the contrast fabric twice the finished width plus 2cm (¾in.). This band can be on the straight or bias grain.

Join the garment seams and join the contrast band, making it the same size, and fold it wrong side

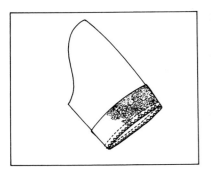

inside and press. Place the band to the garment with raw edges together and seams matching. Tack and stitch together 1cm (⅜in.) from the edge. Neaten the raw edges. Press so that the band extends. Top-stitch or decorate the join if you wish.

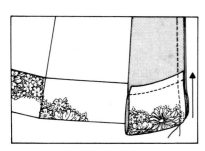

If the garment seams are angled, or if the garment is in several shaped sections, leave the garment seams open for at least 8cm (3in.) and cut a band of fabric to fit each section with the edges sloping to match the garment. Attach the bands and then complete the seams, stitching from the bottom to ensure the edges are level.

CROSSWAY OR BIAS STRIPS

These are narrow strips of fabric cut at an angle to the selvedge. Strips cut at an angle of 45° are on the true cross or 'crossway' and they have maximum 'give'. Bias strips are those cut at less of an angle and they 'give' less. In this book the words 'on the cross' and 'crossway' are used to describe both types.

Both types are used for binding for rouleau, and for piping. Cut the width suitable for the purpose, allowing no more than 6mm (¼in.) seam allowance on each edge. It is worth folding a small piece of fabric to a suitable finished width and then measuring it so that you can cut the strips accurately, as it is difficult to trim them afterwards. When using true cross strips on a straight edge they are easier to handle if you stretch them slightly under the iron after cutting. This will help prevent puckering.

To cut strips either place the fabric on a cutting board and follow one of the diagonal lines with your scissors, or fold the fabric at an angle so that the weft yarns lie over the selvedge, or warp yarns. Cut along the fold, open out the pieces of fabric and cut the strips using an adjustable marker as a guide.

Joining crossway and bias strips
There is rarely sufficient spare fabric to cut very long strips so here is an easy way to make joins. Make sure the ends of the strips are cut exactly on a thread. Turn in and press 5mm (¼in.) at each end. Lay the strips end to end wrong side up. Pick up each pair of ends, place the creases together precisely and pin. Stitch on the crease, press the join

open and trim the edges. Having made all the joins press the strip.

CUFF LINKS FROM BUTTONS

A decorative fastening for shirt cuffs using pairs of dome buttons. Prepare the sleeve by putting in only 4 tucks, there are 5 for other fastenings, making a faced slit opening and attaching the cuff evenly without an extension.

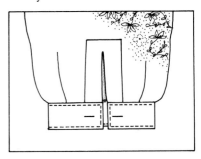

Make a horizontal buttonhole in each end of the cuff. Use double thread, waxed, and join a pair of buttons with 6 threads 5mm (¼in.) in length. The buttons will be difficult to hold so pin one of them to the ironing board after making

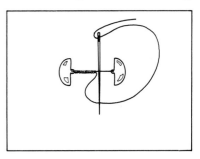

the first two threads. Work close loopstitch over these threads to make a rigid connection between the buttons.

CUFFS

The long-sleeved shirts and the gathered dress have openings at the wrist and cuffs attached. Establish the correct length of the sleeve, make the openings. Stitch the seams. Attach interfacing to the wrong side of the cuffs; use soft or medium Vilene (Pellon) in the dress cuffs; use soft Fold-a-Band (Fuse 'n' Fold) in the shirt cuffs. Mark the cuff extension. Fold over and press the seam allowance on one edge. Put in the tucks or insert gathering thread in the edge of the sleeve.

Pin cuff to sleeve right sides together and with cuff extension at the back of the sleeve, pull up the

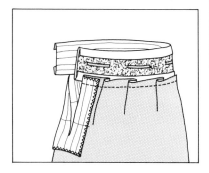

gathers. Tack and machine on seam line or using the Fold-a-Band edge as a guide. Trim edges and press turnings into the cuff.

Fold each cuff end right sides together and stitch across the end and on to the extension part, turn, stitch along lower edge of extension. Trim edges and corners, turn cuff right side out and press

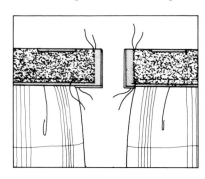

the ends. Turn under remainder of cuff edge, tack down and finish by hemming along the edge into the machine stitching. Press; top-stitch the cuff.

An alternative method that can

be used if the cuff is to be finished with edge-stitching is to attach the cuff to the wrong side of the sleeve and turn it on to the right side. Finish by machining the edge instead of hand sewing it.

CUTTING BOARD

A very useful piece of equipment even if you already have a table that is suitable for cutting out. Open out the board and place it on the table, bed or floor. Use it for folding and laying out the fabric accurately, for finding the straight grain on odd-shaped scraps of fabric, for cutting straight pieces such as frills, bands and waistbands; and for cutting crossway strips using the diagonal lines. The board can also be used as a sewing surface as it protects your table from scratches and you can carry everything away easily instead of clearing up individual items. If you sit in an armchair to sew, fold the board across your knees.

DARTS

Transfer the size and shape of the darts on the V-neck top after cutting out, using tailor's tacks, chalk or fabric pen.

Fold the fabric right side inside, match the dart sides and insert two pins to hold. Insert the pins from the right with the fold to the right so that it can be stitched, removing the pins as you reach them.

Fasten off the thread ends: on Tana lawn and crêpe de chine bring the stitching to an end exactly on

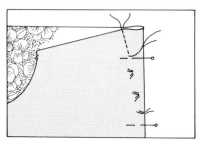

the fold at the point of the dart and thread the ends into a sewing needle and oversew along the fold for a little way. On other fabrics reverse the machining carefully for a short distance.

Press the stitching then press the dart to one side with the bulk lying down towards the waist.

If you normally have a fitting adjustment to make to bust darts, tack them and fit before stitching. Remove tailor tacks.

DOUBLE BINDING

A method of binding that works very well on fine fabrics like crêpe de chine and lawn because it produces a firm edge. It is also effective for binding two layers of fabric as it brings the edge up to the same thickness. We used it on the bandeau top, cummerbund, pockets etc.

Cut crossway strips four times the required finished width plus two seam allowances of 6mm (¼in.) each. Fold the strip wrong sides together, first making all joins as it

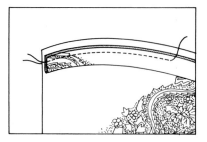

is difficult to do this later. Place the folded strip on the right side of the garment, tack and machine taking 1.5cm (⅝in.) seam allowance on the garment but only 6mm (¼in.) on the binding. Trim edges to 3mm (⅛in.). Roll the binding to the wrong side

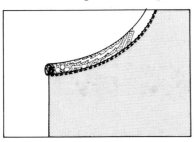

and hem, taking the needle under the machine stitches and into the fold. This binding can also be finished on the right side of the garment by attaching it to the wrong side first and folding it over until it covers the machine stitching.

With both applications you should control the folded edge carefully because it stretches very easily, although this fact can be used to advantage when binding a convex edge as it can be eased round the edge but remain flat.

DOUBLE COLLAR AND CUFFS

Collar
An attractive variation on a shirt or dress shown on the tartan Jubilee button-through dress (page 112). A contrasting colour can be used for the second collar.

Cut two complete collars but trim 6mm (¼in.) from the outer edge of the upper one. Put interfacing in the large collar, then make up both of them and press. Place the small

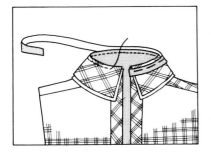

collar on top of the large one and machine them together close to the neck edge. Attach to the neckline of the garment using a bias strip or neck facings. The under or contrast collar will extend 6mm (¼in.) beyond the top collar.

Cuffs
Cut two pairs of cuffs but cut 6mm (¼in.) from the outer edge of one pair. Interface the small cuffs. Stitch round the outer edge of the smaller

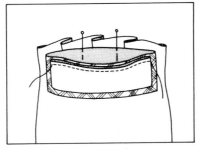

cuffs, trim, turn right side out and press. Repeat with the larger pair of cuffs. Place each small cuff centrally on the larger one and tack, with all raw edges level, tacking through the small cuff and one layer of large cuff. Work a row of machining through these layers to prevent them slipping apart. Attach cuffs to sleeve in the usual way.

DRAWSTRING AND CASING

If you wish to define the natural waist or a low waist on the straight dress in either the long or short versions, you could add a casing with drawstring. Complete the dress except for the hem, put it on and tie a tape measure or belt round the intended waist. Mark round the dress at intervals at the bottom edge of the tape with tailor's chalk, fabric pen or pins. Take off the dress and insert a row of tacking on the marked waistline. Cut a piece of soft iron-on Vilene 10cm (4in.) long and 2.5cm (1in.) wide and press it to the wrong side of the dress at centre front. Make two 3cm (½in.) vertical bound or hand-sewn buttonholes

2.5cm (1in.) apart below the waist mark at the centre front, or attach two metal eyelets.

Make a length of rouleau a little longer than the size of the dress waist. Cut and join sufficient crossway strips to go round the dress. Neaten the edges. Alternative fabrics that could be used for this casing are lawn, bias binding pressed open, and knitted nylon seam binding.

Place on the wrong side of the dress with the upper edge level with the waist marking. Turn in the

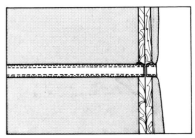

ends over one of the side seams and oversew them together. Machine just within the neatened edge with a straight or small zigzag stitch.

Thread a rouleau tie through the casing and knot each end.

The casing for elastic or drawstring on the trousers and shorts is simply made by turning down the edge to the depth shown on the pattern.

ELASTIC BELT

A quick, easy belt that looks good in Tana lawn. Use wide elastic webbing, measure it tightly round your waist so that the ends just meet. Cut a piece of straight fabric twice the width of the elastic plus 2cm (¾in.) and 1½ times the length. Fold it right side inside and stitch the raw edges. Turn the tube right side out and press with the join in the middle. Slot the elastic through. Machine across each end and again 2.5cm (1in.) inside the end and also neaten the ends. Stitch a clasp to the ends, or use Velcro if you wish to use the clasp on other belts.

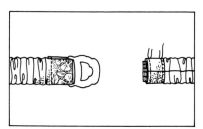

ELASTIC WAISTBAND

A decorative waistband that can be used with the full skirts. It is quick to do, and makes fitting easy. Use ordinary elastic, or elastic webbing which is soft and available in several widths. The waistband looks best if it is 3.5cm (1½in.) or wider, and gathered on to the skirt. The elastic is then threaded through it.

Measure the elastic to fit round the waist, well stretched; cut it allowing 2cm (¾in.) for a join. Cut a strip of fabric twice the width of the elastic, plus its thickness, plus

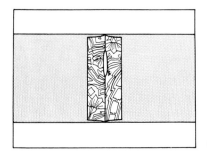

two seam allowances. Make it 1½ times the length of the elastic. Fold the fabric right sides together and stitch across the end, leaving a gap

the width of the elastic. Press open the join. Gather the skirt and attach the band, arranging the join above the left seam of the skirt and the gap on the wrong side. Fold the band to the inside, turn under and hem the inner edge of the band, making sure the finished width is even and

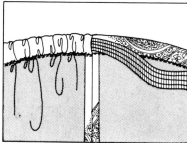

exactly the width of the elastic. Thread the elastic through the waistband. Join the ends of the elastic by overlapping and stitching strongly.

ELASTICATED WAIST AND WRIST

Use on shorts and trousers, long sleeves of child's dress, etc.

Elastic webbing can be stitched directly to the wrong side of a garment using zigzag stitch or stretch stitch. Use a narrow elastic and one row of machining on a sleeve or where very little grip is required, but use wider elastic attached with two rows of stitching at a waistline.

Measure the elastic firmly round the body, add 2cm (⅜in.) and cut. Join the ends. Divide the elastic into 4 equal sections using a fabric pen. Mark the position of the elastic on

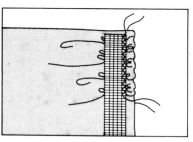

the garment with a row of tacks. Divide it into 4 sections. Place the garment under the machine, wrong side up, with the elastic on top. Stitch for 1cm (⅜in.) to anchor it then continue stitching but stretching the elastic, matching up the section markings.

An alternative method if the elastic is likely to be uncomfortable against the skin is to join the elastic, pin it stretched to the wrong side of the garment near the edge, fold the fabric down over it for 1cm (⅜in.) and machine along the edge. Fold the edge down by the width of the elastic and machine two rows of stitching, stretching it so that the fabric lies flat.

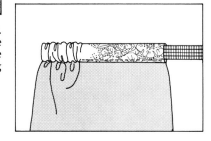

EXTENDED SHOULDER SLEEVES AND SEAMS

Use this method of inserting sleeves in the shirts, the straight dress and the cowl top.

Make wrist openings, if any, in the sleeves. Complete yokes. Matching sleeve head point to shoulder marking, place sleeve to

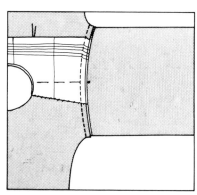

armhole right sides together (or wrong sides together for a French seam), stitch the seam, trim and press turnings towards sleeve. Neaten the seam.

Fold garment with right sides together, match underarm seam from hem through underarm to wrist. Stitch the seam. If using French seams make them as narrow

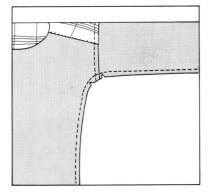

as possible. With open seams snip the turnings at the underarm so that the seams lie flat when they have been pressed open.

FACED SLIT OPENING

A flat edge-to-edge opening that can be used in the sleeves of the gathered dress and the button-through dress made in Varuna wool or Jubilee.

Cut out the sleeves, marking the position for the opening. Cut a rectangle of fabric on the straight grain 15cm (6in.) long by 4cm (1½in.). Neaten the edge all round. Cut a strip of Bondaweb 14cm

(5½in.) long and about 1.5cm (⅝in.) wide. Press it to the centre of the rectangle on the wrong side. Peel off the paper backing.

Fold the rectangle and cut it in half. Place each of the pieces right side down to right side of sleeve, matching centre of strip to marked opening. Tack. Turn sleeve over and stitch on each side of the mark

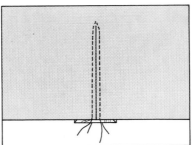

making a point at the top. The rows of stitching should be 3mm (⅛in.) apart. Remove tacks and carefully cut between the stitches. Roll the facing to the wrong side and press

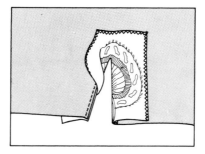

the edge. Take care when pressing as the Bondaweb will melt and the facing will adhere to the sleeve; fraying is eliminated by this method of finishing.

FACINGS

Shaped edges such as the neckline of the straight dress and the neck and armholes of V-neck top can be faced. Use matching or contrast fabric. Cut out the facing pieces in fabric. Attach interfacing to the garment if necessary, on the wrong

side. Cut it using the facing pattern pieces but making it 3mm (⅛in.) narrower.

Join and finish the garment seams. Place the facing pieces on the right side with right sides down, lining up the raw edges. Insert several pins diagonally along the facing. At garment seams allow the ends of the facing to stand

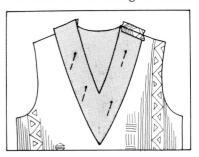

upright together. To join the facing pieces first press the ends over so that the folded edges meet them, lift those edges and join them, stitching in the crease made by the iron. Press open the joins and trim.

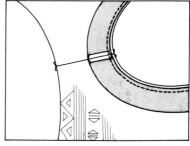

Tack the facing to the garment and machine on the stitching line. With a V-neck, start at the bottom of

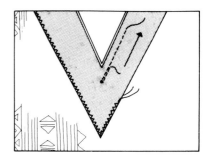

the V, marking the exact centre with chalk or fabric pencil. Be sure to end the stitching at that point.

Trim and neaten the outer edge of the facing. Trim and snip the facing and garment edges and, in the case of Varuna wool and Country cotton, layer them as well.

Roll the facing to the wrong side. It helps to push the toe of the iron under the facing, on the right side of the garment, to obtain a crisp, straight join. Tack the edge and

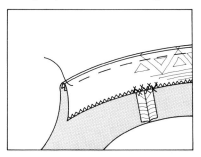

press. Hold the facing in position on the inside by working herringbone stitch over the edge where it crosses seams. Also, on Country cotton, Varuna wool and Jubilee, a few pieces of Wundaweb can be slipped under the facing. Press well.

FACINGS FINISHED ON THE OUTSIDE OF A GARMENT

This type of edge can be used on the long shorts, on sleeves and necklines.

Use either matching or contrast fabric. If the fabric has a large or one-way design, make sure the facings are cut with that design correctly placed for the remainder of the garment. If piping, lace, etc. is to be inserted under the facing then prepare it beforehand. If interfacing is needed, cut it and attach it to the right side, making sure it is at least 6mm (¼in.) narrower than the width the facing will be when it is finished.

To ensure that seams will not show at the edge, stitch the garment seams but stop the machining at the

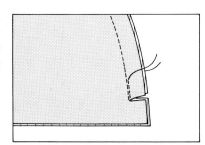

seam line at the garment edge. Snip the seam allowance to the end of the stitching. Press and neaten the seam. Push the unstitched section through to the right side and stitch the seam line. Press open and trim.

Join the seams on the facing, press open and trim the edges. Attach lace, piping etc. to the outer edge, stitching it to the seam line on the right side, and rolling the edge so that the decoration extends. Tack and press – if the facing edge is

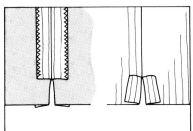

plain, turn it in and tack. Place the facing right side down to wrong side of garment, matching edges and seams, and tack. Measure an even distance from the stitching at the outer edge, mark the neck stitching line with chalk or fabric pen. Machine. Trim and snip the edges. Roll the facing to the outside of the garment. Baste in position. Tack the edge to hold it and machine or slip hem along the edge.

FACING PATTERNS, HOW TO MAKE THEM

Facing patterns are provided in the book for all the styles shown that require them but if you want to vary

the shape of a neckline or if you wish to face a sleeve or hem with a contrast or simply change the shape of any edge, you will need a new facing pattern.

Use paper or light sew-in Vilene to make the pattern pieces.

Draw the new line you want on your pattern but do not cut it. Place the new paper or Vilene over the top and trace the new edge and all nearby seams and edges for a distance of a little more than 6cm (2¼in.). For instance, on a neckline trace part of the shoulder seam, centre front and centre back as well

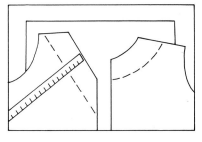

as the new neckline; on a sleeve trace the seam edges; on shorts trace the leg seam edges and so on. Trace back and front patterns. Mark the straight grain and any balance marks and also any note referring to the centre back and centre front. Remove the original pattern.

Mark the remaining edge of the new facing by measuring 6cm (2¼in.) evenly from the new garment edge and cut out the pattern pieces. Pin to fabric and cut.

If interfacing is required use the same facing pattern pieces but cut the interfacing a little narrower by trimming the outer edge.

FAGGOTING

A lacy ladder effect achieved by working stitches between two hemmed or bound edges. It can be done by hand or machine. Hand faggoting is not particularly strong so on children's clothes it should be worked by machine, following the instructions in your sewing machine manual.

To work faggoting by hand, complete the garment edge and tack it to paper. Make a length of rouleau the same length and tack it to the paper an even 6mm (¼in.) away. Work herringbone stitch between

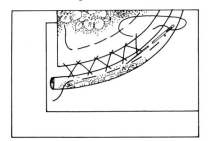

the two edges. If additional decoration is required, rows of feather stitch could be added to the garment or suitably coloured beads might even be threaded on to the needle between connecting stitches for a really bold effect.

FEATHER STITCH

A decorative stitch in straight lines that can be worked beside shirt bands, between tucks on the V-neck top, parallel with hems and frill edges, and it can also be used for attaching lace.

Use two strands of Anchor Stranded Embroidery thread or Soft Anchor thread, or any other suitable embroidery thread. Begin with a back stitch on the under side then work on the right side, taking

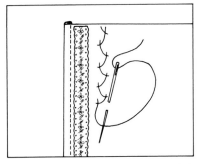

vertical stitches alternately to left and right, and keeping the thread under the needle as the stitch is taken.

FLAT TUCKS

Stitched folds of fabric that can be made to any width that looks right on the garment. Flat tucks can be used on the hems of the gathered skirt, on the child's dress and apron, and across the tops of patch pockets. Experiment with the width and distance between the tucks on spare fabric; either cut out the garment allowing sufficient extra length or make the tucks before cutting out. The tucks on the patch pockets on the drop-waisted V-neck dress (page 105) were carefully calculated.

Convenient widths of flat tuck are half the width of the machine foot or the width of one toe of the foot. If wider tucks are required mark the width by sticking a piece of basting tape to the machine.

Mark the position of the fold of the first tuck with chalk or tacking. Fold the fabric wrong sides inside and press. On striped or check fabric it is unnecessary to mark the line. Place the fabric under the machine foot with the fold to the right. Stitch with matching or contrasting thread. Prevent slippage and wrinkling on crêpe de chine by inserting a row of tacking near but not on the proposed stitching line.

Press the row of stitching, open out the fabric and press the tuck to one side, running the iron against the stitching under the tuck and finally pressing it flat. Fold the fabric ready for the next tuck, placing it flat on the pressing surface. Set your adjustable marker to the required width and adjust the folded edge of fabric, pressing it with the iron to form the fold of the next tuck. Continue pressing and

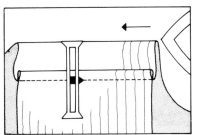

stitching in this way until finished.

Ribbon or embroidery can be added between tucks. Vertical tucks can be pressed in groups in opposite directions with buttons or embroidery between them.

FRENCH KNOTS

Work French knots in clusters on corners of collars, cuffs, pockets, belts, or use them in rows with feather stitch or alongside lace edging. Use matching or contrast thread.

Use two strands of Anchor Stranded Embroidery or similar thread and a crewel needle. If you wish to mark the position of the knots do so using a fabric marking pen. Begin with a back stitch on the under side of the fabric at a point where one of the knots will be, and bring needle through to upper side of fabric. Take one short stitch, leave the needle in the fabric and wind the thread round the point of the needle once or twice, holding the thread fairly close to the eye of

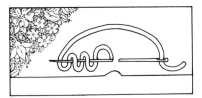

the needle. Pull the needle through until the loops of thread have settled on the surface of the fabric. Pass the needle to under side and either fasten off the thread or take the needle to the position of the next knot. Do not press.

FRENCH SEAMS

This is a neat narrow seam to be used on fine fabrics that fray and on transparent fabrics. French seams have been used on all the Tana lawn and crêpe de chine outfits.

It is not suitable for outer wear so confine its use to shirts, children's clothes, and items of lingerie only.

Tack the layers of fabric with wrong sides together keeping the tacks away from the edge. Machine with a straight stitch a little less than 1cm (⅜in.) from the edge, i.e. 6mm (¼in.) from the seam line. Remove tacking.

Press the stitching. Open out the fabric and press both edges to one side. Turn fabric over and press again to ensure a good seam line.

Trim the raw edges to within 3mm (⅟₁₆in.) of the machining.

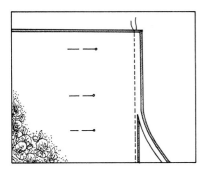

Turn fabric over and hold with right sides together and the join on the edge. Press very carefully on the edge using the toe of the iron. Tack, a little over 6mm (¼in.) from the edge. On short seams e.g. shoulders or short sleeves, this tacking may be

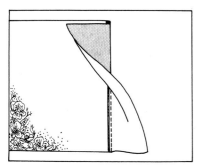

omitted but it is essential on longer seams to prevent the fabric bubbling.

Work another row of machining 6mm (¼in.) from the edge. You are likely to find that you can use your machine foot as a guide for this rather than measuring it. The second row of stitching should

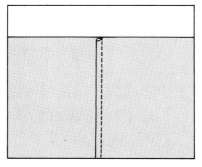

conceal the raw edges, so check that it will do so by inserting the point of a pin 6mm (¼in.) from the edge and holding the seam up to the light enabling you to see the edges inside.

GATHERED DRESS YOKES

Join shoulder seams of yoke and yoke lining. Press open. Stitch raglan seams of dress, insert gathering threads. Matching centre fronts, centre backs and sleeve head points, pin backs and front yokes to right side of dress sections. Pull up the gathers and even them out. There is a lot of fullness in the dress but it can be controlled by using plenty of pins inserted vertically before tacking. Stitch yoke to dress. Remove tacking, trim seam edges.

Place yoke lining to right side of yoke. Match centre back and

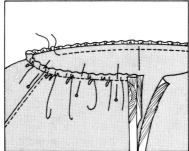

shoulders. Match centre front to the top of the centre front seam opening. Stitch round the neck and down centre front to meet the yoke seam stitching. Trim and snip neck

edges, turn yoke right side out bringing lining into position. Baste round neck edge, along shoulders

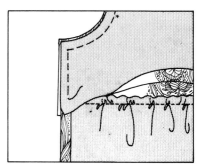

and round the curve of the yoke to hold the lining and yoke flat. Turn under edge of yoke lining and hem into the machine stitching.

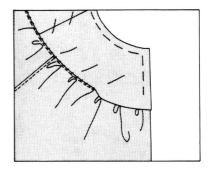

An alternative method is to attach the yoke as an overlaid seam and machine on the outside. This is the easiest way, especially if you are unused to handling curved edges.

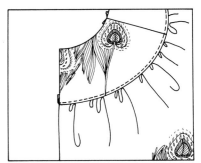

Turn in, tack and press outer edge of yoke, snipping it so that it lies flat. Attach and finish lining yoke in the same way as before.

GATHERING THREADS

Gathering threads may be made by hand, starting with a knot and making running stitch, but they are quicker made by machine using synthetic thread for strength. Set your machine to the longest straight stitch and stitch slightly less than 1.5cm (⅝in.) from the edge of the fabric with the right side up. Start and finish well within the fabric ends and anchor one end of the stitching by reversing for two or three stitches which makes it easier to pull up.

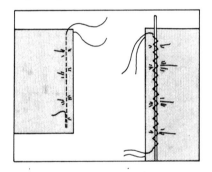

On very firm fabric or where you have large pieces to gather, insert a stronger gathering thread by couching a medium thickness crochet cotton on to the wrong side of the fabric using a zigzag stitch.

When attaching a long gathered circular section, for instance a skirt frill, you can insert one or two rows of shirring elastic to reduce the length of the frill evenly. It is then stretched to fit the garment edge.

Always remove all gathering threads after completion. Snip the thread at intervals or anywhere it is caught and the threads will ease out.

HEMMING

A very small neat hand-stitch used to hold down a folded edge. Make it as invisible as possible on the outside of the garment by picking up one thread of the fabric only before passing the needle into the

fold. Slant the needle slightly forward to achieve even stitches. If there is a convenient row of machining, attaching a binding for example, then pick up the stitch not the fabric.

HEMS

Turning up a skirt
Sometimes a hem can be made at an early stage in the construction of the garment but with most adult clothes the length is critical and should be the final stage in making up. Put on the skirt or dress, adding the belt you intend to wear with it. Wear the right shoes, not simply for heel height but because the style of the shoe can also affect the length.

Turn up and pin part of the hem at the front. It can help to take a measurement from another garment as a guide. Look in a mirror; adjust until you are satisfied.

Insert two pins on the fold and remove the others. Get someone to insert pins at that distance from the floor all round the skirt. This can be done using an adjustable hem marker on a stand, or a long ruler, or even a length of wood. If you have a marker that has a container of chalk you can mark the hemline yourself if you are careful not to twist your body out of position. When marking an ankle length skirt or dress, stand at the top of the stairs and let your helper sit on a lower stair for comfort.

With the straight gathered skirt and also with the straight dress you will be able to turn up the hem evenly without help with marking.

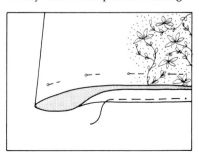

Take off the garment. Arrange the skirt on the table right side out but with the hem edge ready to turn up. With the pins appearing on the fold turn up the raw edge and tack near the fold. Keep the fabric on the table as it is liable to stretch if lifted. Remove pins. If you wish to check the level and length of the skirt hold up the hem surplus with pins, try on the skirt and adjust it, and re-tack if necessary.

After tacking, press the fold. Decide on the most suitable depth for the hem. On most fabrics 4-6cm (1½-2¼in.) is suitable but on Tana lawn and crêpe de chine it will help the skirt to hang better if the hem is deeper than this. Allow extra when cutting out these fabrics. Finish the hem on Tana lawn and crêpe de chine by turning under the raw edge 1-1.5cm (⅜-½in.) and tacking it. Press very lightly and hand slip hem or blind hem the edge by

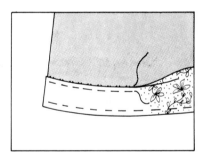

machine. Use this finish on the child's dress so that it can be easily let down. On Varuna wool, Country cotton, Wandel and Jubilee fabrics draw a chalk line at the depth of the finished hem, and work a row of straight machining on the line through the hem surplus fabric

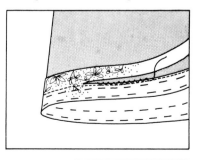

only. Trim the fabric close to the stitching, work zigzag stitch over the edge. Tack the edge flat to the garment. Complete by working hand catch stitch under the edge or work blind hemming by machine. Remove tacking and press but do not exert any unnecessary pressure over the sewn edge.

HEMLINE FRILLS (FLOUNCES)

A frill or flounce can be added to a skirt hemline to make it longer, or it can replace part of the length given of the garment. In this case reduce the length of the main pieces when cutting out.

Measure the length of the garment edge and plan to make the frill at least 1½ times that length. Allow more when using Tana lawn. Work out the depth of the frill so that it balances the remainder of the garment and so that it gives the effect you want.

Cut pieces of fabric on the straight grain the depth you need plus 13mm (½in.) for a narrow hem and 1.5cm (⅝in.) at the edge to be gathered. Join the pieces to make a circle or a long strip using narrow seams. Stitch a narrow hem along one edge using a hand or machined hem, plain or decorative. Add any other decoration to the frill such as lace, ribbon tucks.

Narrow frills (ruffles)
These can be made as above, but they are easier to handle and crisper if they are made from double fabric. If they are to be attached to neckline, armhole, front edge or band they may also be cut on the cross.

Cut pieces of fabric twice the width you require plus 3cm (1¼in.) and of sufficient length. Join the pieces using open seams. Fold in half with wrong side inside and press.

If you are adding decoration leave one join unsewn. Open out the frill and work it on single fabric. Refold the fabric and join the final seam.

Gathering
Divide the frill into equal sections, short frills into 4, long ones into 8, marking the fabric with tailor's chalk or a fabric pen. Insert a gathering thread 1.5cm (⅝in.) from the raw edge in each section, fastening off one end of each for ease of pulling up. If you have a machine attachment that gathers or pleats, use it on long frills but try it out on a spare piece of fabric first, adjusting the amount it draws up until the reduction is **correct. You** are unlikely to be able to get it exactly right so the resulting frill should be longer than necessary rather than shorter.

Divide the garment into sections.

Attaching frills
Working on one section only match two sets of marks, put frill to garment right sides together, edges meeting, and pin. Pull up the thread until the frill fits. Wind the thread round a pin, even out the gathers and pin at short intervals across the seam. Adjust the pins and the gathers as many times as necessary.

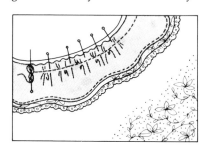

Tack, removing the pins as you come to them and using very small stitches. Fasten off the tacking. Move on to the next section and continue until the frill is attached.

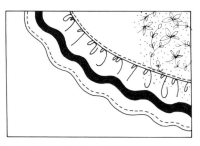

An alternative and slightly easier method is to make the join as an overlaid seam. This is often best if the frill has been pleated by machine as it is easier to ease in any surplus. This seam is now stitched from the right side, machining the edge of the fold. The previous seam should be stitched with gathers uppermost on the tacking. Stitch slowly in both cases, using the point of a bodkin to even out any bunches or pleats in the fabric.

Remove tacks and gathering thread. The raw edges can be trimmed and neatened together but a better finish is to trim the gathered edge only, then fold the garment edge down over it and hem.

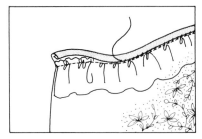

If the frill is only on part of the garment edge, e.g. the armhole, attach it in the same way but then use a facing or a crossway strip machined on top and turned to the wrong side to allow the frill to extend.

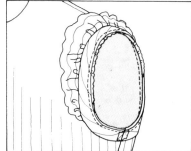

Another attractive way of attaching a frill is to hem both edges, adding decoration, then gather it a quarter of the way in from the top edge and apply it to the

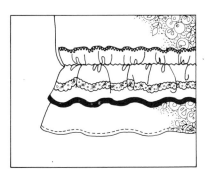

right side of the garment. The frill can extend below the garment or the two edges can be level or stepped. Stitch the frill with a small zigzag or machine embroidery stitch as desired.

HEMMED OPENING

A neat, flat opening for fine fabrics; use it on the sleeves of a shirt or gathered dress made in Tana lawn or crêpe de chine.

Mark the position of the opening where indicated on the pattern.

Thread a small needle with a short length of thread, cut the sleeve from the wrist at the opening position and roll the raw edge into the smallest hem you can manage. Take a couple of hemming stitches in the fold, roll the next part, hem and so on. As you approach the end of the slit you will find the hem becoming narrower until at the end

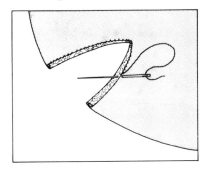

of the slit you will find the hem becoming narrower until at the end there is nothing to roll. Fold over a small amount of fabric once and work several close oversewing

stitches over it to prevent fraying. Press.

If you find it difficult to roll the edge, moisten your fingers for a better grip.

Attach the cuff so that the opening meets edge to edge.

HERRINGBONE STITCH

A stitch with a cross stitch effect. It is worked over an edge to keep it flat, for example where facings cross seams on the inside of a garment. Work from left to right inserting the needle horizontally from right to left, picking up 3mm (⅛in.) of fabric on the needle alternately above and below the edge of the upper layer of fabric.

HOOKS AND EYES

Hooks can be used to fasten the waistband and belts or cummerbund. Use size 2 or 3 for strength and use the metal bar with the hook. In other positions such as necklines use very small hooks with size 00 or 000.

Place the hook in position and attach with a pin. Sew with single thread, lightly waxed and start by working 4 stitches to hold the head of the hook to the fabric. Leave the pin. Pass the needle through the fabric and work close buttonhole stitch round the loops of the hook. Fasten off with two backstitches.

Pin the opening together and insert a pin where the thread loop is to be sewn. When using a metal eye or bar fasten it into the hook and

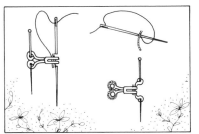

pin it to the fabric to make sure it is in the correct position. Sew it with close buttonhole stitch round each loop.

Make thread loops by making a short bar of three stitches in the fabric then work loopstitch over the thread. Take care not to pick up any fabric on the needle.

KNIFE PLEATS

The knife pleats in the straight skirt will remain crisply in place if they are carefully stitched and handled.

Cut out the skirt and mark the pleat lines and pleat depth point. Place the side panel sections on the centre section, right sides together, and pleat lines matching from hem to waist. Tack. Using a large straight

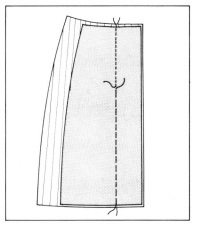

machine stitch sew from the hem up to the top of the pleat. Using a normal length stitch sew from the top of the pleat to the waist and fasten off the thread ends. Remove tacking and press the stitching flat. Press the pleat by opening it out and pressing it open lightly, then press both pleat edges towards the centre of the skirt. Press well on both sides.

Baste the pleat edges together and stitch at the raw edges, ruling a straight line with tailor's chalk for accuracy. Trim the edges close to the stitching.

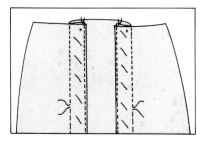

Complete the construction of the skirt. On reaching the hem, remove the large stitching in the pleats, open out the fabric and turn up the hem. Make sure the pleat seam is pressed open in the hem. If you are making the skirt in Varuna wool press a length of light Fold-a-Band

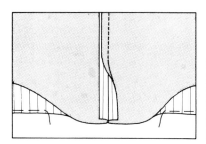

to the pleat, aligning the perforations exactly over the crease. Trim the Fold-a-Band level with the bottom of the skirt hem. After

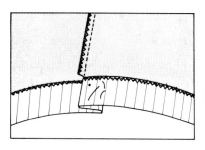

completing the hem, snip the pleat seam so that it swings free and neaten the edges from there up to the waist line. Fold the pleat back into position, baste across it at the hem and re-press, placing a folded piece of fabric against the ridge of the pleat to prevent an impression appearing on the outside of the skirt.

LACE EDGING

Use lace edging flat or gathered on frills, cuffs, collars and yokes. Finish the garment edge then either put the lace over the fabric with the

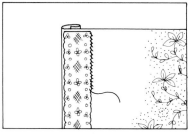

picot edge level with the hem edge and hem the straight edge to the fabric, or oversew the picot edge and hem edge together with the lace extending beyond the garment.

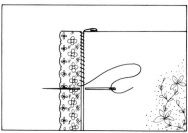

Lace edging often has a distinctive thread running through it near the straight edge which can be pulled up to gather it.

Divide the lace and the garment edge into 4 or 8 sections, pin at those points and pull up the gathering thread. Tack and machine with a straight stitch or with a small zigzag or embroidery stitch. If there is no thread an easy

way to gather lace is to attach it by hand with back stitch, picking up an extra fold of lace on the needle every third stitch. The folds flatten into even gathers.

If you are inserting lace edging where a frill joins the garment, place the lace on the right side of the frill, gather both together with one thread and attach to the garment.

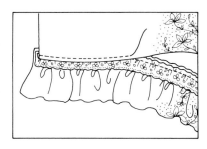

LACE INSERTION

Straight insertion lace can be applied in rows parallel with hems, yokes, shirt front band, etc. Ribbon or embroidery can be added on each side of the lace. Both edges of the lace are straight and it may also have slots for threading ribbon. If the lace has finished edges place it on the right side of the fabric and tack along each edge to secure. Join lace by turning in the ends to meet each other and slip-stitch together. Stitch along each edge with a small straight or zigzag machine stitch or

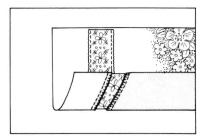

with hemming stitch. Remove tacks. It can be left like this or you may wish carefully to cut away the fabric under the lace. Trim it to within 2mm (⅟₁₆in.) of stitching, neaten with loopstitch.

If the edges of the insertion are unfinished, as is often the case with broderie Anglais, cut the fabric first then turn in each edge and press. Remember to turn in by half the width of the insertion in order to keep the garment the same size.

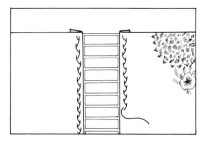

Tack each edge to the insertion and machine or hem by hand, feather stitch, herringbone etc.

LACE SEAMS

The most unobtrusive way of joining lace and mitring is to

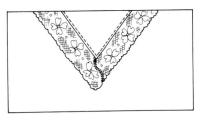

overlap the ends and oversew from the right side through both layers, using thread to match the colour of the lace and following the outline of the design. Trim away excess lace close to the stitching on both sides. If you are unable to join the lace this way then hold the ends with right

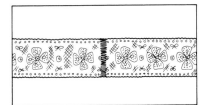

sides together and join with a small zigzag stitch. Trim off surplus lace and press the join to one side.

LAPPED SEAM

A lapped seam is a flat method of joining a non-fraying fabric such as Vilene, or it can be used as a decorative feature on yokes, or for attaching bands of fabric. To make lapped seams in interfacing, either for economy or perhaps as a way of adding extra stiffness to the point of a shirt collar, lap one layer over the other and then work a medium-width zigzag stitch through both layers. To join or apply layers of fabric, trim the edges of the upper fabric with pinking shears, lap one fabric over the other and stitch with a decorative machine stitch.

LINING

Almost any of the adult dresses and skirts could be lined, although it is not necessary to do so if they are full or gathered. Instructions are included for lining the straight skirt and also the button-through dress. If you decide not to line them, omit those stages in construction.

The decision on whether or not to line depends on style and on the type of fabric. Lining will help fitted skirts to hang freely. Varuna wool and Jubilee are likely to stick to underclothes and may be better lined when used for straight or almost straight styles.

Select washable lining fabric. Consult the charts (see pages 10-12) for the quantity required for the garment, remembering that the lining may not be the same width as the garment fabric. Cut out the lining using the same pattern pieces but economise if you wish by considering the following pattern adaptations:

A skirt lining can be cut 2.5cm (1in.) shorter than the pattern.

Omit sleeve lining in a dress.

Eliminate some seams, for example, by pinning together the centre and side patterns of the straight skirt.

Omit pleats by folding back the pleat extension on the pattern and cutting it out to stitch as a seam instead of a pleat. Stitch the seams in the lining, leaving them open as slits where the pleat falls. Make up the lining in the same way as the garment, using open or narrow seams. With fitted clothes take a smaller seam allowance, making the lining slightly looser to avoid too much strain on the lining material. Attach the lining to the garment with wrong sides together, tacking around the top (i.e. waist, yoke, shoulder) so that the two layers hang freely below. It can be helpful to use a dress form when putting the two together. Put the skirt or dress on the form with the lining under the garment, pin at the waist or yoke then tack round through both layers, vertically down each seam almost to the hemline and down centre front and centre back.

Turn up skirt hem and finish; turn up lining hem so that it is between 2cm (¾in.) and 3cm (1¼in.) shorter to ensure that it will not hang below the skirt. The lining

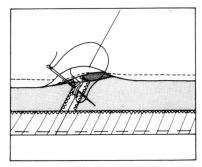

not hang below the skirt. The lining hem should be folded over twice and machined or slip hemmed.

Before removing tacking stitches work a bar tack 1cm (⅜in.) in length between lining and garment, above the hem at the seams. Make the bar by working four stitches between the two fabrics then work loopstitch closely over the threads.

LOOPSTITCH

Use for neatening raw edges of fabric. Work from left to right, drawing the needle towards you and stabbing the point of the needle through the fabric. The thread should be kept under the needle, the stitches should be 3mm (¹⁄₁₆in.) apart and 3mm (¹⁄₁₆in.) deep.

MACHINE FELL (FLAT FELL) OR WELT SEAM

A double-stitched seam that can be used on any of the fabrics except perhaps crêpe de chine and on all the garments in this book. It is decorative but can be used on all the main seams.

The finished width should be no more than 4mm (³⁄₁₆in.) on Tana lawn, a little wider on Country cotton or Varuna.

Place the two pieces to be joined with right sides together and stitch on the fitting line. Press the seam open, then to one side. Make sure

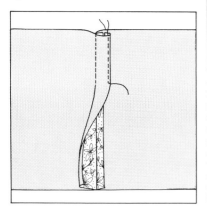

corresponding seams face in opposite directions. Trim the upper seam allowance to less than 1cm (⅜in.) and the one underneath to 3mm (⅛in.). Turn under the upper one evenly, moistening your fingers to help. Tack, but not near the edge. Press and machine.

MITRED CORNERS

A neat way of preparing right-angled corners on fabric that is to be applied to another layer, e.g. patch pockets.

Make sure the corners of the pockets are cut at accurate right angles. With the wrong side up press over first one seam allowance

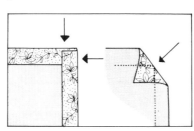

and then the other. Open out the corner and fold the point over again but at an angle of exactly 45°; press the fold lightly. Open out the corner. Turn pocket right side up

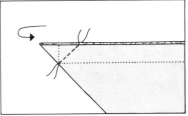

and fold so that the two raw edges meet. Stitch across the corner on the fold. Trim off the corner, turn right side out and press. Mitres are difficult at the first attempt and any folding and refolding, restitching, and unpicking will stretch and fray the corners. Avoid this by experimenting first with a piece of paper to familiarise yourself with the sequence.

NARROW HEM, MACHINED

This can be used on the edges of frills on gathered and circular skirts, on the child's dress and on shirt hems. If possible, leave one seam unstitched at the hem edge for about 10cm (4in.). Attach the hemming foot or shell hem foot to your machine and feed the fabric through, holding the raw edge vertically. The foot will roll a narrow hem.

Alternatively, use the iron to press a narrow fold of fabric on to the wrong side then put the fold under the machine, wrong side up, fold the fabric over once more, as narrow as possible, and machine.

In both cases press the hem and complete the unstitched seam, starting at the hem to ensure the edges are level.

NARROW SEAMS

Seams in Tana lawn, crêpe de chine and other fine fabrics may be better if they are made as narrow seams rather than open because both edges of fabric are pressed in the same direction and neatened together which makes the seam firm. This seam is quick to sew and can be used on main garment seams but is also particularly useful for joins in frills, linings, facings etc.

It is also very suitable for full gathered skirts and where several joins are to be made. Seams on the bias or cross are often best made narrow to allow the fabric to fall freely.

Complete all fitting before working the seams. Accuracy is essential as the surplus is trimmed and the seams cannot be let out later.

There are two ways of making narrow seams. Both methods are suitable for outer clothes and for seams in linings.

1. For use on fine fabrics that do not fray, e.g. Tana lawn, and for bias seams

Pin the two layers with right sides together, keeping the pins well away from the edge. On an area made accurately to size trim the edges, cutting the seam allowance down to 4mm (³⁄₁₆in.), but on large areas such as full skirts, frills etc., do not trim.

Machine using a stitch that combines zigzag and straight stitch, using a zigzag width that

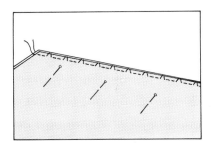

will work over the raw edges as you sew 4mm (³⁄₁₆in.) from the edge. Remove the pins.

Press the stitching then open out the fabric and press the seam to one side. Press on the right side.

2. Use this method on firm or springy fabrics and on those that fray, including Jubilee
Put the layers of fabric together and machine on the seam line with a straight stitch.

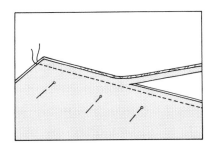

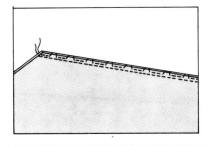

Trim the edges to 3mm (¹⁄₁₆in.) and work a small zigzag stitch or a combination stitch over the edge. Remove pins.

Press the stitching flat then press the seam to one side.

Where a third seam has to be made, make sure that the two that meet are pressed in opposite

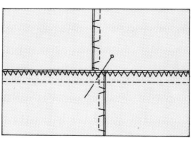

directions to make a flatter join and make the third seam slightly wider and of type (2) above. To be sure the two seams meet exactly insert a pin and stitch the seam with the pin in position.

NEATEN (FINISH)

Most woven fabrics will fray after wear and washing if exposed edges inside the garment are left raw. Tana lawn frays very little but it is fine and needs the firmness that neatening gives. Fraying has to be prevented on other fabrics like crêpe de chine and Varuna wool. Do this by neatening the raw edges, singly or two together, using a small zigzag machine stitch or small blind hem stitch, or by hand using overcasting. If the raw edge is short or difficult to get to on a machine then hand sewing will be easier and in any case provides a softer finish. The use of pinking shears on raw edges often makes fine fabrics curl up at the edge.

NEEDLES

Hand sewing is more enjoyable and the results are better if you use the right type of needle for each process.

Between or egg-eyed Betweens are for all hand sewing. They are short, which enables you to take very small stitches, and your thimble rests comfortably on the end but with the fingers still close to the point and controlling it.

Sharps needles are long and can be used for stitches like needle running, where a lot of fabric is picked up, or where the needle has to be stabbed through the fabric.

Crewel needles have large eyes and are used for embroidery.

NEEDLE RUNNING STITCH

Use this stitch when there are long rows of gathering threads or threads for smocking to be inserted. Thread a long needle, crewel or Sharps, size 7 for lawn and crêpe de chine, 6 for other fabrics, with a long length of sewing thread. Knot the end. Hold the fabric right side up and take the first stitch 2cm (¾in.) in from the edge.

Hold the needle flat on the fabric and move the point sharply up and down, moving along the fabric and picking up tiny amounts of fabric. To keep the stitches even, rest the fabric on your knee and hold it down with your right hand, leaving the fingers holding the needle extended, and hold the fabric taut with the left hand. Keep the fabric flat, and do not pull up the gathers as you work unless you know exactly how close they have to be. Make gathers for smocking like this.

OPEN (PLAIN) SEAMS

This is the seam that is suitable for all clothes and which is therefore most often used. Use it on all the patterns in the book, with Country cottons, Varuna wool, Jubilee, Tana lawn and crêpe de chine. If another seam is chosen it is for reasons of appearance, washing, etc. For instance, use French seams for ease of ironing and to minimise frayed edges, machine fell (flat fell) seams to keep edges flat.

To make an open seam, place one piece of fabric on top of the other, flat on a table with the right sides together and the raw edges matching. Tack or insert a few pins at right angles to the edge. Stitch the seam 1.5cm (⅝in.) from the edge starting at the hem in order to avoid puckers. Reverse the stitching at each end. Press the stitches then open out the layers of fabric. Open the seam edges with your fingers,

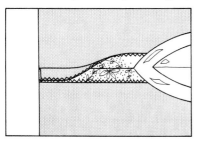

flattening the seam on to the pressing surface and press with the iron until it lies flat. The raw edges should be trimmed straight and neatened. Work the neatening from the hem up as it is easier to handle and prevents fluting and fraying.

OPENING ON CHILD'S DRESS AND ROMPERS

The pattern is made with an extension for the opening below the yoke. If the garment is to have hard wear attach a strip of iron-on interfacing to the wrong side 3cm (1¼in.) wide and with one edge level with the garment edge.

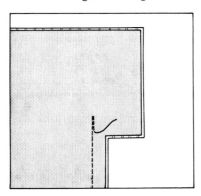

Stitch the garment seam at the back. Fold back the extension on the right back and stitch across the bottom to the end of the seam stitching. Snip to the corner of the stitching. Trim the edges and turn the corner right side out.

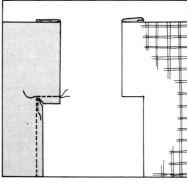

On the under side fold the extension back in line with the seam stitching, press. Turn under the raw edges on both sides of the opening and across the bottom.

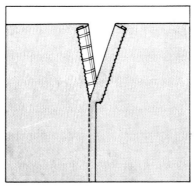

Hem or machine in place so that it withstands the strain of repeated washing.

Lap right over left and pin. On the wrong side hem the bottom 2cm (¾in.) of the opening to the under layer for strength. On the right side hem the bottom of the opening to the under layer and hem along the edge for 2cm (¾in.), working a bar tack at the top of the stitching.

If you are making the pinafore or dress alone simply press back the extension on both sides and stitch to make an edge-to-edge opening.

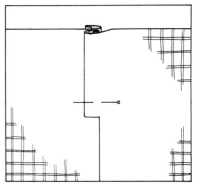

On completing the dress or rompers you may wish to sew one or two press studs to the opening to keep it in place in wear.

OVERLAID SEAM

Use on yokes and shaped edges. It is particularly useful for attaching the yoke of the gathered dress. It can also be used to join a frill to a main section of the garment. At least one row of stitching is visible on the outside. The advantage of the seam is that you are making it with the right side of the fabric uppermost, controlling the finished effect, and this is particularly useful if you are inserting a frill, piping, etc. in a seam.

Fold under and press the edge of the yoke or upper layer of fabric. Lay it over the under layer,

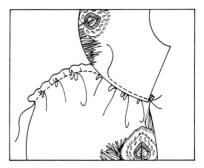

arranging gathers, etc. evenly. Be sure to take the correct seam allowance on both edges. Tack. Machine using a plain or decorative stitch or, on baby clothes, feather stitch can be used. On the inside trim and neaten all edges together.

PATCH POCKETS

If the fabric has a large or geometric print, assemble the main part of the garment before cutting out the pockets. Take a spare piece of the fabric and place it on the garment, altering the area of print until it looks right. The pocket can either be perfectly matched with the garment or a distinctive effect can be created by deliberately not matching it.

After cutting out the pockets reinforce the upper edge by pressing lightweight Fold-a-Band to the wrong side with the edge level with the raw edge. Neaten the edge including the Fold-a-Band. You may wish to reinforce the large patch pockets if you are making them in Tana lawn; if so press soft iron-on Vilene to the wrong side before attaching the Fold-a-Band. Mitre the two bottom corners. Turn in the side edges and press. Turn down the top edge on the perforations in the Fold-a-Band, tack and press.

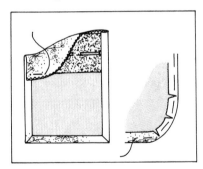

Put on the garment and pin one pocket in a position where it looks right and where you can reach it. Take off the garment and, if there are to be two pockets, fold the garment at the centre and mark the position of the pocket by working a tailor tack or by marking with chalk or fabric pen at one side and corner.

Tack the pockets in position. Tack across the top and then all around,

keeping the stitches well within the edge. Stitch in place either on the edge or the width of the machine foot from the edge. If you have made tucks in the pocket before

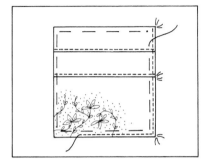

cutting it out, make the width of stitching the same as for the tucks. With crêpe de chine and possibly with Varuna wool, you may prefer to work a hand slip stitch just under the edge to attach the pocket. Make sure the top corners are strongly sewn with a triangle of machining or with a small bar tack hidden under the corner.

Remove tacks. Press from the wrong side of the garment and then the right side.

PETER PAN COLLAR

Attach yokes as for other collars. Interface one collar piece, place together with second collar, tack and stitch round outer edge. Trim and snip the edges. Turn collar right side out and press.

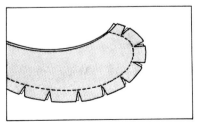

Attach front bands to shirt or dress, fold band right sides together at the neck and stitch across top of band to the join. Trim the turnings

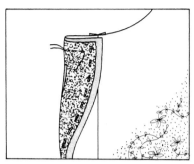

and snip at the end of the stitching. Turn the corner right side out and press. Tack the band in place.

Matching centre backs and bringing the front ends of the collar

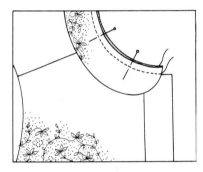

to exactly the centre of the band, pin and tack collar to neckline. On slippery fabrics also machine collar to neckline. Cut a crossway strip 3cm (1¼in.) wide and tack it on top of the collar with raw edges together. Machine, taking 1.5cm

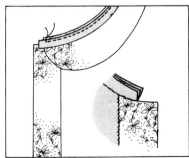

(⅝in.) seam allowance and taking care to finish the stitching precisely at the end of the snip in the band. Trim all edges; using the toe of the

iron press turnings down towards yoke. Press crossway strip down. Turn under the edge of the strip and hem below shirt neckline. Tuck the

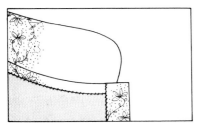

end of the strip under the shirt band. Finally complete the stitching on the inside of the band.

Plan the spacing of the buttons so that the top one appears below the neck but about mid-way down the collar. Attach a press stud at the corner of the band under the collar.

PIN

Use as few pins as possible, insert them at an angle on the bias of the fabric to avoid bumps, pick up a small amount of fabric only and do not push the pin in too far. Never pin if more than two fabric layers are involved as it will create inaccuracy between upper and lower layers. When stitching remove each pin just before you come to it to ensure the fabric is quite flat. Replace pins in pin box or drop on to magnet.

PIN TUCKS

Narrow raised tucks stitched by machine using a grooved foot and twin needle. Two reels of thread are threaded through the machine, separating only at the tension disc and at the needle where one thread passes through each eye. Insert the spool in the usual way. Work the tucks on single fabric without interfacing attached and try them out on a spare piece of fabric first because on some materials they produce wrinkles if worked on the weft. On Country cotton or Varuna wool a raised effect can be created

by running fine crochet cotton under the fabric.

Use groups of pin tucks on the blouse cuffs inside the front band, on pocket tops and down the centre of the V-neck top. Work them before cutting out the garments to size. In the case of cuffs and pockets ensure matching pairs by tucking a piece of fabric for both and then cut it in half. Pin-tucked areas can be emphasised with ribbon or embroidery.

Mark a chalk line or line of tacking on the straight grain of the fabric. Attach the grooved foot and twin needle and thread the machine with matching or contrast sewing thread. Set the machine to a small straight stitch or an embroidery stitch for a more elaborate effect. Stitch the first tuck running the edge of the foot against the marked line. Work the second tuck with the foot resting on the first to ensure that it is parallel. Work subsequent tucks in the same way, always stitching in the same direction. Press lightly on the wrong side only. Cut out the section of garment.

PIPING

A folded piece of matching or contrast fabric can be used in seams at shoulders, yokes, waists, front band on shirt, edge of cuffs, etc. Inserted to extend beyond the edge of the garment it has the advantage of making it firmer as well as being decorative. Examples of its use in this way include the romper yoke and collar, shirt front band, yoke and collar of robe, and there are many other places where it can be used with good effect.

Cut strips of fabric on the cross 1.5cm (⅝in.) wide. Join if necessary. Fold with wrong side inside and press the folded edge, stretching the fabric slightly.

Place on right side of garment with fold lying towards main area of fabric. Tack within about 3mm (⅛in.) of the folded edge extending over the seam line. Keep the tacking out of the way of the fold. Stitch

strip in place exactly on the garment seam line. If you are unsure of doing this accurately mark a line on the fabric first using tailor's chalk or fabric marker pen and place piping strip against it.

Put second piece of garment in position right side down on top of piping. With raw edges together tack through all layers. Turn this assembly over so that the line of

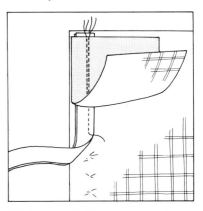

stitching is visible. Stitch again on top of or very close to the first row of stitching.

If the piping is in a seam press the layers in one direction, trim and neaten. If it is in an edge, trim the raw edges, snip curves and roll the layers of garment until the wrong sides are together and the piping

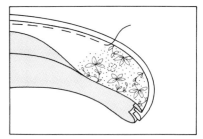

extends. Tack close to the piping to hold the edge firm. Press.

PRESS

This involves applying the iron to the process or stitching just completed. Use the toe of the iron and manipulate it, pressing down on the fabric and then using the iron as a whole, pressing rather than sliding the iron, until, when the iron is removed, the fabric remains in its new position. Always press the right side of the fabric as well as the wrong for perfect results but protect crêpe de chine from shine by using a dry muslin cloth under the iron. Consult the fabric chart for pressing instructions for specific fabrics.

PRESS STUDS AND SNAP FASTENERS

Keep corners of shirts, yokes, etc. flat by attaching a press stud. Always use very small fasteners, preferably size 000 or 00. Attach the knob section to the outer layer of the garment and the socket to the under layer. Mark the exact position, slip the knob on to a pin and place it on the fabric. Use single sewing thread and take a stitch under the press stud and then one stitch in two of the holes to stop the press stud moving. Remove the pin. Work 3 buttonhole stitches in each hole, and pass the needle to the under side to fasten off.

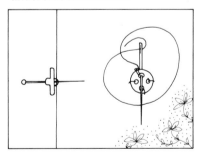

Find the correct position for the socket by inserting a pin through the centre of the knob into the socket and then into the layer of fabric underneath. Make a stitch under the socket, take a stitch in two of the holes, remove the pin and complete by working 3 buttonhole stitches in each hole.

Stud fasteners (snaps) with fancy tops could be used on some versions of the shirt.

PRICK STITCH

A hand stitch that is worked from the right side. It is similar to back stitch but the needle is inserted very near where the thread emerges so that only dents are visible and not stitches.

QUILTING

Quilted fabric can be used for small areas such as the yokes of the gathered dress and the child's dress, or for the entire garment. An example of this is the jacket made in quilted Varuna wool (see page 99). Quilted fabric can be bought by the metre or you can make your own. Do the quilting before cutting out the garment; if you require a small area only then cut the fabric roughly to shape but at least 8cm (3in.) larger all round than the pattern piece. For padding use washable polyester wadding. The thickness is denoted by the weight; 2 oz per metre 115cm (45in.) wide is sufficient for most indoor clothes and for small areas of quilting. If you want the padding thinner it can be peeled in half. Use lining material or cotton lawn to back the quilting. This avoids the necessity for a separate lining although with yoke, cuffs etc., it is not necessary because the inner layer of fabric will cover the wadding.

Place the backing material wrong side up on the table, put the wadding on top and the fabric on top of that, right side up. Keeping it on the table work lines of basting all over it 5cm (2in.) apart, keeping the thread loose and the ends unfastened. Mark the lines for stitching with tacking or with a fabric pen. Diamonds are easiest to sew. Discover the most suitable size by trying it out on spare fabric.

To stitch by machine use the quilting foot; it has short toes which enable you to see the lines, it also reduces bubbling and the toes do not become caught in the tacking. If you have a quilting bar, attach this too; its use means you do not have to mark stitching lines.

Make all lines in the same directions, working one set of diagonals and then the other.

Hand quilting is very satisfying to those who enjoy hand sewing. Geometric patterns can be made or a padded effect can be created by widely spaced single back stitches, perhaps with beads added or, with a distinctive print, outline the motifs. Use a Sharps needle, long pieces of thread in order to avoid too many joins, and use running stitch or prick stitch.

When the quilting is complete, pin on the pattern and cut out. Make up using open or welt seams. Finish edges with binding.

RIBBON OR BIAS DECORATION

Strips of contrast fabric can be added to a garment to form bands round a skirt, or they can run parallel with a yoke line or pocket top.

Cut strips of fabric on the cross or bias 2cm (¾in.) wide. Stretch under the iron and turn in each edge towards the centre and press the folds. Alternatively pass the strip through a bias-making tool and press.

Mark the position for the decoration using tailor's chalk or fabric pen. Place strip in position right side uppermost and tack. If all garment seams have been joined,

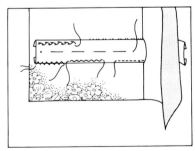

snip one seam and push the ends of the strip through to the inside. Re-stitch the seam.

Attach the strip with zigzag or machine embroidery stitch or with feather stitch or other hand embroidery stitch, or sew it invisibly with slip hemming.

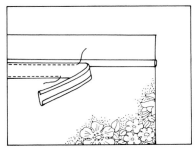

Alternatively put fabric piping under the edge and machine on each edge of the strip to hold in place.

Ribbon can be used in the same way but no preparation is necessary. Select washable satin ribbon 3mm (⅛in.) or 6mm (¼in.) wide and attach with small straight machine stitch using the quilting foot for good visibility and control. To attach ribbon by hand, work hemming stitch along each edge with thread of a perfectly matching colour.

ROLLED HEM

A very narrow hem finished by hand or machine. Use on crêpe de chine and Tana lawn for shirt hems, frills, etc. Use on edges that do not require the weight that a deep hem provides, e.g. sleeves; on hems where there is already enough fabric to ensure the article hangs properly, e.g. circular skirt; and where a deeper hem would look unattractive.

The finished hem should be as narrow as the fabric will allow. The edge must be cut accurately, trimming away all but enough to roll. Calculate the exact amount by rolling the edge of a spare piece of fabric and measuring it. Cut the garment edge to the correct length.

Stitching by hand
Thread a size 7 or 8 Between needle with a short length of thread, knot

the end. Roll the fabric edge towards you using the thumb and forefinger of each hand. Work

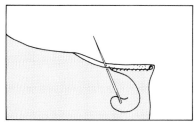

hemming stitch along the fold. Roll a little more and stitch. Continue like this, moistening your finger tips in order to grip the fabric. If the fabric does not fray a small slip stitch can be used; it shows less than hemming. It helps if the entire edge is straight or curved, but if you do have angled corners to stitch roll

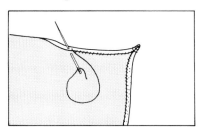

and hem the two edges but hold them together and prevent the corner from fraying by taking a couple of stitches right through the corner.

Stitching by machine
Put the hemming foot or shell hem foot on your machine; adjust to a stitch suitable for the fabric. Trim the edge of the fabric and stitch the hem, feeding it evenly into the foot. Practise this first on spare fabric to learn how to hold the fabric and to find out how deep the finished hem is and therefore at what level to trim the edge of the garment.

ROULEAU (TUBING)

Narrow tubing made from fabric cut on the cross or bias and used for decoration as bows, ties, button

loops, hanging loops, etc. It should be made as narrow as the fabric will allow. Experiment to find a suitable width by folding a small piece of fabric and measuring it. It is difficult to reduce the width after cutting and if it is too narrow you will not be able to use it.

Cut the crossway strips twice the finished width of the rouleau plus two seam allowances of 6mm (¼in.). Stretch the strip by running the iron along it. Fold right side inside and measure from the fold the amount you calculated as the correct width. Insert the point of a pin to mark it. Place the strip under the machine foot with the fold to the right. Line up the pin point in front of the needle, lower the foot and look at the position of the fold. It is likely that the fold will be level with the edge of the machine foot on many machines. If so, remove the pin and use that as the guide for keeping straight. If not, try moving the needle position, moving the strip to line up the pin again. Having found a point to watch closely as you guide the fabric, set the machine to a slight zigzag stitch to add 'give' to the stitch, or even use a stretch stitch. Use synthetic thread to ensure that the stitching will not break when the rouleau is put under strain. As you stitch keep the fabric folded evenly and pull it slightly as it goes under the machine.

Trim the raw edges a little. Turn the rouleau right side out using a rouleau needle. Slip it into the tube,

sew the eye to the raw edge at the top with several stitches, using the thread ends. Ease all the fabric on to the needle and pull it through. Cut off the needle, trim the ends of the tube neatly.

The ends can be finished by pushing in the raw edges for 1cm

(⅜in.) or so, or turn in, gather and sew on a bead or round button, or simply tie a knot.

ROULEAU LOOPS

These are loops made from bias or from purchased binding to fasten over covered or dome buttons or large beads. They have been used on the yoke and cuffs of the gathered dress, on the jacket and on the shoulders of the cowl top and straight dress.

Work out the required length of each loop by experimenting with a strip of fabric pinned and passed over a button. Add 2.5cm (1in.) to each for stitching the ends into the seam and calculate the total. Cut the strip of bias fabric 2.5cm (1in.) wide. Fold it right sides together and stitch, making the rouleau as narrow as possible. The exact width will depend on the type of fabric being used. Trim a little and turn it right side out using a rouleau needle.

If you want a more rigid loop it can have piping cord inserted in it. To do this cut a length of thin cord twice the length of the fabric and wrap the fabric round wrong side out. Use a machine piping foot and

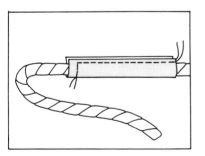

stitch across the end to hold the cord and then along its length close to the cord. Turn the loop right side out by pulling the cord and easing the fabric over it. Trim off surplus cord.

Mark off the loops in equal lengths. If they are to be close together arrange the rouleau on the right side of the garment, winding

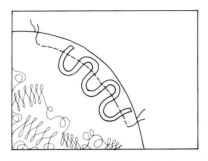

it to join loops. With single or spaced loops cut the rouleau to size and put in position. Machine in place on the garment seam line. Finish the edge with the facing, binding etc., stitched on top and turned to the inside so that the loops extend.

ROULEAU NEEDLE

A long needle with a ball end used for turning fabric tubing, belts, straps, etc.

RUCHED TRIMMING

A decoration made from ribbon or fabric that can be added to the hem and yoke of the child's dress, the neckline or armholes of V-neck top, the hemline slit of the straight dress etc.

Allow 1½ times the length of the edge to be decorated.

If you are using fabric, cut a crossway or bias strip 5-6cm (2-2½in.) wide and the length required, fold it right side inside and machine along the edge 3mm (⅛in.) from the raw edges. Turn it right side out using a rouleau needle. Press with your fingers, with the join lying down the middle of the strip. Turn in and oversew the ends. If you are using ribbon, cut to length and turn narrow hems at the ends.

Insert a gathering thread by machine-stitching on the right side down the centre of the strip or ribbon. Mark the position for applying it on the right side of the

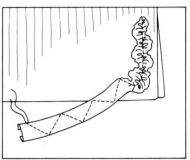

garment using tailor's chalk or fabric pen. Tack trimming in place, pulling up the gathers evenly. Stitch in place with a small zigzag stitch worked over the gathering thread.

For a different effect insert the gathering thread by hand but zigzagging across the trimming. Pull it up and tack to the garment. Attach by working back stitch over the gathering thread or use a row of embroidery.

Do not press this decoration.

RUCHING

This is a form of decorative gathering and is the result of rows of machine gathering extending into the garment. It can be used on the skirt of the child's dress, on the gathered dress, and anywhere else where there is plenty of fullness, but if the area is likely to be strained in wear the ruching should extend into a seam so that the ends of the gathering are held firmly.

Mark the area to be ruched as a rectangle on the right side, marking the four corners with chalk or fabric

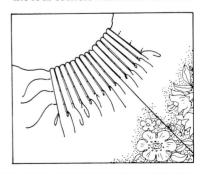

pen. Insert horizontal parallel rows of gathering with fabric right side up. Pull up the threads evenly on the right side until the edge is the correct size to fit the corresponding piece of fabric. Pass all threads to the wrong side and knot in pairs.

The ruching can be reinforced with a piece of lawn the size of the rectangle. Turn in the edges and hem to the wrong side, leaving the edge nearest the raw edge of the garment to be included in the seam at that point. Do not press.

SCALLOPED COLLAR

An attractive variation for the collar of the child's dress or the round collars on the shirt, drop-waist dress or gathered dress.

Pin the collar pattern to the fabric but re-mark the outer edge making the collar wider. Do not alter the size of the neck edge. It can be made any width up to the length of the shoulder seam, and the outer edge can be any shape. If you are uncertain of the amount to add cut it out in paper or interfacing first and pin it to the garment.

Cut out the collar in fabric, place interfacing between the two layers and baste together with fabric right side out. Mark the outer edge using a fabric pen. Finish the raw edge with scallops worked using a machine embroidery stitch or hand loopstitch. Cut away the surplus fabric.

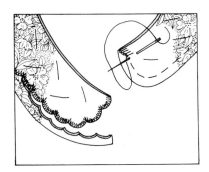

Attach the collar to the neckline of the garment using facings or bindings.

Cuffs may be made in the same way. Cut them 1cm (⅜in.) wider, mark the line on which to sew, cut away the surplus after stitching.

SCALLOPED EDGE

A method of finishing the hems of sleeves, full skirts etc. The size of the scallops should be in proportion to the area on which they are made and to the sophistication of the garment. For example those on a hemline could be up to 15cm (6in.) in width but those on a small child's dress in lawn would look best kept to no more than 5cm (2in.).

Having decided on the approximate width and depth of a scallop, take a piece of paper exactly equal to the length of the edge of the garment, without seam allowances; its depth should be the intended depth of the scallop plus 10cm (4in.). Fold the paper over and over until you have a rectangle close to the size you need. Use a plate or saucer and draw one scallop with its outer edge 2.5cm (1in.) from the edge. Run a toothed tracing wheel over the line to mark all layers. Cut

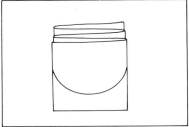

the scallops. Pin the paper to the garment and outline the scallops with tacking. Cut a strip of fabric on the straight grain the same length and width as the paper. Make a seam to join the ends, place it right side down to the right side of the garment and baste in position. Machine from garment side following the outline. Neaten the edge of the facing. Trim away all surplus fabric and snip the edge well. Roll the facing to the inside, roll, tack and press the edge.

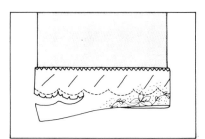

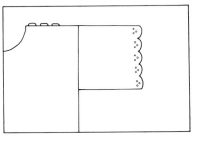

Anchor the facing on the inside of the garment by working small herringbone stitch, where it crosses seams and also slip-stitching just under the edge. On Country cotton and Varuna wool put in short pieces of Wundaweb at intervals instead

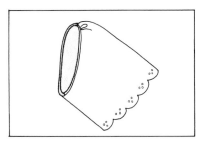

of slip-stitching. If the area is small, for example a sleeve, it would be best to cut a second sleeve and use that as the facing.

SCISSORS

Use a small pair of scissors with short pointed blades for snipping threads and fabric edges. They cannot be used for trimming or cutting as the fabric slips out from between the blades. The most comfortable scissors to use are those with large holes for thumb and second finger, where the forefinger is used to support the scissors and control the snip. Open the scissors only as far as is necessary, and snip with the tips of the blades.

SEAM LINE

The patterns allow 1.5cm (⅝in.) on all seam edges so the seam line or line on which you stitch is that distance from the raw edge unless you make any adjustment. If you are not confident about guessing the distance, most machines have a mark beside the foot which is 1.5cm (⅝in.) from the central needle position. Alternatively, mark the fabric with tailor's chalk or fabric pen. Do not use tacking for marking as it becomes trampled under the stitching. Note that seam lines on the illustrations in this book are shown by tufts of tailor's tacks.

SEAM POCKETS

Pockets can be put into the side seams of several of the garments including trousers and shorts, skirts and dresses. There is one tissue pattern for a seam pocket which you could use for all seam pockets, cutting two of them for each pocket. The shape of the pocket opening has been added to skirt seams for ease of placing in position and also so that the join is hidden. If you decide to put pockets somewhere else or at a different level add the same shape and length of extension to the seam edges when you cut out the garment.

For a pocket bag that stays flat in wear you can attach light iron-on Vilene to two pocket pieces. Avoid getting adhesive on your pressing surface as follows:

Reserve the fabric for the pockets but cut out only one pair. Use the paper pattern and cut two in Vilene. Press the Vilene to the wrong side of the reserved fabric. Cut round the edge.

Place the interfaced pockets right side down to the right side of the garment back and then match the

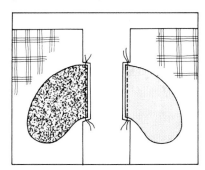

extensions. Stitch. Attach the other pocket bags to the garment front. Press all pocket bags to extend. Stitch the garment seams above and below the pocket, fastening off the stitching well. Change to a large

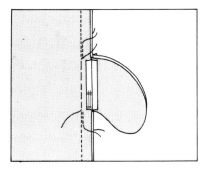

machine stitch and stitch across the pocket opening. Press the bags towards the front of the garment.

Trim the seams of the pocket bags; snip the garment seam on the back only to the end of the seam stitching above and below the

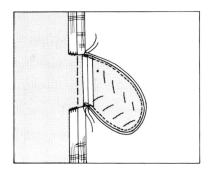

pocket bag so that the pocket seam lies flat. Neaten the snipped edges.

Baste the pocket bags together, stitch and neaten round the outer edge. Remove stitching across pocket opening.

SETTING IN SLEEVES

The sleeves in the rompers and in the child's dress are set into a standard shaped armhole and, although the sleeve head is gathered, it should be handled in the same way as a plain classic sleeve.

Set in the sleeves as the final process if possible to avoid unnecessary crushing. Complete the garment as far as possible and make up and finish the sleeves. Insert a gathering thread over the sleeve head.

Hold both the garment and the sleeve with right sides out and match the underarm seams. Pin. Hold the sleeve and armhole edges together for about 3cm (1¼in.) on either side of the pin, and tack.

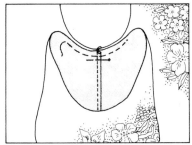

Fasten off the tacking and remove pins. Tack the other sleeve in the same way.

Put your hand inside the bodice, take hold of the edge of the head of the sleeve and the armhole edge of the bodice, at the shoulder and, holding them together, pull them through until you have the bodice folded back wrong side out over the sleeve. Insert a pin at the sleeve head.

Turn the sleeve head and armhole edges over until the sleeve head is visible and on top. Do not pull out

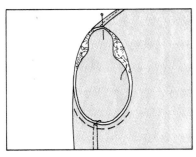

the entire sleeve but leave it where it supports the seam while you handle it.

Pull up the gathering thread until the sleeve rests on the armhole. Even out the gathers. Insert several pins across the gathers. Tack with small stitches. Stitch the armhole

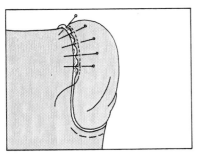

with the sleeve uppermost so that you can control the gathers. Stitch beside the gathering thread so that it can be removed afterwards. Neaten the armhole.

SHEARS

Use large shears for cutting out, opening them as far as is comfortable and cutting firmly right to the tips of the blades.

SHELL EDGING

A decorative hem finish for frills, sleeves, etc., on Tana lawn and crêpe de chine.

To produce the effect by machine, attach a shell hem attachment and set to zigzag stitch. Trim the edge straight and make all the seams except one. Feed the fabric through the hemmer holding the edge vertically and taut. Join the final seam.

An alternative method that may be used on lawn is to set the machine to blind hem stitch, turn under one narrow fold of fabric and feed it into the machine, so that when the needle moves to one side it clears the fold, drawing in the edge and making a shell effect.

To make a shell edge by hand, turn a narrow hem on the fabric and tack and press. With wrong side up stitch the hem with three hemming stitches then take the needle right

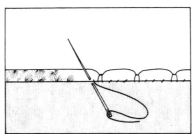

over the hem twice, pulling the thread to draw the fabric in a little. Continue with this stitch. Remove tackings. Do not press.

SHIRRING

This is elasticated gathering that can be used at the wrists of dresses, ankles of trousers, etc. It will not withstand too much strain and it may become slack with constant washing, but it can be replaced if this happens. The ends of shirring are not strong so join all seams on the garment and even finish the hem before shirring. It is not possible to assess how tight the shirring will be as this depends on the tension on the elastic and on the type of fabric being used. Each row that is inserted makes it tighter so continue adding it until the fabric has been reduced to a suitable size.

Wind the shirring elastic on to the machine spool by the same method as for winding thread. The elastic must be wound this way in order to give it tension so it cannot be wound successfully by hand. Note that if you have a machine that only winds spools by passing the thread through the eye of the needle, you will not be able to do shirring by this method.

Put the spool in the machine. Thread the top with a synthetic thread and set the stitch to a large straight stitch.

With the fabric right side up, work a row of machining in the desired position, starting nearest to the hem edge. On completing one row raise the foot, swivel the fabric, work two stitches, turn the fabric

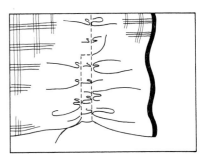

back again, lower the foot and work a second row. Continue like this until you have sufficient rows. Pass thread ends to the wrong side and

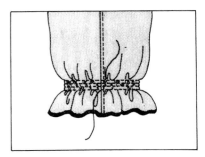

use them to oversew the ends of elastic to the seam allowances. For reinforcement a short piece of bias binding or tape can be hemmed over these ends.

Hold the shirred section in the steam from boiling water to shrink the elastic and draw the gathers tighter to provide firmer grip.

An alternative method is to hold the elastic on the wrong side of the fabric, pulling it taut while you work a small zigzag stitch over it.

Repeat steam treatment if slackened in wear.

SHIRT BAND COLLAR

Complete yoke and front bands. Attach interfacing to one collar piece, or both if you want a really crisp finish. If you are inserting contrast piping stitch it to one collar piece on the right side. Tack collar

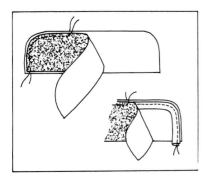

pieces right sides together and stitch round outer edge. For perfectly matching corners make a cardboard template from the pattern. Mark a dotted curve on the fabric using a fabric pen. Trim and

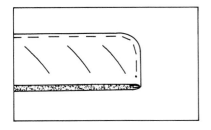

snip round edge. Roll collar right side out, tack the edge and press. Baste down the centre of the collar to keep the layers together.

Matching centre backs and interfaced side of collar to right side of shirt neckline, bring collar ends precisely to the corners of the front bands. Tack collar to shirt. Snip neck edge several times so that it lies flat and machine; it is easier to stitch accurately with shirt on top

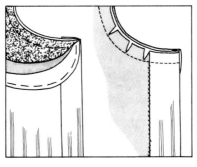

and collar underneath. Trim and snip the neck turnings and press them into the collar. Bring raw edge

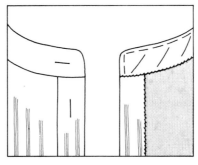

down over neck join, turn under and hem into machining.

When spacing the buttons make one horizontal buttonhole in the band and the top buttonhole in the band about 2.5cm (1in.) below the neck seam.

SHIRT FRONT BANDS

The bands for the front of the shirt have been made the correct width to be interfaced with light Fold-a-Band (Fuse 'n' Fold). This has the advantage of central perforations on which to make the centre fold and accurate straight edges to use as a stitching guide.

The easiest way to make the bands is to pin the pattern to the fabric when laying out all the pattern pieces but do not cut the bands. Cut two pieces of lightweight Fold-a-Band equal in length to the band pattern piece. Press each piece to the wrong side

of the fabric you have reserved; it is easy to line up the perforations in the Fold-a-Band on the straight grain, or on a particular part of the print on the fabric that you need to

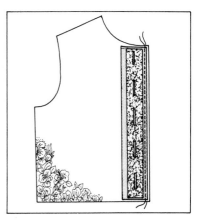

match with the front of the shirt. Press with a warm iron then press again using a damp muslin pressing cloth.

You may consider trimming the ends of the Fold-a-Band back to the seam line at the neck and hem to reduce bulk and in crêpe de chine this is a good idea, but in most other fabrics it works well to leave the interfacing in to the end of the band because it provides support in the neck seam and at the hem it is easier to make sharp corners.

Tack the bands to the shirt fronts right sides together and stitch just off the edge of the Fold-a-Band. Trim seam edges, press edges

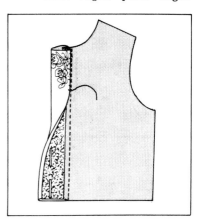

towards band. Fold fabric over the other edge of the Fold-a-Band and bring it over on to the wrong side of the shirt, folding it on the perforations. Baste through the band. Hem into the machining to finish.

An alternative method for top-stitched shirts is to attach the bands to the wrong side, bringing the second edge to the right side of the

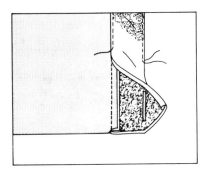

shirt to cover the machine stitching. Baste in place and machine along both edges of the band.

When using the pattern to make a dress which is lined as in the

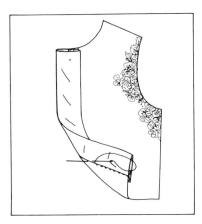

button-through dress in tartan Jubilee (page 112), press open the join between front and band then bring the other edge over to lie flat inside the dress to reduce bulk. Work prick stitch in the seam join from the right side. The edge of the lining will eventually cover the raw edge on the underside. If unlined, neaten the raw edge.

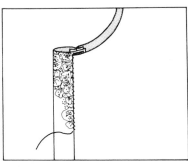

The centre front lines of the shirt, the position on which buttonholes are made and buttons are attached, is exactly in the middle of the bands when complete.

SHIRT HEM

Turn up a narrow hem on the shirt and hem by hand or machine it. On the lightweight fabrics such as Tana lawn work any top-stitching.

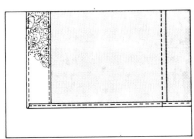

Complete the front bands right to the hemline and turn up and stitch the hem across to the front edge.

On Varuna wool and Jubilee open out the front band at the hemline, turn up the hem along the bottom, trimming away the raw

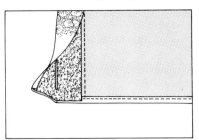

edge to 3mm (⅛in.) inside the band. Complete the hem stitching, fold the band back into position and slip-stitch the edges together at the bottom. Complete the hemming along the band. This method should be used on the hem of the button-through dress but with a deeper hem on the main part of the dress.

SHIRT COLLAR

The classic shirt collar uses the band and the pointed collar patterns. Interface one band and one collar to the stiffness required, building up several layers of light iron-on interfacing rather than using a heavy interfacing. The collar points only can have an extra piece of interfacing attached. If a tie is to be worn attach interfacing to both bands for additional crispness.

Put collars right sides together, tack and stitch outer edge. Mark the corners before stitching with a fabric pen to give a clear point on which to turn. With fabrics that fray, including crêpe de chine and Jubilee, change to a smaller machine stitch for 2cm (⅜in.) or so

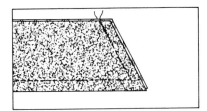

at the corner. Trim and snip the turnings, turn collar right side out, roll the edge, tack and press. If you are top-stitching the shirt do it now on the collar edge.

Matching centre backs, place

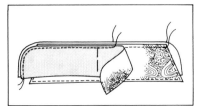

pointed collar between bands with neck edge of collar to upper edge of band. Tack along edge and round ends. On fabrics that slip, including crêpe de chine, machine the collar to one band piece then attach second band.

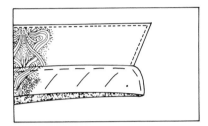

Trim and snip all raw edges, pull collar above band and press. Tack below the join and baste down the middle of the collar.

Matching centre backs, pin interfaced band to shirt neck. Make sure the ends meet the front bands precisely. Snip the neckline at intervals so that it lies flat, and stitch. You may find it helps if you

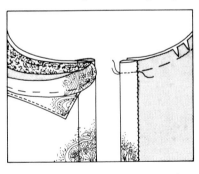

anchor the collar band ends with a few stitches before stitching right round the neck.

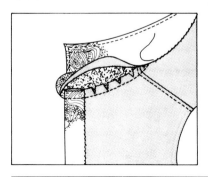

Trim and snip the turnings, press them up into collar. Turn under the raw edge and hem into the machine stitching to finish. Top-stitch the band.

When spacing the buttonholes place one horizontally in the middle of the band, and the first vertical

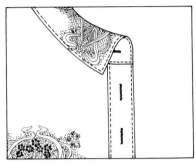

buttonhole no more than 2.5cm (1in.) below the neck join or the opening will gape.

SHIRT YOKE

After cutting out mark the centre back on yoke and back shirt; mark shoulder line on yoke. Pin or tack the back tucks. Matching centre backs tack back yoke to back shirt right sides together. Place yoke lining right side to wrong side of shirt matching centres. Tack.

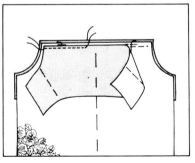

Machine across yoke through all layers. Trim the seam allowances, remove all tacking, press turnings towards yoke. Press the right side to ensure there are no creases in the yoke.

Stitch front yoke edges to fronts

of shirt right sides together, trim and press turnings towards yoke. Baste through yoke and lining to hold the layers together around

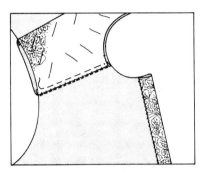

neck and armholes. Fold under raw edges of front yokes, tack and hem into the machine stitches.

If you insert piping in the yoke seams, machine it to the yoke

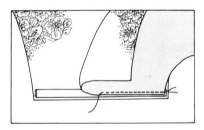

edges, stitch the seams, attach yoke lining with a second row of stitching using the first as a guide.

An alternative and slightly quicker method of attaching the front yokes to eliminate the hand sewing is to tack the yoke to the fronts, bring the yoke lining around but wrong side up and place it right side down on the inside of the seam

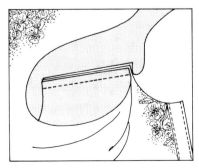

already tacked. You will have to pull the yoke lining and match up the neck and armhole edges carefully, tack and machine. Trim the linings and press.

SLEEVE BANDS

The three-quarter sleeves on the gathered dress have bands below the elbow. Cut the Fold-a-Band to length given and press to the wrong side of the fabric. Cut out, allowing turnings. Join the ends of the band; press open the join. Press over one long edge of the band. Insert gathering threads in the sleeve. Pin the band to the sleeve matching the

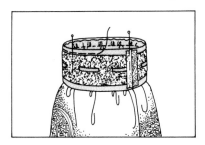

seam to the sleeve seam. Pull up gathers to fit band. Tack and machine. Bring pressed edge of band to inside of sleeve and hem to back of gathers.

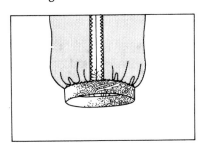

SLIP HEMMING

Similar to hemming but a weaker, looser stitch. After picking up a thread slip the needle into the fold for about 1cm (⅜in.) before bringing it out to take the next

thread. Use slip hemming on garment hems.

SMOCKING

Smocking, which is surface embroidery, can be worked on the child's dress or pinafore. The gathers or pleats must be even for successful results so use a home smocking machine which will insert the gathering threads very quickly, or use strips of smocking dot transfer applied to the wrong side of the fabric. Use dots, or space the needles on the machine, 6mm (¼in.) apart. Leave at least 2cm (¾in.) of fabric free at each end of the gathered area, more if you can. To gather by hand use a Sharps No.6 needle and pieces of thread the length of the fabric. Start with a knot and pick up each dot on the needle.

After working all rows trim the thread ends evenly. Pull up the threads so that the fabric is against the iron then loosen them so that the tubes of fabric have small spaces between them. Anchor the ends of thread in pairs by winding them round pins.

Embroider the surface by working a variety of stitches to form a pattern. Stem stitch, sometimes referred to as outline stitch, is commonly used for the top and bottom rows of the design. Another effective stitch is cable stitch, which makes honeycomb and trellis patterns. Work from left to right, picking up the surface of the pleat and inserting the needle horizontally. The tension should be firm and even throughout. Practice will ensure this.

On completion remove the gathering threads, pin the smocking to size and press by holding a steam iron against the wrong side and leave to dry.

SNIP (CLIP)

This means using small scissors to make a series of nicks in the edge of

the fabric to relieve strain or allow it to lie flat. The snips should stop short of the seam line and they should be angled – the edges will lie flatter and you will be less liable to cut through any stitching. Edges are snipped either before sewing to make a process easier to handle, e.g. the curve of a collar on to a neckline, or after stitching to make the edges lie flat, e.g. after attaching a facing, collar, etc.

STITCH

The word stitch in this book means working the permanent machine stitching or hand sewing that is the next stage of the process. If you are machining, using either zigzag or straight stitch, the stitch should be the same size on the entire garment. Remember to reverse at each end of the line to prevent it pulling undone. If you are hand sewing start with a knot (on crêpe de chine work a couple of back stitches and cut off the knot) and make the smallest, neatest stitches possible. Consult the chart on page 56 for correct needle size. Fasten off the thread with two back stitches.

TACK/BASTE

This is stitching using tacking thread with a No. 5 or 6 Between needle and a knot in the end. Make straight stitches about 1cm (⅜in.) long, shorter if fabric is gathered. Where possible keep the fabric flat on the table for accuracy, lifting it only for sewing shaped areas. Remove stitches by pulling on the knot. Use a bodkin to loosen the thread if necessary and re-use the length of thread. Never use sewing thread for tacking as it is harsh and may leave marks, it is difficult to remove as it will only break under extreme pressure, and – worst of all – it is expensive. It is always worth taking the trouble to tack or baste especially if the process is tricky, if the fabric is gathered or shaped, or if it is the first time you have attempted a process.

TIES

Flat ties are used to fasten the child's pinafore, and they could be used on the jacket in place of buttons. The ties can be made from either bias or straight fabric. Decide on a suitable length by tying strips of fabric together.

Cut the strips to twice the finished width plus two seam allowances; this will be about 4cm (1½in.). Fold each one right side inside and press lightly. Stitch down the edge. Stitch across one end at an angle or straight. Press the stitching, turn ties right side out using a rouleau needle. Ease out the corners with the point of a bodkin. Roll the edges and press with your fingers so that the join is on the edge. Press.

Attach ties to the garment by putting them on the outside with all raw edges level with garment edge. Machine to hold in place. Attach the garment facing, or yoke lining etc.,

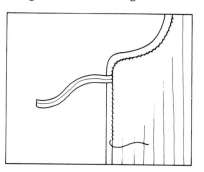

in the usual way which, when turned to the inside, will enable the ties to extend beyond the edge of the garment. If the edge is to be

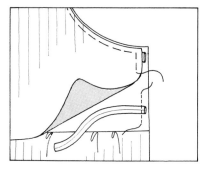

finished with binding, attach that first then push the end of the tie under the binding on the wrong side before doing the final hemming.

A decorative way of attaching ties is to machine the end to the outside of the garment. Cut pieces of fabric,

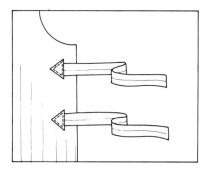

turn in the edges square or angled and cover the end of the tie. Tack and stitch in place.

TRIM

This means cutting away any surplus fabric after a final row of stitching has been worked and before proceeding with the next process. Hold the edge to be trimmed in the left hand and cut with medium-sized scissors. Cut away the maximum the fabric will stand, leaving 6mm (¼in.) on fraying fabrics but less on those that do not fray.

VELCRO

Velcro is one way of fastening the waistbands on the skirts. Use at least 5cm (2in.). Trim the Velcro to the length of the waistband overlap, then cut a further 2mm (¹⁄₁₆in.) from the hook side to ensure that when fastened the hooks are always covered by the soft loop side of the Velcro.

Attach with hemming using a short piece of lightly waxed thread, or use a small zigzag machine stitch.

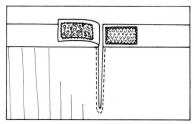

Use suitably-sized Velcro circles to fasten cuffs, belts, etc., and they can also be used underneath buttons in place of buttonholes. Peel the Velcro circle from the paper backing, place on the fabric where the adhesive will hold it while you

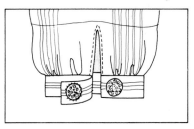

hem round the edge. The second circle of Velcro can be attached to the lower part of the garment by working a triangle of machine stitches across it.

WAISTBAND

Select a waistband stiffening that is suitable for the fabric and sufficiently firm for you. A waistband pattern is provided with the full-size tissue patterns in the back of the book and this is for use with all the diagram-pattern skirts in the book as well as with the straight and pleated skirts. The pattern is the correct width to take 5cm (2in.) wide Fold-a-Band (Waist-Shaper), with the advantage of central perforations to produce a central fold as well as stitching guides for the edges. Other waistband stiffenings include petersham and iron-on waistbanding, and you can select from several widths and then adjust the pattern width.

If the paper pattern is the correct length to fit your waist plus sufficient overlap for the type of fastening you wish to use, cut out the waistband in fabric and attach stiffening. Attach Fold-a-Band by pressing it firmly to the wrong side with perforations exactly in the middle. Attach petersham and other stiffening by machining along each side, with one edge in the middle of the fabric. Another and more accurate way of making the waistband is to dispense with the pattern and measure Fold-a-Band round your waist instead,

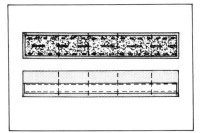

allowing 5-7cm (2-2½in.) overlap, and cut. Press to the wrong side of a spare piece of fabric and then cut out the waistband using the edge of the Fold-a-Band as a guide and adding some extra seam allowance all round. Note: if you use a wider waist stiffening follow this method of measuring.

Mark off the amount of extension you allowed and divide the remainder into four, using tailor's chalk or fabric pen. Complete the skirt except for the hem. Tack lining in place and attach hanging loops. There are two ways of attaching the waistband. One method attaches it to the right side of the skirt and is finished on the inside by hand, the other attaches it to the wrong side, the edge of the band being brought over to the right side, turned under and machined. The choice of method will depend on whether you prefer visible machine stitching or not. If the fabric is Tana lawn or Country cotton, fold one edge over the stiffening, tack and press. On heavier fabric trim 6mm (¼in.) from one edge and neaten. Put waistband to skirt with the right sides together, match centre and side seams, arrange the overlap at either right or left skirt back according to preference, and pin.

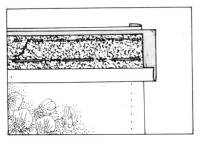

If the skirt is gathered, pull up gathers to fit band and wind thread ends around pins. If you are making a straight skirt make sure the skirt has been fitted carefully and the waistband made exactly to size, then ease the skirt on to the band. Tack waistband to skirt, stitching just off the edge of the stiffening or, in the case of Fold-a-Band, along the perforations. Try on and adjust

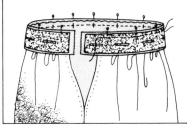

if necessary. Machine waistband to skirt, stitching with the band uppermost. Check frequently to make sure the skirt beneath is lying flat.

Remove tackings, trim the seam allowances and press them towards

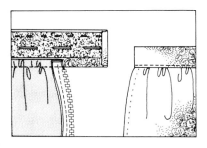

the band. Fold the ends of the band right sides together and pin with edges level. Machine across the end to the top of the zip and, on the

extension side, along the lower edge of the band. The stitching should meet the stitching attaching

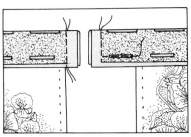

the band to the skirt. Trim edges and corners and turn right side out. Fold band along the middle and press, bringing the inner edge on to the machine stitching. On lightweight fabric fold under and tack, finish by hemming into the machine stitches. Remove tacking and press. Add top-stitching all round if you wish.

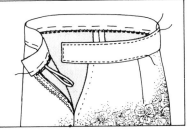

On heavier fabrics attach the band in the same way and stitch the ends but snip the waistband level with edges of the skirt opening to allow the neatened edge to lie flat over the waist seam. Tack flat and machine or prick stitch by hand below the waistband.

The alternative method of attaching the waistband is quicker to sew but requires a little more care in order to obtain a neat finish on the right side. Attach waistband to wrong side of skirt, trim seam allowances and press them towards the band. Tuck in and press on to the stiffening all other edges of the waistband. Fold waistband down the middle, bring the edge on to the right side of the skirt. Pin and tack making sure the ends are level and the edge covers the machine stitching. Machine along the edge of band and all round outer edge if you wish.

WAIST JOIN

This process is used to attach the V-neck top to the skirt to form the drop-waist dress, to join the short version of the blouse to the skirt, and to attach the yoke on the children's clothes. In each case construct the bodice except for inserting the sleeves, and finish the skirt except for the hem. With the drop-waist dress or other adult clothes with waists the garment should be fitted and adjusted for width, as well as position of the waistline. It is easier to make such adjustments on the wrong side, so put on the dress inside out and pin to alter it. Make sure centre front and centre back are marked on bodice and skirt.

Insert gathering threads along the upper edge 1.5cm (⅝in.) from the edge, one across the front ending 1cm (⅜in.) from the side seams and another across the back. If there is an opening in the back of the skirt insert a gathering thread each side, reversing the stitching at the edge of the opening to fasten the thread.

Have the bodice of the garment right side out, turn the skirt so that it is wrong side out and put bodice inside skirt. Arrange the two so that the side seams are level and pin

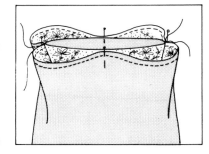

together. Match centre fronts and centre backs and pin. Insert all pins vertically under the gathering thread.

On the children's clothes match the centre on the yoke with the centre back of the skirt; this is in line with the centre back seam at the base of the opening.

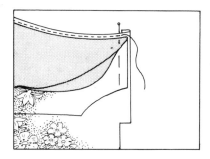

Pull up the gathering thread, working on one quarter of the waist and easing the gathers along the thread until the skirt fits the bodice. Wind the thread end round a pin to hold. Pull up the other end of the thread and wind around a pin. Even out the gathers smoothing the

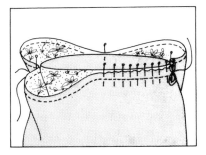

fabric vertically to settle the gathers into even tubes of fabric. Insert pins frequently, picking up a small amount of fabric only. Tack each quarter, stitching on the gathering thread and removing the pins as you reach them. Fasten off the tacking; pin and tack the next section. Repeat until waist join is tacked. Try on and if adjustments are necessary the tacking will have to be removed and the process started again. Check that all pins are out and stitch the join. Machine with the gathered side uppermost; allow the stitching to fall below the tacking and work slowly, easing the gathers under the needle evenly and checking frequently to make

sure the bodice underneath is lying flat.

Remove the gathering threads. Trim the seam allowances and neaten with zigzag stitch. Alternatively trim the gathered edge only, fold the bodice edge over twice and hem. The yokes of the children's clothes are double, so after trimming the edge of the yoke the lining is turned under and hemmed down on to the skirt. Press.

WELT SEAM

A double-stitched seam that may be used on all fabrics and all the garments in the book. It is decorative and can be used on yokes as well as on functional main seams.

The finished width should be no more than 4mm (³⁄₁₆in.) on crêpe de chine and lawn, a little wider on Country cotton or Varuna.

Place the two pieces to be seamed right sides together and stitch on the fitting line. Press the seam open, then to one side. Make sure corresponding seams face in opposite directions. Trim the upper seam allowance to less than 1cm (⅜in.) and the one underneath to 3mm (⅛in.). Turn under the upper one evenly, moistening your fingers to help flip it under. Tack but not near the edge. Press and machine.

ZIP FASTENER (ZIPPER)

Use fine metal or nylon zip fasteners on all fabrics. Do not use pins but always tack in place or use basting tape.

Edge-to-edge method
Use this method on the gathered and circular skirts. Make an open seam in the garment, neaten the raw edges including where the zip is to be inserted. Use a large stitch and sew up the gap left for the zip. Press the seam open. Place zip right side down on top of the seam with

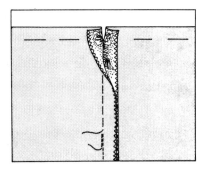

the teeth exactly over the centre and slider a little below the seam line. Tack along both zip tapes.

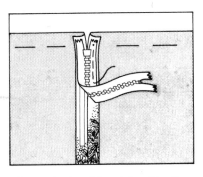

Alternatively stick a strip of basting tape each side of the opening, peel off the backing and press the zip to the tape with the teeth carefully on the seam line.

Sew in the zip from the right side. Use hand prick stitch or machine it

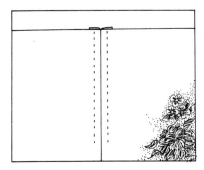

using the zip foot. Sew from the bottom of the zip towards the slider on each side. A pucker or bump at the bottom can be avoided by sewing only beside the teeth and not across at the base.

Press by running the toe of the iron over the stitching and up to the zip but not over it.

Covered method
This method provides a fold of fabric to cover the zip teeth. Use in the straight and A-line skirts.

Stitch the skirt seam leaving the correct length of opening. Press; neaten the seam edges. Decide which edge will be the fold of the

fabric covering the zip and turn it in and press it on the seam line. It will help to keep the stitching flat and the opening neat if a narrow strip of light iron-on Vilene is slipped under this fold, but it is optional.

On the other edge, the one that will be hidden, turn under the raw edge – not on the seam line but 2-3mm (⅛in.) beyond it. Press the fold (and on Varuna wool it will require tacking as well). Put the zip under this edge and hold it so that

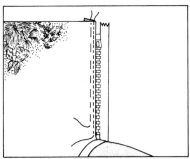

the fold of the fabric is close against the teeth. The slider should be 17mm (¾in.) below the top of the opening. Tack fabric to zip. Attach zip foot to machine and stitch as

close as possible to the teeth. Remove all tacking and press by running the toe of the iron over the line of the stitching.

Bring the pressed fold of fabric over the zip, line up the fold with the seam line beneath, that is 2-3mm (¹⁄₁₆in.) beyond the zip teeth; oversew the fold to the fabric beneath with tacking thread, or

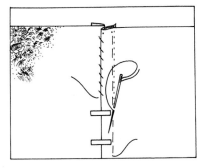

hold with basting tape. Tack again beside the teeth to hold the fold to the zip tape. Work hand prick stitch to finish, mark a line on which to stitch with tailor's chalk or fabric pen. Remove tacks, press stitching.